D1035536

025.43   76 7303
BLOOMBERG, MARTY
   INTRO TO CLASSIFICA-
TION & NUMBER BUILDING
IN   DEWEY

Please leave Transaction Cards in this
pocket.

Marking and mutilation of books pro-
hibited by law. Borrower is responsible
for all material checked out under his
name.

SCOTT COUNTY LIBRARY
Shakopee, Minn. 55379

An Introduction to Classification and Number Building in Dewey

LIBRARY SCIENCE TEXT SERIES

Introduction to Public Services for Library Technicians. By Marty Bloomberg.

Introduction to Technical Services for Library Technicians. By Marty Bloomberg and G. Edward Evans.

A Guide to the Library of Congress Classification. By John Phillip Immroth.

Science and Engineering Literature: A Guide to Reference Sources. 2nd ed. By H. Robert Malinowsky, Richard A. Gray, and Dorothy A. Gray.

The Vertical File and Its Satellites: A Handbook of Acquisition, Processing and Organization. By Shirley Miller.

Introduction to United States Public Documents. By Joe Morehead.

The School Library Media Center. By Emanuel T. Prostano and Joyce S. Prostano.

The Humanities: A Selective Guide to Information Sources. By A. Robert Rogers.

The School Library and Educational Change. By Martin Rossoff.

Introduction to Library Science: Basic Elements of Library Service. By Jesse H. Shera.

Introduction to Cataloging and Classification. 5th ed. By Bohdan S. Wynar, with the assistance of John Phillip Immroth.

An Introduction to Classification and Number Building in Dewey

Marty Bloomberg and Hans Weber

Edited by John Phillip Immroth

1976

Libraries Unlimited, Inc.
Littleton, Colo.

76 1303

Copyright © 1976 Libraries Unlimited, Inc.
All Rights Reserved
Printed in the United States of America

LIBRARIES UNLIMITED, INC.
P.O. Box 263
Littleton, Colorado 80120

Library of Congress Cataloging in Publication Data

Bloomberg, Marty.
    An introduction to classification and number
building in Dewey.

    (Library Science text series)
    Bibliography: p. 193
    Includes index.
    1. Classification, Dewey decimal. I. Weber,
Hans H., 1935-   joint author. II. Title.
Z696.D7B58   025.4'3   76-26975
ISBN 0-87287-115-0

TABLE OF CONTENTS

Chapter 1
The Dewey Decimal Classification

Chapter 6
Class 400–499 (Language)

Chapter 7
Class 500–599 (Pure Sciences)

Chapter 8
Class 600–699 (Technology–Applied Sciences)

Chapter 9
Class 700–799 (The Arts)

Chapter 10
Class 800–899 (Literature)

Chapter 11
Class 900–999 (General Geography and History
and Their Auxiliaries)

Chapter 12
Book Numbers

Appendix
Additional Problems

PREFACE

The purpose of this text is to provide a concise introduction to the Dewey Decimal Classification. The text is intended for library technical assistants, clerks, and paraprofessionals. It should also be a useful introduction for library school students and for librarians who have had little experience using the Dewey Decimal Classification.

This text is limited to a presentation of fundamental introductory materials; no attempt is made to cover every aspect of the Dewey Decimal Classification.

The first chapter presents a general introduction to the Dewey Decimal Classification. The next ten chapters cover the main classes of the Dewey Decimal Classification and the use of the classification schedules. The final chapter presents introductory materials on book numbers. Numerous figures, examples, and problems are included to amplify the text.

The materials in this text are based on the following editions of these cataloging tools: *Dewey Decimal Classification and Relative Index*, 18th ed. (Lake Placid Club, N.Y., Forest Press, 1971. 3v.), and *Abridged Dewey Decimal Classification and Relative Index*, 10th ed. (Lake Placid Club, N.Y., Forest Press, 1971). Examples from the tables, schedules, and Relative Index are "reproduced from Edition 18 (1971) of DEWEY Decimal Classification by permission of Forest Press Division, Lake Placid Education Foundation, owner of copyright." The reader is cautioned against attempting to apply the material presented in this text to any edition of the above works other than the specific editions cited, since some variation exists between different editions. The volume and page references in the text (e.g., "DDC, Vol. 2, p. ___," or "Abridged DDC, p. ___") refer to the 18th edition and the 10th abridged edition, respectively.

Throughout the text the Dewey Decimal Classification will be abbreviated DDC. The DDC over the years has been called "Dewey," "Decimal Classification," "DC," "DDC," and "Dewey Classification." Any of these terms may be used in other books or periodical articles, but they all refer to the same classification system.

The authors want to thank the many librarians who offered valuable suggestions to improve the text. Special appreciation goes to Mr. Richard Sealock, Executive Director of the Forest Press, for permission to reproduce parts of the *Dewey Decimal Classification and Relative Index* (18th ed.) and the *Abridged Dewey Decimal Classification and Relative Index* (10th ed.). Our thanks also go to the H. W. Wilson Company for permission to reproduce an entry from the *Junior High School Catalog*; to LJ/Xerox Bibliographies for permission to reproduce an LJ card; and to Josten's Library Service Division for permission to reproduce a Josten's catalog card. The Forest Press, in granting permission to make quotations from the 18th edition of the Dewey Decimal Classification, is not responsible for the accuracy of the built numbers or the interpretation of the instructions and rules.

Last, but by no means least, our thanks to Linda Evans, who typed the manuscript. Any errors in the text are the authors' responsibility.

HW

University of Houston

MB

California State College,
San Bernardino

EDITOR'S FOREWORD

The authors of this book, Marty Bloomberg and Hans Weber, tell the reader in the Preface that the purpose of this text is to provide a concise introduction to the Dewey Decimal Classification. The methodology of their concise introduction is at least two-fold, and this approach may be discerned in each of the ten chapters devoted to the individual main classes of DDC.

First, each of these chapters provides a detailed survey of the contents of the class in a section called "Details of the Class." This survey should serve the reader as a travel guide or road map to the DDC. It is suggested that the reader compare each of these sections to the actual DDC schedules. The "Details of the Class" sections lead the reader through each class and make him aware of the major contents, the basic organization, and the arrangement of each. These summaries, written objectively and uncritically, provide an essential overview of each main class in DDC.

Second, the authors provide a carefully constructed sequence of number building examples, problems, and solutions for each of the ten major classes. In these sections they consistently and meticulously analyze the way to approach the examples and the problems first through the Relative Index, thus demonstrating to the reader how to use the Relative Index effectively as a starting point in the classification of a subject. This methodical use of the Relative Index is perhaps the most significant single technique presented in this text. All too often the student of DDC tends to skip the index and go initially to the schedules. Such an approach is as erroneous as trying to class directly from the index without using the schedules. This text shows how to use the Relative Index to get to the appropriate location in the schedules and then how to build the correct number. Further the authors do clearly explain the number building process in both the schedules and the auxiliary tables.

In addition to covering the ten major classes of DDC, this text contains a sound introductory chapter that discusses the physical format, general characteristics, and special characteristics of DDC. A chapter on book numbers is also included.

Those who use this text should have a set of the DDC tables, schedules, and Relative Index available, for much of the value of this text will be lost if it is not used in close conjunction with the DDC—the 18th edition, the 10th abridged edition, or, better still, both of these. Number building in DDC should be a pleasurable activity; it should, in fact, be fun. Building a DDC number is like solving a puzzle, and this text does much to lead the student to find the correct solution.

JPI

CHAPTER 1

THE DEWEY DECIMAL CLASSIFICATION

INTRODUCTION

The purpose of this chapter is to present a general introduction to the DDC. The chapter begins with a concise history of DDC, including biographical information about Melvil Dewey, information on the editions of DDC, and a discussion of the reasons for the success of this classification system. The second section deals with the physical format of the DDC in relation to the introductory materials, auxiliary tables, schedules, and the Relative Index for both the 18th edition and the 10th abridged edition. The general characteristics of DDC are discussed in the next section of this chapter, with an explanation of the hierarchical structure of DDC and examples of the main classes, divisions, sections, and further subdivisions. The decimal nature of the DDC notation is illustrated by examples, as is the basic categorization of the classification by disciplines and not simply by subjects. Following this section on general characteristics is a detailed section on the specific characteristics of the 18th, or full, edition of the DDC. The seven auxiliary tables and their mnemonic features are discussed, and many examples are given. As these individual tables are being discussed, it is recommended that the reader have the first volume of the 18th edition available for consultation and comparison to this text, so that he can become familiar with these tables while reading about them. The seven tables are: 1) Standard Subdivisions, 2) Areas, 3) Individual Literatures, 4) Individual Languages, 5) Racial, Ethnic, National Groups, 6) Languages, and 7) Persons. The notes and instructions within the schedules comprise the second part of this section. Scope notes and class-here notes are defined, and examples are given. Number building and the concept of the base number are then introduced. Centered headings and the Relative Index complete the discussion in this part of the section. The following section deals with the specific characteristics of the 10th abridged edition. The next two sections include important practical applications of DDC. First, there is an explanation of the segmentation or recommended shortening of DDC numbers assigned by the Decimal Classification Division of the Library of Congress. Second, many valuable sources of printed DDC numbers are cited, including commercial cataloging services and standard bibliographic sources. The last section of this introductory chapter presents the general principles of book classification. These principles, although applicable to many classification systems, are most appropriate to DDC. This chapter concludes with an important note to the reader on the structure and content of the remaining chapters, which cover in detail the individual classes and the application of DDC number building.

HISTORY OF THE DEWEY DECIMAL CLASSIFICATION

The DDC is the most widely used classification scheme in the United States. Between 1873 and 1876 Melvil Dewey developed the DDC, which was in part based on an earlier scheme devised by W. T. Harris. The DDC was an immediate success; at the present time nearly all public libraries and school libraries and over half of the academic libraries in the United States use the classification. It is also popular throughout the world and has been translated into many languages.

Melvil Dewey

Dewey was born in Adams Center, New York, in 1851. He graduated from Amherst College, where he later became an assistant librarian. As an Amherst student in 1873, Dewey conceived the idea for the classification scheme that would bear his name. In 1876 the DDC was published with the title *A Classification and Subject Index for Cataloguing and Arranging the Books and Pamphlets of a Library.* Dewey's name did not appear on the title page, but it was clearly stated in the copyright notice on the verso of the title page.

The first edition of 1,000 copies was 44 pages long and included eight pages of introduction, twelve pages of schedules, and eighteen pages of index. Although some contemporaries found the new classification too lengthy and subjected it to severe criticism, the DDC was an immediate success and revolutionized library classification.

Dewey, besides contributing to library classification, was one of the organizers of the American Library Association and the first editor of the *Library Journal.* He was active in the Spelling Reform Association, formed a library supply house and the Library Bureau, and founded the first library school in 1887.

The Editions of the DDC

The DDC is now in its 18th edition, published in 1971. From the "too lengthy" 44 pages of the 1st edition, the DDC has grown to 2,692 pages in three volumes. Undoubtedly future editions will increase in length. In recent times the DDC has been revised about every eight years, with the 19th edition scheduled for publication in 1978 or later.

There is an abridged version of the DDC, now in the 10th edition. The abridged edition is designed primarily for use in school and small public libraries. Earlier abridged editions were structured so that a library could eventually change to the unabridged edition as their collections grew. The 10th abridged edition, however, is structured as a completely independent volume intended for libraries that probably will never be large enough to use the unabridged edition.

Success of the DDC

The success of the DDC was immediate. Even today, some one hundred years later, no other classification scheme has been found sufficiently superior to justify the cost of implementing it in most libraries. A scholar of library classification, W. C. Berwick Sayers, credits the DDC's success to its "cardinal virtues [which] are universality and hospitality, a simple expansible notation, which is now almost an international classification vocabulary, excellent mnemonic features, first class machinery for its perpetuation, and an admirable index."[1]

Some of the strengths of the DDC that account for its initial success are: (1) It allows materials to be shelved in a *relative location* as the collection expands. Before the DDC was introduced, libraries used a "fixed location" for materials in which each item was assigned to a certain location set aside for a subject. Frequently the shelves themselves were numbered, and each item was assigned to a specific location or spot on a particular shelf. (2) The notation is simple and easily understood. (3) The scheme is easily expanded to accept new areas of knowledge. And (4) the DDC schedules provide clear and concise directions for use and for number building.

Given these reasons for the initial success of the DDC, we are now concerned with why the DDC continues to be so popular. Some of the reasons are: (1) It is already being used by many libraries throughout the world. In the United States the DDC is used by 98 percent of the public libraries, nearly all school libraries, and over 50 percent of college, university, and special libraries. (2) The DDC is being continuously revised by a permanent office established in the Library of Congress in 1933. This office has been responsible for editing both editions of the DDC since the 16th (1958). Between editions the DDC is kept up to date with *Dewey Decimal Classification Additions, Notes and Decisions*, a publication issued when necessary. Some current changes are reported regularly in *Cataloging Service*, a bulletin issued by the Processing Department of the Library of Congress. (3) Numerous centralized cataloging services provide catalog cards with pre-assigned DDC numbers, and many Library of Congress cards also provide a DDC number. In a recent six-month period, over 50,000 DDC numbers were assigned to books cataloged by the Library of Congress. And (4) "there is a continuing lack of a general classification scheme sufficiently excellent to convince librarians of the need for reclassifying their stacks."[2] "Thus the DC survives and thrives because," as Sayers has written, "despite the arguments of its critics concerning real or imaginary faults, it is still the best classification for public and probably for college libraries. No other system has been able, in practice, to offer a decisive challenge or prove its theoretical superiority for the arrangement of such collections."[3]

---

[1] W. C. Berwick Sayers, *A Manual of Classification for Librarians*, 4th ed. (London, Andre Deutsch, 1967), p. 151.

[2] C. D. Needham, *Organizing Knowledge in Libraries: An Introduction to Classification and Cataloging*, 2nd rev. ed. (London, Andre Deutsch, 1971), p. 95.

[3] Sayers, *A Manual of Classification*, p. 163.

FORMAT OF THE DDC

18th Edition

The 18th edition of the DDC is published in three volumes with 2,692 pages: Volume 1, Introduction and Tables; Volume 2, Schedules, and Volume 3, Index.

Volume 1 includes a general preface, a lengthy Editor's Introduction to the principles and use of the DDC, a glossary of terms used in classification, Melvil Dewey's introduction to the 12th edition of DDC, seven auxiliary tables used for building numbers, a table of relocated and discontinued numbers, a table of "Three-Figure Numbers Not in Use," and summaries of the ten main classes, the one hundred divisions, and the one thousand sections. Before using the DDC it is essential to read the Editor's Introduction. This text does not attempt to cover many of the details of the DDC, which are discussed in the Editor's Introduction. The glossary, with over seventy definitions, can be helpful to the cataloger.

Volume 2 includes the classification schedules for the ten main classes of the DDC. A brief introduction explains the format of the schedules and the meaning of special features such as brackets, italics, asterisks (*), and daggers (†) found in the schedules. Throughout the schedules are notes and instructions on how to use the schedules; these will be discussed below.

The schedules consist of a series of numbers or a combination of numbers and letters that constitute the notation of the scheme (Fig. 1-1).

Fig. 1-1. Classification Schedule

574

.1   Physiology

               Class here comprehensive works on physiology and anatomy

               Class microphysiology in 574.8

                    For anatomy, see 574.4; pathological physiology, 574.21; development and maturation, 574.3

                              SUMMARY

                    574.11   Circulation
                       .12   Respiration
                       .13   Nutrition and metabolism
                       .14   Secretion and excretion
                       .16   Reproduction
                       .17   Histogenesis
                       .18   Movements and control mechanisms
                       .19   Biophysics and biochemistry

Often the schedules includes instructions and informational notes on the use and application of the classification scheme.

Volume 3 contains the Relative Index, which is discussed later in this chapter. Following the Index are two tables: "Obsolescent Schedules" (the 340's and 510's from the 17th edition, which were completely revised in the 18th edition); and a "Tables of Concordance" comparing the law (340's) and mathematics (510's) schedules of the 17th and 18th editions.

10th Abridged Edition

The abridged edition is published in one volume, with 529 pages. Preceding the schedules is a Publisher's Foreword, a preface describing some special features of the abridged edition, an introduction to the structure and use of the DDC, a glossary of terms used in classification, four auxiliary tables used for building numbers, and two tables; "Relocations and Discontinued Numbers" and "Variations between Abridged 10 and Edition 18." These preliminary materials are followed by the classification schedules, then by the Relative Index and information on how to use it and on the abbreviations used in the Index. Following the Relative Index are two tables: "Obsolescent Schedules" (the 340's and 510's from the 9th edition, which were completely revised in the 10th edition), and "Tables of Concordance," comparing the law (340's) and mathematics (510's) schedules of the 9th and 10th editions.

GENERAL CHARACTERISTICS OF THE DDC

Hierarchical Structure

The DDC is a hierarchical classification, which means that it develops progressively from the general to the specific in disciplinary and subject relationships. Even so, the overall arrangement is not necessarily theoretical or logical. The DDC is built on the premise that no one class can cover all aspects of a given subject. The basic arrangement is by discipline, and a given subject may appear in any number of disciplines. The various aspects of a specific subject are brought together by the Relative Index. The most general numbers are the ten *main classes*:

000	Generalities
100	Philosophy and related disciplines
200	Religion
300	The social sciences
400	Language
500	Pure sciences
600	Technology (applied sciences)
700	The arts
800	Literature (belles-lettres)
900	General geography and history

Each of the main classes from 1 through 9 is assigned to a broad discipline or group of related disciplines. The 0 class (000–099) is somewhat of an exception, because generalities are not necessarily related disciplines—e.g., newspapers, encyclopedias, library science. Notice that the numbers are always written as 100, 200, 300, etc., because a DDC number *always* consists of three digits to the *left* of the decimal.

Each main class has ten *divisions*. The division, called the "second degree" of subdivision in the DDC, is represented by the second digit of the notation— 010, 020. Below are excamples of the ten divisions in two of the main classes:

000	Generalities
010	Bibliographies and catalogs
020	Library and information sciences
030	General encyclopedic works
040	not used
050	General serial publications
060	General organizations and museology
070	Journalism, publishing, newspapers
080	General collections
090	Manuscripts and book rarities

300	The social sciences
310	Statistics
320	Political science
330	Economics
340	Law
350	Public administration
360	Social pathology and services
370	Education
380	Commerce
390	Customs and folklore

Each of the 10 divisions in turn is divided into 10 *sections*. The section, called the "third degree" of subdivision in the DDC, is represented by the third digit in the notation—011, 012. Below are the *sections* in the 010 *division*:

010	Bibliographies and catalogs
011	General bibliographies
012	Of individuals
013	Of works by specific classes of writers
014	Of anonymous and pseudonymous works
015	Of works from specific places
016	Of specific disciplines and subjects

01<u>7</u>   General subject catalogs

01<u>8</u>   General author and date catalogs

01<u>9</u>   General dictionary catalogs

The hierarchical system in the DDC is based on the ten main classes, the 100 divisions and the 1000 sections. The hierarchical progression from the general to the specific is incorporated in the notation, which is lengthened by one digit for each successive division:

<u>6</u>00   Technology (applied sciences)

6<u>4</u>0   Domestic arts and sciences

64<u>6</u>   Sewing, clothing, personal grooming

646.<u>7</u>   Personal grooming

646.7<u>2</u>   Personal appearance

646.72<u>4</u>   Care of hair

646.724<u>2</u>   Professional hairdressing for women and girls

Decimal System

The DDC is a *decimal* classification system. All knowledge is represented by *ten* broad subject classes (000, 100, 200, etc.). Each of these main classes is divided into *ten* divisions (010, 020, 030, etc.). Each of the ten divisions in a main class is divided into *ten* subdivisions (010, 011, 012, etc.). The subdivision then can be further subdivided decimally (016.<u>52</u>).

The DDC numbers are arranged decimally, which means that the order of progression is:

612
612.001
612.01
612.014
612.0142
612.3
612.31
612.4

Notice that subdivision .31 comes *before* subdivision .4 because in a decimal system .31 is the smaller number. The example above shows the order in which works with these numbers would stand on the shelves and the order in which the shelflist cards would be filed.

Classification by Discipline

"No other feature of the DDC is more basic than this: that it scatters subjects by discipline" (DDC, Vol. 1, p. 18). The Editor's Introduction to the DDC further states that "the primary basis for DDC arrangement and development of subjects is by discipline . . . while subject, strictly speaking, is secondary" (DDC, Vol. 1, p. 17). One of the functions of classification is to bring together on the shelves materials on the same subject and on related subjects. It needs to be emphasized, however, that no classification accomplishes that function perfectly. It is important to remember that *all* material on a subject is seldom if ever classed together. The following example shows that materials on different aspects of railroads are classed throughout a collection:

Aspects of Railroads	DDC Number
1) Technical aspects of railroad building	625.1
2) Railroad economics	385.1
3) Model railroading	625.19
4) Railroad law	343.095
5) Government control of local railroads	350.875
6) Railroad safety	614.863
7) Bibliography of railroads	016.385 or 385.016
8) Railroad passenger station architecture	725.31
9) Fiction about railroads	808.839356

Thus, throughout the DDC various aspects of a topic or discipline may be placed in different numbers. For example, child hygiene is classed in 613.0432 (applied sciences), child psychology is classed in 155.4 (philosophy and related disciplines), and sociology of children is classed in 301.4314 (social sciences). No attempt is made to place all aspects of a topic in one number in the schedule. Although all of the works are about "children," they are classified according to their subject emphasis—hygiene, psychology, and sociology.

The device that brings together the various aspects and relationships of a topic is the Relative Index, which is discussed later in this chapter.

SPECIFIC CHARACTERISTICS OF THE DDC—FULL EDITION

Tables and Mnemonic Features

The seven tables in the full DDC are important devices—they aid in number building, and they serve a mnemonic (memory) function. In the DDC the mnemonic feature involves using the same combination of numbers to represent the same topic or to have the same meaning throughout the schedule (i.e., the standard subdivision –05 means periodicals in 52<u>0.5,</u> in 624.2<u>05</u> and in 660.<u>05</u>). The result of adding the notations (numbers) from these tables to the numbers in the classification schedules is that given combinations of numbers have a consistent meaning in various contexts. The notations in these tables are used *only* in conjunction with numbers from the classification schedules. The notations from the tables are *never* used alone. The dash (–) before the notations in the tables emphasizes the fact that they must be added to another number. The dash is omitted when the notation is added to a number from the schedules.

Standard Subdivisions (Table 1)

Standard subdivisions (Table 1) provide notations to identify works in a particular format, physical form, or "mode of treatment." Examples of treatment by format or physical form are dictionaries, encyclopedias, and periodicals; other "modes of treatment" can be an historical or geographical approach to a subject, or a philosophical or theoretical approach (Fig. 1-2).

Fig. 1-2. Standard Subdivisions (Table 1)

SUMMARY

–01	Philosophy and theory
–02	Miscellany
–03	Dictionaries, encyclopedias, concordances
–04	General special
–05	Serial publications
–06	Organizations
–07	Study and teaching
–08	Collections
–09	Historical and geographical treatment

In the examples below, more than one "0" is often used for a standard sub-division—such as –03, –003, or –0003. The number of "0's" used in a standard subdivision will vary in order to avoid conflicting with other numbers in the schedule. If more than one "0" is required, there will always be appropriate instructions in the schedule.

–01   **Philosophy and theory.** Treatment of the subject from a theoretical or philosophical point of view.

7<u>01</u>	philosophy of fine and decorative arts
350.<u>0001</u>	philosophy of public administration
20<u>0.1</u>	philosophy of religion

Even though the standard subdivisions generally can be used with any number in the schedules, it is *always* necessary to check the schedules to see if there are special directions for a particular classification number. The number combination —01 does *not* always signify a philosophical treatment. For example, 350.001 is the number for bureaucracy, 350.01 is the number for foreign affairs departments, and 543.01 is the number for reagents in general chemical analysis.

—02 **Miscellany.** A brief or outline treatment of a topic, such as an outline, manual, or synopsis. Included here are tabular and illustrated treatments of a topic.

502	miscellany in pure sciences
802	miscellany about literature
366.002	miscellany about associations

An example of a case when —02 does *not* mean a miscellany is 658.02, which is the number for management of enterprises of specific sizes and scopes.

—03 **Dictionaries, encyclopedias, concordances**

720.3	a dictionary or encyclopedia of architecture
611.003	a dictionary or encyclopedia of human anatomy
503	a dictionary or encyclopedia of the pure sciences

An example of a case when —03 does *not* mean a dictionary or encyclopedia is 343.03, which is the number for law of public finance.

—04 **General special.** This standard subdivision is reserved for special aspects that have general application to a particular discipline. It is used *only* when there are specific instructions in the schedule.

231.04	God, Trinity, Godhead, general special topics
263.04	days, times, places of religious observance, general special topics
591.04	zoology, general special topics

An example of a case when —04 does *not* mean general special is 343.04, which is the number for tax law.

[**Editor's note**: The concept of "general special" is a regularly used device in the Library of Congress classification; it is now being used in DDC as well. For example, a work on the days, times, and places of religious observance for students of English literature could be classed 263.04; in this case the general special concept of the —04 would be students of English literature.]

—05 **Serial publications.** Treatment of a subject or discipline in a periodical format—articles, papers, etc. Also used to identify yearbooks and annuals.

720.5 periodical on architecture

342.005 periodical on constitutional law

531.05 periodical on mechanics

An example of a case when —05 does *not* refer to a serial is 343.05, which is the number for kinds of taxes by base.

—06 **Organizations.** Provides for official publications of international, national, state, and local organizations. Such publications include reports, proceedings, regulations, and membership lists. Includes governmental, non-governmental, professional, and business organizations.

720.6 an architectural organization

531.06 an organization devoted to mechanics

906 an historical organization

An example of a case when —06 does *not* refer to an organization is 361.06, which is the number for counseling and related social welfare services.

—07 **Study and teaching.** Works on how to study and how to teach. Includes general works and works on how to study or teach specific subjects.

707 study and teaching of fine and decorative arts

591.07 study and teaching of zoology

630.7 study and teaching of agriculture

An example of a case when —07 does *not* refer to a work on study and teaching is 350.7, which is the number for internal administration in public administration.

—08 **Collections and anthologies.** Includes collections of originally separate essays, lectures, or articles. Does not include collections planned as composite works.

080 a collection of individual works (e.g., Harvard Classics)

531.08 a collection on mechanics

350.0008 a collection on public administration

An example of a case when −08 does *not* refer to a collection or anthology is 344.08, which is the number for law of educational and cultural exchanges.

−09   **Historical and geographical treatment.** Treatment from an historical or geographical view. Also for historical periods not limited geographically.

> 720.9   a history of architecture
>
> 531.09   a history of mechanics
>
> 350.0009   a history of public administration

An example of a case when −09 does *not* mean an historical or geographical treatment is 350.9, which is the number for malfunctioning of government.

The standard subdivisions provide possibilities for further division within each subdivision. For example, standard subdivision −06 provides the following more specialized subdivisions:

−06   Organizations

−061   Permanent government organizations

−063   Temporary organizations

−065   Business organizations

Earlier, the number 720.6 was given for an architectural organization. It is possible to use number 720.63 to identify a temporary organization related to architecture.

Standard subdivisions can be added to any number in the schedules unless instructions in the schedule indicate otherwise. Some restrictions on the use of standard subdivisions are discussed in section 3.37 in the Editor's Introduction to the DDC (DDC, Vol. 1, pp. 33-34).

Again, each standard subdivision is preceded by a single −0 (e.g., −03), in many places in the schedules there are directions to use a double or even triple −0 to introduce a standard subdivision (e.g., 342.005, 350.0008). This is necessary to preserve the hierarchical order when the −0 division is used for other special purposes. Some examples will illustrate the principles of the application of standard subdivisions:

(1)   **Standard subdivisions as part of a complete number.**

In some parts of the DDC schedules, a concept or format ordinarily expressed as a standard subdivision has its own number—e.g., 803 is a dictionary of literature, not 800.3 or 800.03.

(2) **Standard subdivision introduced by a double −0 when a single −0 is used for a specific purpose.**

An example of the double −0 is found at 342. The instructions say to use 342.001−342.009 for standard subdivisions. Here the single −0 is used for specific topics—e.g., 342.04 (structure of government), 342.05 (legislative branch of government). Therefore, a serial publication on public law is classed in 342.005.

(3) **Standard subdivision introduced by a triple −0 when a double −0 is used for a special purpose.**

An example of the triple −0 is found at 350. Here the instructions say to use 350.0001−350.0009 for standard subdivisions. Here the double −0 is used for specific topics—e.g., 350.001 (bureaucracy) and 350.009 (special commissions, corporations, agencies, quasi-administrative bodies). Therefore, a dictionary of public administration is classed in 350.0003.

Areas Table (Table 2)

The notations in this table, the largest auxiliary table, allow a number to be expanded to indicate a geographical significance. Throughout the DDC schedules there are instructions to "add area notation" to build a more specific classification number. Where no specific instructions are given in the schedules for adding the area notation, the standard subdivision −09 for historical and geographical treatment can be added to the base number, and then the area notation can be added to −09. The summary of the areas table is given in Fig. 1-3.

Fig. 1-3. Areas (Table 2)

SUMMARY

−1	Areas, regions, places in general
−2	Persons regardless of area, region, place
−3	The ancient world
	−4−9 The modern world
−4	Europe
−5	Asia Orient Far East
−6	Africa
−7	North America
−8	South America
−9	Other parts of world and extraterrestrial worlds Pacific Ocean Islands (Oceania)

The area notation −1 is used for areas not limited by continents, countries or localities. Included are the treatment of a subject by region, areas, places, and groups in general. Also included here are such geographical features as frigid zones, land forms, oceans and socioeconomic regions. Area notation −2 is used for biographical materials. Therefore, a collection of biographies of people in elementary education would be classed in 372.9<u>22</u>. Instructions in the schedule at 372.91—.99 tell the classifier to add "Areas" notation —1—9 from Table 2 to base number 372.9:

372.9	base number for geographical treatment of elementary education
<u>22</u>	area notation for collective biography (from Table 2)
372.922	collective biography of elementary educators

Notation —3 is used for the ancient world. Notations —4 to —9 are used for specific continents, countries, and localities in the modern world. Each area is further subdivided; for example, —73, the notation for the United States, has the following subdivisions:

—73	United States
—74	Northeastern United States
—75	Southeastern United States
—76	South central United States
—77	North central United States
—78	Western United States
—79	Pacific Coast States

Each area notation is further subdivided for more localized areas, and the numbers are correspondingly longer:

—79	Pacific Coast States
—794	California
—7949	Southern (California) counties
—79493	Los Angeles County
—79494	Los Angeles City

The following examples show the two methods used to add an area notation to a base number. At some places in the schedule there are instructions to add the area notation to the base number. A general work on the Roman Catholic Church will be classed in number 282. Instructions at 282 say to "add Areas notation 4—9 from Table 2 to base number 282" (Fig. 1-4).

Fig. 1-4. Classification Schedule

282	**Roman Catholic Church**
	Class Oriental churches in communion with Rome in 281.5—281.8
.09	Historical and geographical treatment
	Class treatment by continent, country, locality in 282.4—282.9
.4—.9	Treatment by continent, country, locality
	Add "Areas" notation 4—9 from Table 2 to base number 282

A work on the Roman Catholic Church in the city of Los Angeles will have number 282.79494:

282		Roman Catholic Church
	79494	area notation for Los Angeles city (from Table 2)
282.79494		Roman Catholic Church in the city of Los Angeles

If specific instructions are not given for geographical treatment in the schedules, the standard subdivision −09 (historical and geographical treatment) can be added to any base number that can be logically developed. Then to −09 (or −009 or −0009, depending on whether a single, double, or triple −0 is required) add the proper area notation. For example, 332.1 is the general number for banks and banking, and there are no instructions for adding area notation. Thus, a work on banking in the city of Los Angeles would be classified in number 332.10979494:

332.1		banks and banking
	09	standard subdivision for historical and geographical treatment (from Table 1)
	79494	area notation for Los Angeles city (from Table 2)
332.10979494		banks and banking in the city of Los Angeles

Individual Literatures (Table 3)

The notations in Table 3, Subdivisions of Individual Literatures, are used only with base numbers 810–890. There are special subdivisions of the standard subdivisions −08 for collections of literature and −09 for history, description, or critical appraisal of literature. For example, a work on idealism in French literature is classified in number 840.913. The number is built by adding the notation −0913 for idealism from Table 3 to the base number 84 for French literature. A work on women writers in France will have number 840.99287; 84 is the base number for French literature, and −099287, from Table 3, is the notation for literature written by women. In addition, Table 3 contains the standard mnemonic notation for individual literary forms. The following form divisions apply to all numbers in the 800's:

- −1 poetry (811 American, 821 English)
- −2 drama (812 American, 822 English)
- −3 fiction (813 American, 853 Italian)
- −4 essays (814 American, 834 German)
- −5 speeches (815 American, 845 French)
- −6 letters (816 American, 846 French)
- −7 satire and humor (817 American, 867 Spanish)
- −8 miscellaneous writing (818 American, 868 Spanish)

This table will be discussed in more detail in Chapter 10.

Individual Languages (Table 4)

The notations in Table 4, Subdivisions of Individual Languages, are used only with base numbers 420–490. The following form divisions apply to all numbers in this class:

−1   written and spoken codes (42<u>1</u> English, 43<u>1</u> German)

−2   etymology (42<u>2</u> English, 43<u>2</u> German)

−3   dictionaries (42<u>3</u> English, 44<u>3</u> French)

−4   unassigned

−5   structural system, grammar (42<u>5</u> English, 43<u>5</u> German)

−6   prosody (42<u>6</u> English, 45<u>6</u> Italian)

−7   nonstandard language (42<u>7</u> English, 46<u>7</u> Spanish)

−8   standard usage (42<u>8</u> English, 45<u>8</u> Italian)

For example, a work in English on reading will be classified in number 428.4. The number is built by adding the notation −84 for reading, from Table 4, to the base number 42 for the English language. A work on spelling in the English language will have number 428.1; 42 is the base number for the English language, and −81 is for words including spelling, from Table 4. This table will be discussed in greater detail in Chapter 6.

Racial, Ethnic, National Groups (Table 5)

The notations in Table 5, Racial, Ethnic, National Groups, are used when directed in the schedules. These notations can be added to base numbers in the schedules and to notations from other tables (this is just like adding geographical notations from Table 2 to standard subdivision −09 from Table 1). The summary of this table is:

−1   North Americans

−2   Anglo-Saxons, British, English

−3   Nordics

−4   Modern Latins

−5   Italians, Romanians, related groups

−6   Spanish and Portuguese

−7   Other Italic people

−8   Greeks and related groups

−9   Other racial, ethnic, national groups

A work on Jews as non-dominant aggregates will be classified in number 301.451924. The number is built by adding −924, the notation in Table 5 for Jews, to base number 301.451 for aggregates of specific national, racial, and ethnic groups. This table will be discussed further in Chapter 9.

Languages (Table 6)

The notations in Table 6, Languages, are used as directed in the schedules. These notations can be added to base numbers in the schedules and to notations from other tables. This table is particularly important in the classes 400 and 800. A summary of these language mnemonics is:

−1   Indo-European languages

−2   English and Anglo-Saxon languages

−3   Germanic languages

−4   French and related languages

−5   Italian, Romanian, Rhaeto-Romanic

−6   Spanish and Portuguese

−7   Italic languages

−8   Hellenic languages

−9   Other languages

The Bible translated into Serbo-Croatian will be classified in number 220.59182. The number is built by adding −9182, the notation in Table 6 for the Serbo-Croatian language, to the base number 220.5 for the Bible. This table will be discussed in more detail in Chapter 2.

Persons (Table 7)

The notations in Table 7, Persons, are used as directed in the schedules. These notations can be added to base numbers in the schedules and to notations from other tables.

−01   Individual persons in general

−02   Groups of persons in general

−03−08   Persons with nonoccupational characteristics

−03   Persons by racial, ethnic, national background (using Table 5 for subdivisions)

−04   Persons by sex and kinship characteristics

−05   Persons by age

−06   Persons by social and economic characteristics

−08   Persons by physical and mental characteristics

−09	Generalists and novices (for example, librarians are −092)
−1−9	Specialists

−1	Persons occupied with philosophy
−2	Persons occupied with religion
−3	Persons occupied with social sciences
−4	Persons occupied with linguistics
−5	Persons occupied with pure sciences
−6	Persons occupied with applied sciences
−7	Persons occupied with the arts (for example, −78, musicians)
−8	Persons occupied with creative writing and speaking
−9	Persons occupied with geography, history, related disciplines

From −09 to −9 this table is based on the ten main classes of DDC.

A manual on sex education for school children will be classified in number 301.4180544. The number is built by adding −0544, the notation in Table 7 for school children, to base number 301.418, for sex instruction. This number can be analyzed as follows:

301.418	manuals on sex instruction
05	persons by age
054	children
0544	school children
301.4180544	a manual on sex instruction for school children

The Classification Schedules–Notes and Instructions in the Schedules

Throughout the DDC schedules (and tables) there are instructional notes to aid and direct the classifier. We will discuss here the "scope note" and the "class here note."

Scope Notes and Class Here Notes

The scope note usually appears after a major classification number, stating exactly what is to be classed in the number. One example of a scope note is found at 604.6, the number for waste technology (Fig. 1-5).

Fig. 1-5. Classification Schedule, Scope Note

604

.6 **Waste technology**

> Methods and equipment for salvaging and utilizing waste materials; products manufactured from waste materials [*formerly 679.9*]
>
> Class utilization of a specific waste material, manufacture of a specific product with the subject, e.g., scrap metals 669.042

The first note defines the scope of the subject to be classed in the number. The second note suggests alternative numbers for more specialized aspects of waste technology.

Another example of a scope note is found at 541.28, the number for quantum chemistry (Fig. 1-6). This note defines the term and lists special topics that are also to be classified in the number.

Fig. 1-6. Classification Schedule, Note

541

.28   Quantum chemistry

           Use of wave and other quantum mechanics for study of chemical structure and reactions in terms of motion of electrons

           Including molecular and atomic orbitals, magnetic resonance spectroscopy, other spectroscopy used for study of chemical structure and reactions

An example of a "class here" type note is found at 358.17 (Fig. 1-7). The first note directs the classifier to use 358.17 for comprehensive works on missile forces, warfare, and defense. The second note gives directions for building numbers for specialized subtopics. The last note is a "class elsewhere" direction relating to major aspects of a broader topic.

Fig. 1-7. Classification Schedule, "Class here" Note

358

.17   Guided (Strategic) land missile forces and warfare

           Class here comprehensive works on missile forces, warfare, defense

           Add to 358.17 the numbers following 623.4519 in 623.45194−623.45196, e.g., long-range surface-to-surface missile-launching forces 358.1754

           Class air missile forces in 358.42−358.43, naval missile forces in 359.981

Always read all the notes before using a DDC number. The notes are essential for number building and for determining where to classify materials. Failure to read and carefully follow the notes in the DDC schedules will result in incorrect classification or incorrectly built numbers.

Base Number and Number Building

The base number is a sequence of numbers that does not vary but remains the same in any sequence. To a base number digits from other parts of the schedule or from the tables can be added as instructed. For example, at 499 in the schedule several base numbers are listed to which other digits from the schedule and tables can be added (Fig. 1-8).

Fig. 1-8. Classification Schedule, Base Numbers

499   **Other languages**

           Add "Languages" notation 99 from Table 6 to base number 4

           Base number for *Tagalog (Filipino): 499.211

           Base number for *Indonesian (Bahasa Indonesia): 499.221

           Base number for *Javanese: 499.222

           Base number for *Malay (Pidgin Malay, Bazaar Malay): 499.28

           Base number for *Malagasy: 499.3

           Base number for *Esperanto: 499.992

           Base number for *Interlingua: 499.993

*Add to base number as instructed under 420−490

The base number for all languages is 4, as it is for the entire class. All numbers are added to base number 4. The base number for Tagalog is 499.211. Instructions tell the classifier to add to the base number as instructed under 420—490. Thus, in any sequence the base number does not vary, as the following examples show:

499.21101	philosophy and theory of Tagalog
499.211152	spelling and pronunciation of Tagalog
499.2113	dictionary of Tagalog

The base number for American literature is 81:

810	American literature in English
811	American poetry
811.5	20th century American poetry
813	American fiction

It is from the base numbers that the classifier builds more specific numbers for the materials being cataloged. Number building is the process of developing a number by the addition of numbers or segments of numbers from other parts of the schedule, from the tables, or both.

Centered Heading

At various places in the DDC schedules the hierarchical structure cannot be closely observed; this is shown by a span of numbers in the schedule. These spans of numbers, called "centered headings," represent a concept for which no more specific number exists; the concept is therefore assigned to a span of numbers. The "centered headings" are identified in the scheduled by a triangular mark ▶ (Fig. 1-9).

Fig. 1-9. Centered Heading

▶ 381—382 General internal and international commerce (Trade)

Class comprehensive works in 380.1

381 Internal commerce (Domestic trade)

.3 Commercial policy

Class commercial policy with respect to specific commodities and services in 381.4

.4 Specific commodities and services

▶ 381.41—381.43 Products of primary (extractive) industries

Class comprehensive works in 381.4

Note that in Fig. 1-9 comprehensive works on commerce are assigned to 380.1 because no specific number is provided within the span of 381–382 for comprehensive works. In the Editor's Introduction to the DDC "centered headings" are also defined as "steps in the successive divisions of a discipline or subject for which positions in the lengthening digital notations are not available (DDC, Vol. 1, p. 39).

Relative Index

The Relative Index brings together the various aspects and relationships of a topic. It is an alphabetical listing of all the main headings in the DDC schedules, showing also synonyms and, to a large degree, the relation of each subject to other subjects. The DDC defines "relativity" as "that property of the index which reverses the subordination of subject to discipline, thus bringing together from all disciplines the various aspects of individual subjects" (DDC, Vol. 1, p. 60). Earlier it was pointed out that the DDC scatters aspects of subjects by discipline throughout the schedules. The Relative Index brings together the various aspects of a topic, as shown in the following example:

Children

art representation	704.9425
ethics	170.20222
etiquette	395.122
hygiene	613.0432
psychology	155.4
sociology	301.4314

The DDC principle of classification by discipline is demonstrated here: six aspects of the main subject "children" are placed in different disciplines in the schedules and are brought together in the Relative Index. Use of the DDC Relative Index will be discussed in the following chapters, with many detailed examples.

The Relative Index does not include most proper names, names of most cities, countries, animals, plants, chemical compounds, geographical names, organizations, drugs, and manufactured articles. The Relative Index *does* include entries for "every significant term named in the schedules and tables."

SPECIFIC CHARACTERISTICS OF THE 10TH ABRIDGED EDITION

The 10th abridged edition of the DDC is an *independent* volume and "is not . . . in the strictest sense an *abridgment* of the full 18th edition, but a close *adaptation* of it" (Abridged DDC, p. 3). The abridged edition is intended for use in small general libraries with 20,000 or fewer titles and with no expectation of growth beyond that size. This is a change from earlier abridged editions, which were developed on the premise that a library would ultimately grow large enough to use the unabridged edition.

SEGMENTATION OF DDC NUMBERS

In the following chapters we will give examples of building DDC numbers. Many of the numbers will be long—far too long for many small libraries. The same problem of length exists for DDC numbers developed by the Library of Congress and printed on Library of Congress cards. Since 1967, therefore, the DDC numbers on LC cards and in LC printed catalogs have been divided into *segments*. For example, a work on Mexicans in the United States will be assigned number 301.45′16′872073. The segmenting is shown by prime marks, which are *not* part of the DDC number. The DDC number can be divided at each prime mark without losing its meaning. The library, depending on its needs, can select any of these numbers for the above book: 301.45, 301.4516, or 301.4516872073.

DDC numbers are segmented on the premise that a five-digit number is the maximum needed in a small library and a seven-digit number is the maximum needed for a medium-sized library. Numbers are printed in one, two, and three segments. Those that appear in one segment should generally be used without reduction (e.g., 372.6). If a number is printed in two segments, small libraries are advised to use the first segment, while other libraries should use the whole number (e.g., 372.6′32 can be used as 372.6 or 372.632, depending on the library's size). If a number is printed in three segments, the first segment can be used by small libraries, the first two segments by medium-sized libraries, and all three segments by larger libraries (e.g., as shown above, 301.45′16′872073 can be used as 301.45, 301.4516, or 301.4516872073). These are only general suggestions; each library must establish a policy for particular situations.

The DDC numbers in this book have *not* been segmented. The emphasis in these chapters is on number building. While working the exercises, however, the student might give thought to the question of where the numbers could be segmented.

SOURCES OF DDC NUMBERS

Libraries that use the DDC have a choice of sources to help in finding a classification number. Although the library staff can do "in-house" classification, many sources are currently available for pre-assigned DDC numbers. A DDC number is printed on the cards available from a commercial cataloging service such as Josten's or LJ (Xerox Bibliographics). See Figs. 1-10, 1-11.

Fig. 1-10. Commercial Cataloging Service Card (Josten's)

```
016.382  Hogg, Peter C
 44096      The African slave trade and its sup-
Hogg       pression, a classified and annotated
           bibliography of books, pamphlets and
           periodical articles [by] Peter C. Hogg.
           London, Frank Cass [1973]
           409 p.
           (Cass Library of African studies. Gen-
           eral studies, no. 137)


           1.Slave-trade—Africa—Bibliography. 2.
           Slave-trade—Bibliography. 3.Slavery—Bi-
           bliography.      I.(Series) II.Title

           016.382'44'096     Z7164.S6H63 1973
                                            72-90130
```

Fig. 1-11. Commercial Cataloging Service Card
(LJ—Xerox Bibliographics)

Zaffo, George
　　The giant nursery book of things that go; fire engines, trains, boats, trucks, airplanes. Doubleday 1959
　　189p illus

　　"All the moving vehicles that small children love are pictured in action and discussed in the text." — Library Journal

　　1. Picture books for children　2. Transportation　I. Title

B 4-619　　　　　　　　　　　　　　　　　　E; 385
LJ Cards Inc © 1965　　　　　　　　　　　　—p

Before using a commercial cataloging service it is necessary to determine whether they get DDC numbers from the abridged or full edition.

Many bibliographic sources also give DDC numbers. Before using these sources, one should check to see which edition of the DDC is used to build numbers. The more important sources are:

> *American Book Publishing Record* (BPR) (Fig. 1-12, below)
> *Book Review Digest* (Fig. 1-13, page 37)
> *The Booklist*
> *National Union Catalog* (NUC) (Fig. 1-14, page 38)
> *Weekly Record* (WR)
> H. W. Wilson's *Standard Catalog Series: Children's Catalog, Junior High School Catalog* (Fig. 1-15, page 38), *Senior High School Catalog, Public Library Catalog.*

Fig. 1-12. *American Book Publishing Record*

GRAVES, Robert, 1895-   809.7 ◀——
Mrs. Fisher : or, The future of humour / by Robert Graves. Norwood, Pa. : Norwood Editions, 1975. p. cm. Reprint of the 1928 ed. published by K. Paul, Trench, Trubner, London, and Dutton, New York, in series: To-day and to-morrow. [PN6147.G7 1975] 75-43915 ISBN 0-88305-839-1 lib. bdg. : 12.50
1. Wit and humor—History and criticism. I. Title. II. Title: The future of humour. III. Series: To-day and to-morrow.
Prepared from C.I.P.

FEMINIST literary   809'.933'52 ◀——
criticism : explorations in theory / Josephine Donovan, editor. Lexington : University Press of Kentucky, c1975. 81 p. ; 22 cm. Includes bibliographical references. [PN98.W64F4] 75-12081 ISBN 0-8131-1334-2 pbk. : 4.00
1. Criticism. 2. Women in literature. 3. Women authors. I. Donovan, Josephine, 1941-
Contents omitted.

Fig. 1-13. *Book Review Digest*

PAINE, ROBERTA M. Looking at architecture.
127p il $6.95; lib bdg $5.81 '74 Lothrop
720.9 Architecture—History—Juvenile literature
ISBN 0-688-41553-9; 0-688-51553-3 (lib bdg)
LC 73-17718
"Through black-and-white photographs and reproductions this explores great buildings of the world—the pyramids, the Parthenon, the Great Wall of China, Gothic churches, the Taj Mahal, Versailles Palace, the capitol in Washington, D.C., Moshe Safdie's Habitat '67, etc. [It] also includes a glossary of building materials, [and] notes on the architects. [Bibliography. Index.] Grades four to seven." (Library J)

Horn Bk 50:149 O '74 200w

"Although Paine's personal opinions (about skyscrapers, building codes, etc.) surface in the discussion of 20th-Century architecture, this is otherwise an objective account which gives much interesting and useful information on different building techniques." V'Anne Didzun
Library J 99:2275 S 15 '74 90w

" 'Find me China!' came the cry from my 8-year-old, and wonder of wonders, here was a children's architecture book that had China. 'Is Africa there?' and sure enough, there was Nigerian architecture. Books on architecture for children are rare, and cross-cultural global ones as agreeable as this, even rarer. What Paine's . . . approach loses in historic continuity, it gains in richness. . . . The explanations are clear and the photographs fine; the book is well priced. Alas, however, for the last quarter of the book dealing with contemporary architecture. Paine . . . must be awed to the point of visual paralysis to devote a half-dozen pages to Moshe Safdie, sound though his work be, with nary a word for the Bauhaus, Le Corbusier, Louis Sullivan, Gropius, Frank Lloyd Wright, et al. Nevertheless, these startling exclusions . . . should not lessen the value of the 100 preceding pages." J. H. Kay
Nation 219:314 O 5 '74 250w

Reviewed by Paul Goldberger
N Y Times Bk R p8 Je 2 '74 550w

Fig. 1-14. *National Union Catalog*

Nicholls, Bronwen.
  Move! / ₍by₎ Bronwen Nicholls ; photographs by Chris-
topher Nicholls, John Lancaster ₍and₎ John Tweg. — South
Yarra, Vic. : Heinemann Educational, 1974.
  90 p. : ill. ; 24 cm. — (Australian theatre workshop ; 8)   Aus
  ISBN 0-858️-077-8 : $3.50
  1. Drama in education. 2. Movement (Acting)   I. Title.
  PN3171.N5   1974   792'.07'1294   75-306866
                                                          MARC

Nichols, Marion.
  Encyclopedia of embroidery stitches, including crewel /
Marion Nichols. — New York : Dover Publications, 1974.
  xii, 218 p. : ill. ; 29 cm.
  Includes index.
  ISBN 0-486-22929-7 : $4.95
  1. Embroidery.   I. Title.
  TT770.N48   746.4'4   72-97816
                                              MARC

Nichols, Peter, 1927–
  Chez nous ; a domestic comedy in two acts / by Peter
Nichols. — London : Faber, 1974.
  83 p. ; 21 cm.   GB 74-26057
  ISBN 0-571-10583-1 : £2.00. ISBN 0-571-10602-1 pbk.
  I. Title.
  PR6064.I 2C5   822'.9'14   75-302079
                                              MARC

Fig. 1-15. *Junior High School Catalog**

Knight, David C.
The tiny planets; asteroids of our solar
system; with 21 photographs and diagrams.
Morrow 1973 95p illus $4.50, lib. bdg. $4.14
                                    523.4 ◄────
1 Planets
ISBN 0-688-20072-9; 0-688-30072-3
  A historical and scientific study of asteroids including chapters on their discovery
and history, their orbits and natural characteristics
  "This volume will prove fascinating reading
for the more sophisticated science student who
has already made some study of the solar system. The topic of asteroids is rarely covered
with much detail in more general volumes on
the solar system. 'The Tiny Planets' is a most
enjoyable answer to this need. . . . Most certainly this is not a book for beginners. The
information is quite sophisticated while the
absence of many pictures and the presence of
long chapters assume mature reading skills."
Appraisal

*Reprinted by permission. Copyright ©1975 by The H. W. Wilson Company.

PRINCIPLES OF BOOK CLASSIFICATION

Classifying books has been defined " . . . as the art of assigning books to their proper places in a system of classification in which the various subjects of human inquiry, or the descriptions of human life in its various aspects, are grouped according to their likeness or relation to one another."[4] In practice, however, this is not an easy task. Catalogers use the following general principles when selecting a DDC number:

1) Class a book, or any other material, where it will be most useful to the patron. This can usually be accomplished by placing similar materials together. This may also be accomplished by the use of broad or close classification depending on library needs.

2) Class a book first by subject and second by form, except in the field of literature. For example, an encyclopedia of art will be classed in art and not with general encyclopedias. The subject, art, is more important than the form, an encyclopedia. (Thus, in DDC the work would be classed in 703 for fine arts, not in 030 for general encyclopedias.)

3) Class a work of literature first by its original language and second by its form. For example, a work on French poetry translated into English will be classed in the number for French poetry, not for English poetry, because the original language is French. After the original language of the work has been determined, it is then classed by form (drama, poetry, fiction, essays, speeches, and letters).

4) Class a book that covers two or three subjects under the first subject treated unless another subject receives more prominent attention. A book that treats first chemistry and then physics but that gives equal treatment to each is classed with the first subject treated—chemistry.

5) Class a book that covers more than three subjects in a general subject embracing all of the subjects. For example, a book treating mathematics, astronomy, physics, and chemistry will be classed with comprehensive works on pure science. A work treating arithmetic, algebra, trigonometry, and geometry is classed with comprehensive works on mathematics.

6) Class a book in the most specific number possible in the classification scheme. For example, a history of the American Civil War will be classed in a specific number for the Civil War and not in a more general number. A work on the banjo is classed in the specific number for the banjo and not in a general number for string instruments. Classifying a book in too general a number defeats the purpose of classification, since it places books on specific topics in meaningless order.

7) In general, class a book first by subject if there is a choice between subject and geographical location. For example, a book on German architecture is classed in the number for architecture, not in the number for geography of Germany.

---

[4]William Stetson Merrill, *Code for Classifiers; Principles Governing the Consistent Placing of Books in a System of Classification*, 2nd edition (Chicago, American Library Association, 1939), p. 1.

8) Class biographies, autobiographies, diaries, and reminiscences either together in a general biography number or with specific disciplines. For example, a biography of a lawyer is classed either in a general number covering biographies of people regardless of occupation or in a number in law used for biographies of lawyers, judges, etc.

9) Class a book according to the author's intent in writing it. For example, if an author produces a book of drawings of dogs the cataloger must examine the book to see if the book is meant to emphasize the drawing of different breeds or techniques of drawing dogs. Depending on the author's intent, the book could be classed in a number for dogs or a number for techniques of drawing.

THE REMAINING CHAPTERS

The next 10 chapters cover the main classes of the DDC. The materials in each chapter are presented in 7 sections: "Introductory Note," "Outline of the Class," "Introduction to the Class," "Details of the Class," "Number Building," "Problems to Solve," and "Answers to Problems." In each chapter the section called "Details of the Class" is devoted to a narrative description of the disciplines and topics covered by the sections in each main class. The reader should study carefully the "Details of the Class" and not jump directly to "Number Building." Familiarity with the DDC schedules is a valuable aid in classification and should not be underestimated. Experienced catalogers often rely more on a knowledge of the DDC schedules than on the Relative Index.

The DDC numbers built in the "Number Building" sections may be longer than some libraries need. These numbers, however, were selected primarily because they provide experience in using the DDC. In practice most libraries would, in fact, use shorter numbers. To use the DDC properly and be aware of its potential, one should know how to build longer numbers even if a particular library uses no more than six- or seven-digit numbers. For the most part, the examples in the "Problems to Solve" section require only six- or seven-digit answers.

To avoid any possible confusion and to emphasize number building, the segmentation marks have been omitted from the numbers in Chapters 2 through 11. The "Additional Problems" section at the end of the text, however, does provide segmentation marks with the answers. If the reader is interested in the possible placement of segmentation marks for any DDC number used in this text, he could check *American Book Publishers Record* (BPR), which includes the segmentation marks. In some cases the exact number may not be found, but the number is usually close enough to be helpful. Remember to check BPR from 1971 onward, because earlier years did not use the 18th edition of DDC and the numbers might be different.

As pointed out earlier, the reader must have a set of the DDC available as he proceeds through this text. By following each step in the DDC number building process, he will become familiar with the Relative Index, the schedules, and the various tables as they are used in the examples.

The DDC is subject to interpretation in determining where certain works should be classified. The examples and problems that follow were selected to classify in a particular class. In real cataloging situations many works are difficult to classify and can with justification be placed in any of several places in the DDC schedules. Even experienced catalogers often disagree on where a particular work should be classified. Classification is as much an art as a science. The emphasis in the examples and problems that follow is not only on selecting the proper class, but on number building once the proper class has been decided upon.

CHAPTER 2

CLASS 000–099
(GENERALITIES)

INTRODUCTORY NOTE

The structure of this chapter and the next nine chapters follows the arrangement and method noted at the end of Chapter 1. "Outline of the Class" and "Introduction to the Class" give the general subject scope and limitations of the class. The section that follows these, "Details of the Class," should be read carefully and compared to the DDC schedules for this class. This section is designed to highlight the coverage of material in the class and should lead the reader through the individual pages of the schedule. It is important to remember that this class deals with general material and not specific subject- or discipline-related material. For example, a general encyclopedia goes in this class, but an encyclopedia of philosophy would be classed in the philosophy class (100's); works about a general museum go here, but works about an art museum would go in the 700's, the class for fine arts. The section on number building demonstrates the application of Standard Subdivisions, the Areas Table, and the Languages Table to this class. This section clearly explains how to use the Relative Index of DDC in classification problems. Although many long DDC numbers are built in this section, all are simply constructed and explained by detailed examples. The examples can be followed through the DDC schedules. The last section of this chapter allows the student to assign five simple DDC numbers in this class.

OUTLINE OF THE CLASS

000	Generalities
010	Bibliographies and catalogs
020	Library and information sciences
030	General encyclopedic works
040	Not used
050	General serial publications and their indexes
060	General organizations and museology
070	Journalism, publishing, newspapers
080	General collections
090	Manuscripts and book rarities

INTRODUCTION TO THE CLASS

This class, called General Works in earlier editions of DDC, is devoted almost entirely to areas considered to be very general in nature (general encyclopedic works) and to a few areas that are more specific but are still general in nature (library science, journalism, and newspapers). These latter areas were placed here to some extent for historical editorial reasons. Today it would be possible to consider journalism, publishing, and newspapers (070) as more properly belonging in Communication Services (383–384).

The ten main divisions of this class are all concerned with the use and application of knowledge in general. Because this is the first chapter on the actual use of the DDC, the authors have provided a large number of figures to help the reader— examples from the schedules, from the Relative Index, and from various tables.

DETAILS OF THE CLASS

The first division includes the numbers 000 to 009. Here are found general works of knowledge (001). Some subdivisions are for scholarship and learning (001.2), general humanities (001.3), methodology and research (001.4), information and communication (001.5), data processing (001.6) and a place for controversial and spurious knowledge, unexplained phenomena, and hoaxes (001.9). The only other assigned subdivision is for systems theory, analysis and design (003).

The second division includes the numbers 010 to 019. This division is devoted to bibliographies and catalogs of books of individuals, classes of writers, and specific places and subjects. Also included here are library catalogs.

The next division, 020 to 029, is concerned with library and information science, defined by the DDC as "the science and art utilized in identification, collection, organization, exploitation of books, other printed and written records, audiovisual materials" (DDC, Vol. 2, p. 470). Some of the subdivisions of this division include general library matters, library goals and development, library facilities, personnel matters, library use and operations, use of books and documentation (i.e., abstracting, indexing, and information retrieval).

The division 030 to 039 is used to classify general encyclopedic works, encyclopedias in various languages, and works about encyclopedias.

Currently no subject is assigned to 040 to 049.

General serial publications, their indexes, and books about serials are assigned to 050 to 059. Periodicals on specific subjects are assigned to subject areas. For example, a chemistry periodical would be classified in 540.5.

The division 060 to 069 encompasses the subjects of general organizations and museum science. Included here would be the history, regulations, reports and proceedings of general organizations such as societies, foundations, associations, and congresses. Domestic, foreign, and international associations are included. Associations concerned with specific areas are classified with subject areas (for example, the proceedings of the American Chemical Society would be classified in 540.6). General rules of order are included here (060.42). The last subdivision, 069, is used for museology or museum science and the related services, facilities, and collections.

Journalism, publishing and newspapers are covered by division 070 to 079. Examples of subjects included here are news media (070.1); writing and editing for newspapers, periodicals, radio and television (070.4); activities associated with publishing (070.5); and the historical treatments of newspapers and journalism (070.9). The remaining numbers are assigned to geographical treatment of newspapers and journalism.

The division 080 to 089 is devoted to general collections of essays, addresses, lectures, and quotations. Some emphasis is placed on works from various geographic areas and in various languages.

The last division, 090 to 099, is concerned with manuscripts and book rarities. Book rarities include books distinguished by printing date, edition, typography, binding, illustrations, ownership, content, and format.

NUMBER BUILDING, 000–099

The following examples will help illustrate the use of the 000–099 class and the application of Standard Subdivisions (Table 1) and the Areas Table (Table 2). Using a copy of the DDC with this section will help the reader follow each step in the process of building a classification number.

Obviously it is not possible to give examples that cover every possible classification problem or that show how to build every number. The examples for this schedule, and for each of the following schedules, were developed to help illustrate in general how to build a classification number.

Example 1

Where would you classify a general book on electronic data processing? The first place to look is the Relative Index. The index should be used to help you get to the proper place in the schedules. Do not classify directly from the index. The Relative Index provides several approaches to the problem. Under the entry "Computers" there is a reference to "Electronic data processing" (Fig. 2-1).

Fig. 2-1. Relative Index

Entry ⟶ Computers
documentation use   029.7
"See" Reference ⟶ electronic data proc. *see*
     Electronic data
     processing
   electronic eng.
     prod. econ.   338.476 213 819 5
      s.a. spec. aspects e.g.
      Finance
     tech. & mf.   621.381 95
      s.a. spec. uses e.g.
      Data processing
      other mf. aspects see
       Manufacturing firms
     marketing *see* Marketing

If you first looked under "Data" you might be confused unless you read carefully and found the term "Electronic data processing" under "Data—cells—electronic data processing" and a reference to see "Inputs—electronic data proc." (Fig. 2-2).

Fig. 2-2. Relative Index

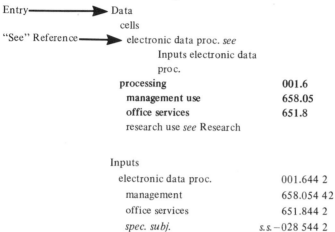

Entry⟶	Data	
	cells	
"See" Reference⟶	electronic data proc. *see*	
	Inputs electronic data proc.	
	processing	**001.6**
	management use	**658.05**
	office services	**651.8**
	research use *see* Research	
	Inputs	
	electronic data proc.	001.644 2
	management	658.054 42
	office services	651.844 2
	spec. subj.	*s.s.* −028 544 2

The number cited at "Inputs—electronic data proc." (001.644 2) is in the correct general area, but it is more specific than required. The number cited with "Data processing" (001.6) is the general number for data processing, as you will find when you check the schedule.

Go to the entry for "Electronic data processing," which is the exact term you want. Here there is a reference to number 001.64 (Fig. 2-3).

Fig. 2-3. Relative Index

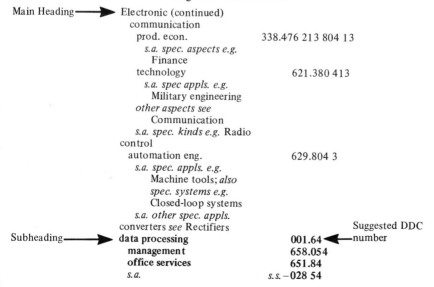

Main Heading⟶	Electronic (continued)	
	communication	
	prod. econ.	338.476 213 804 13
	s.a. spec. aspects e.g.	
	Finance	
	technology	621.380 413
	s.a. spec appls. e.g.	
	Military engineering	
	other aspects see	
	Communication	
	s.a. spec. kinds e.g. Radio	
	control	
	automation eng.	629.804 3
	s.a. spec. appls. e.g.	
	Machine tools; *also*	
	spec. systems e.g.	
	Closed-loop systems	
	s.a. other spec. appls.	
	converters *see* Rectifiers	Suggested DDC
Subheading⟶	data processing	001.64◀—number
	management	658.054
	office services	651.84
	s.a.	*s.s.* −028 54

Now go to the schedule to check the number (Fig. 2-4).

Fig. 2-4. Classification Schedule

001

.6	**Data processing**	
	Class data processing in a specific discipline or subject with the discipline or subject using "Standard Subdivisions" notation 0285 from Table 1, e.g., data processing in banking 332.10285	
.61	Systems analysis	
	Including preparation of system flow charts	
.62	Nonmechanized	
.63	Automatic	
	Including puncht-card data processing	
	For electronic data processing, see 001.64	
⟶ .64	Electronic	
.640 4	Specific types of computers	
⟶ .640 42	Analog	
.640 44	Digital	

001.64 is the correct number for a general work on electronic data processing. Notice that the numbers in the schedule get longer as the subject gets more specific. For example, a book on electronic data processing using an analog computer would have the number 001.640 42 (Fig. 2-4).

In the Relative Index for the abridged edition, the entry under "Data processing" cites number 001.6, which is as far as you can go for this edition. Notice that in the abridged edition the Relative Index entries "Electronics" and "Computers" have no subheadings for "Data processing."

Carrying our example one step further it is possible to build a number for data processing in a specific discipline or subject. In the schedule at 001.6 (see Fig. 2-4) there are instructions to use standard subdivisions (Table 1) notation −0285 and to class data processing in a specific discipline or subject with the discipline or subject. The example in the schedule—data processing for banking—is a good one. The subject is the application of data processing to banking, so banking is the primary subject. Thus, the DDC number for banking (332.1) is given first, and the standard subdivision for data processing (−0285) is added to build number 332.10285. Now we will go through the steps as if you had gone to banking as a subject first.

The Relative Index has entries for both "Banks" and "Banking" (Fig. 2-5); each of these entries has the subheading "economics," citing number 332.1.

Fig. 2-5. Relative Index

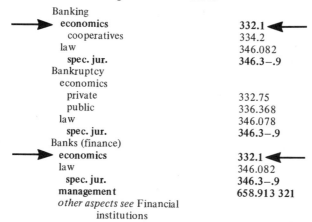

Banking
  economics   **332.1**
    cooperatives   334.2
    law   346.082
    spec. jur.   **346.3–.9**
Bankruptcy
  economics
    private   332.75
    public   336.368
    law   346.078
    spec. jur.   **346.3–.9**
Banks (finance)
  economics   **332.1**
    law   346.082
    spec. jur.   **346.3–.9**
    management   **658.913 321**
    other aspects see Financial
      institutions

Go to the schedule at 332.1, and you will see that it is the general number for banks and banking (Fig. 2-6).

Fig. 2-6. Classification Schedule

332.1–332.3 Financial institutions and their functions

    Class here clearinghouses [*formerly* 332.78]

    Class comprehensive works in 332.1

.1   **Banks and banking**

    Class here comprehensive works on money and banking, on financial institutions and their functions

    Class management of financial institutions in 658.913321

      For specialized banking institutions, see 332.2; *credit and loan institutions,* 332.3; *money,* 332.4; *credit,* 332.7

Now, following the instructions under 001.6 (Fig. 2-4), add the standard subdivision notation –0285 from Table 1 (Fig. 2-7) to the base number for banks and banking:

332.1	banks and banking
<u> 0285</u>	standard subdivision for data processing
332.10285	data processing in banking

Fig. 2-7. Standard Subdivisions (Table 1)

–028 5   Data processing

    Class here comprehensive works on data processing as applied to the subject

    Add to –0285 the numbers following 001.6 in 001.61–001.64, e.g., programing –028542

    Class data processing as methodology in –0183, in research in –072

In the abridged edition, the instructions at 001.6 state "class data processing in a specific subject with the subject, using 'Standard Subdivisions' notation 028 from Table 1." The number for banking in the abridged edition is also 332.1, so the resulting abridged edition notation is

332.1	banking
___028___	data processing (from the standard subdivisions notation)
332.1028	data processing in banking

By following simple directions, you have built a seven-digit number. Further, you should note that this seven-digit number consists of only two parts: first, the base number for banking (332.1), which is stated in the schedules, and second, the standard subdivision for data processing (028).

Using the full edition, you can build a number to reflect an even more specialized work on on-line systems of data processing in banking. Follow the "add to" instructions under —0285 (Fig. 2-7, page 47) to add the numbers following 001.6 in 001.61—001.64 (Fig. 2-4, page 46). The number for on-line data processing systems is 001.64404. Following the instructions at —0285, add the numbers following 001.6 to —0285 to build —02854404. Add this to the base number for banking to build:

332.1	banking
0285	data processing (from Table 1)
4	electronic (from 001.64, as instructed at —0285)
44	input, storage, output
___4404___	on-line systems
332.102854404	on-line data processing systems in banking

Remember that most libraries do not use numbers as long as this example. Our purpose here is to develop number building skills. Small libraries could class a book on on-line data processing in banks at either 332.1 or 332.10285 with satisfactory results.

Example 2

The classification of bibliographies on specific disciplines or topics provides some interesting examples because the DDC allows subject bibliographies to be classed together in 016 or with the subject (Fig. 2-8).

Fig. 2-8. Classification Schedule

016   **Bibliographies and catalogs of specific disciplines and subjects**

If preferred, class with the specific discipline or subject using "Standard Subdivisions" notation 016 from Table 1, e.g., bibliographies of astronomy 520.16; or, if preferred, class with the specific discipline or subject adding 0 to the notation, e.g., bibliographies of science 500.0, of astronomy 520.0, of descriptive astronomy 523.0, of descriptive astronomy of stars 523.80; or, if preferred, class with the specific discipline or subject using book number A1 or Z9.

Add 001—999 to base number 016, e.g., bibliographies of astronomy 016.52

What DDC number would you assign to a bibliography of oceanography? If the subject approach is taken, begin by looking up "Oceanography" in the Relative Index (Fig. 2-9).

Fig. 2-9. Relative Index

Oceanography	551.46
libraries	026.551 46
misc. aspects see Special	
libraries	
museums	
desc. & colls.	551.460 074
museology	069.955 146
s.a. spec. activities e.g.	
Display	

Here you find the number 551.46. Checking the schedule (Fig. 2-10) verifies that this is the correct general number for oceanography.

Fig. 2-10. Classification Schedule

551

551.46–551.49 Water bodies

Class comprehensive works in 551.4

For geologic work of water, see 551.35

Oceanography ➤ .46   Oceans and seas (Oceanography)

Class here salt-water bodies

Standard Sub- ———➤ Use 551.46001–551.46009 for standard subdivisions

divisions note   *For dynamic oceanography, see 551.47; biological oceanography, 574.921–574.928*

If you had looked up "Bibliographies" in the Relative Index, you would have found the number 010. Checking the schedule, however, will show that 010 is too general a number. Always check the schedules and *do not* classify directly from the Relative Index since the Relative Index is only a finding tool for locating the proper area in the schedules. Keep looking through the schedule and you will find 016, the number for bibliographies on specific subjects (Fig. 2-8, page 48).

The instructions at 016 say to use the standard subdivision −016 from Table 1 (the dash means that the number must be appended to a base number and cannot be used alone) with the base number for the subject. Also the instructions under oceanography (551.46) include a "use" note stating that the numbers 551.46001−551.46009 are to be used for the standard subdivisions. This means that the standard subdivisions for oceanography must use a double zero, not a single one. A bibliography of oceanography will have the following number:

551.46		oceanography
0		required digit to introduce standard subdivisions for oceanography
	016	standard subdivision for bibliography (from Table 1, *not* from the schedules
551.460016		a bibliography of oceanography

Another example of when to use two zeroes is found in the instructions under 292 in the schedule. There you are told to use 001–009 for standard subdivisions. Thus a bibliography of classical religion would be classified in 292.0016. See also the instructions under 230 and 516 in the schedules for other examples using two zeroes with standard subdivisions (Figs. 2-11, 2-12).

Fig. 2-11. Classification Schedule

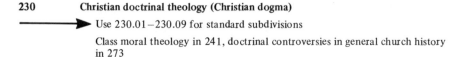

230   **Christian doctrinal theology (Christian dogma)**

Use 230.01–230.09 for standard subdivisions

Class moral theology in 241, doctrinal controversies in general church history in 273

Fig. 2-12. Classification Schedule

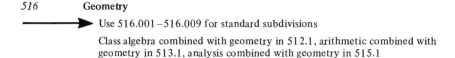

516   **Geometry**

Use 516.001–516.009 for standard subdivisions

Class algebra combined with geometry in 512.1, arithmetic combined with geometry in 513.1, analysis combined with geometry in 515.1

Example 3

The second major method used to classify bibliographies is to class them in 016 in the schedule (*not* –016, the standard subdivision) and add the subject number. The instructions at 016 say to add 001–999 to the base number 016 (Fig. 2-8, page 48). This means you can add any number in the schedule to 016 to provide for the specific subject being classified. Using this method, a bibliography of oceanography could have the number:

016   bibliographies of specific disciplines

__551.46__   oceanography (an example of a specific discipline)

016.55146   a bibliography of oceanography

Notice that the decimal is used *only* after the third digit (016.). When 551.46 is added after the decimal in "016." the second decimal is dropped. A DDC number can have only one decimal and it is *always* after the third digit.

A bibliography of architecture, using this method, will add the number for architecture (720) to base number 016:

016   bibliographies of specific disciplines

__720__   architecture (as explained below, the final zero will be dropped)

016.72   a bibliography of architecture

Notice that you do *not* use 016.720 since the general instructions for the DDC tell you to drop a zero digit on the far right of the decimal unless instructed otherwise (see DDC, Vol. 1, p. 40).

Two other alternatives for classifying bibliographies are suggested in the full edition but not in the abridged edition (Fig. 2-8, page 48). The first alternative is to add a final zero to the subject number. A bibliography of oceanography would then be 551.46<u>0</u>:

551.46	oceanography
<u> 0</u>	to indicate a bibliography
551.460	bibliography of oceanography

A bibliography of architecture would be 720.0. Notice that here you *do not* drop the final zero to the right of the decimal.

A second alternative for classifying subject bibliographies with their disciplines is the use of book numbers A1 or Z9. Using this method, our bibliographies of oceanography and architecture would be classified as follows:

551.46		551.46		720		720
A1	or	Z9		A1	or	Z9

The bibliographies will stand on the shelves either before the general works (A1) or after all other works on the subject (Z9).

The method a library uses to classify bibliographies must be applied consistently throughout the classification schedules. *Do not* use one method for one subject and another method for another subject.

The abridged edition provides only two methods for classifying bibliographies. The first is to add the standard subdivision −016 to the subject number, as in 551.4016 (the abridged edition number for oceanography is 551.4). A bibliography of architecture would be 720.16. The second suggested method is to add the subject number to 016 in the schedule (not −016 in Table 1). Thus, the bibliographies for oceanography and architecture would be 016.5514 and 016.72, respectively.

Example 4

The following examples help show the uses of Table 1 (Standard Subdivisions), Table 2 (Areas), and Table 6 (Languages).

A dictionary of architecture will be classified in 72<u>0.3</u>.The number is built as follows:

720	architecture
<u> 03</u>	standard subdivision for dictionaries (Fig. 2-13)
720.3	a dictionary of architecture

Fig. 2-13. Standard Subdivisions (Table 1)

−03   Dictionaries, encyclopedias, concordances

Do not use 720.0̲3̲ , because you are not instructed to use more than one zero. Examples of numbers that use more than one zero for a standard subdivision are a dictionary of Christian dogma (230̲.0̲3̲) and a dictionary of geometric terms (516.0̲0̲3̲). In both cases there are instructions in the schedule to use a double zero for standard subdivisions (Figs. 2-11, 2-12, on page 50).

The notations in Table 1 are also used to identify serial publications. Periodicals are the best known type of serial. If serials or periodicals are classified by discipline or subject, −05 is added to the base number. For example:

720   architecture

  05   standard subdivision for a serial

720.5̲ architectural serial

Notice that you again drop one zero because you are not instructed to use the double zero. Periodicals concerned with Christian dogma and geometry, however, would have numbers 230.0̲5̲ and 516.0̲0̲5̲, respectively, because the instructions in the schedule provide for the double zeroes (Figs. 2-11, 2-12, page 50).

If all serial or periodical publications are placed together, then they may be classed in number 050 from the schedule (*not* from Table 1) It should be noted that many libraries do not classify periodicals at all; they merely alphabetize them. If 050 is used, the titles can be arranged either alphabetically or by language and then alphabetically within each language. In the full edition the language option allows further number building through the use of Table 6, Languages. (See our discussion of Table 6 in Chapter 1.) A Spanish language periodical would be found in the schedule at 056 (Figs. 2-14, 2-15).

Fig. 2-14. Classification Schedule

056   **In Spanish and Portuguese**

             Add "Languages" notation 61–69 from Table 6 to base number 05, e.g., Portuguese-language serial publications 056.9

Fig. 2-15. Languages (Table 6)

−6	**Spanish and Portuguese**
−61	**Spanish**
−67	**Judeo-Spanish (Ladino)**
−68	**Papiamento**
−69	**Portuguese**
	Including Galician (Gallegan)

The instructions in the schedule at 056 direct you to add the required "Languages" notation 61–69 to base number 05. A Spanish language periodical would be classified 056.1:

05	base number for periodicals (from 050)
__61__	Spanish language (from Table 6)
056.1	Spanish language periodical

Now we will use the Areas Table (Table 2) in classifying a newspaper. What number would you assign to the Chicago *Tribune*? The Relative Index entry "Newspapers" cites number 070 for journalism, publishing, and newspapers. This is as far as some libraries classify newspapers (and, actually many libraries do *not* classify newspapers), since instructions in the schedule allow the alphabetic arrangement of newspapers under 070 (Fig. 2-16).

Fig. 2-16. Classification Schedule

071–079 Geographical treatment of newspapers and journalism

Class here specific general newspapers and works about them

Arrange geographically as below; but, if it is desired to give local emphasis and a shorter number to newspapers and journalism in a specific country, place them first by use of a letter or other symbol, e.g., newspapers and journalism in New Zealand 07N (preceding 071). See also option under 071

If preferred, arrange newspapers alphabetically under 070, using A1 for comprehensive works about them

Class comprehensive works in 070

If you want a more specific number, the abridged edition allows for the use of 071 for newspapers in the United States. The full edition allows for further number building through use of the Areas Table. At 071.3–.9 in the schedule are instructions to add to the base number 071 the numbers in the Areas Table *following* 7 in the notations 73–79, which cover the United States. Look through the Areas Table until you find −773 (Illinois), −7731 (Cook County) and −77311 (Chicago) (Fig. 2-17).

Fig. 2-17. Areas (Table 2)

| −773 | Illinois |
| | |

	SUMMARY
−773 1	**Cook County**
−773 2	**Northeastern counties**
−773 3	**Northwestern counties**
−773 4	**West central counties**
−773 5	**Central counties**
−773 6	**East central counties**
−773 7	**Southeastern counties**
−773 8	**Southwestern counties**
−773 9	**Southern counties**

| −773 1 | Cook County |
| −773 11 | Chicago |

Following the instructions under 071.3–.9, the number for the Chicago *Tribune* will be:

071	newspapers in North America
.7	area notation for North Central United States (i.e., –77; but remember that you use only the numbers *after* the first 7)
.73	area notation for Illinois (from 7<u>73</u>)
.731	area notation for Cook County (from 7<u>731</u>)
.7311	area notation for Chicago (from 7<u>7311</u>)
071.7311	the Chicago *Tribune*—a newspaper

Although this is a long DDC number, it was easy to build by following the directions in the schedule.

Where would you classify a work about the French National Library, the Bibliothèque Nationale? The Relative Indexes in both the full and the abridged DDC have a reference from "National libraries" to "Government libraries" (Fig. 2-18).

Fig. 2-18. Relative Index

Government (continued)	
libraries	
catalogs *see* Library	
catalogs	
gen. wks.	**027.5**
buildings	
architecture	727.825
functional planning	022.315
spec. groups	027.65

The entry "Libraries—spec. kinds" (Fig. 2-19) is also given in both editions, with a reference to numbers 026–027.

Fig. 2-19. Relative Index

Libraries	021
accounting	657.832
financial management	658.159 32
govt. control	
activities	350.852
govt. depts.	350.085 2
s.a. spec. levels of govt.	
law	344.092
spec. jur.	**344.3–.9**
residential int. dec.	747.73
s.a. spec. kinds of bldgs.;	
also spec. dec.	
⟶ spec. kinds	**026–027**

As you look through the schedule at 026–027, you will find the number 027.53–027.59 for specific libraries (Fig. 2-20).

Fig. 2-20. Classification Schedule

027

.5		**Government libraries**
		National, state, provincial
.509		Historical and geographical treatment
		Class specific institutions in 027.53–027.59
.53–.59		Specific institutions
		Add "Areas" notation 3–9 from Table 2 to base number 027.5

The instructions here tell you to add area notation 3–9 from Table 2 to base number 027.5. In Table 2, –4 is the area notation for Europe and –44 for France (Fig. 2-21).

Fig. 2-21. Areas (Table 2)

–44   **France and Monaco**

Class a specific overseas department of France with the subject, e.g., Martinique –72982

For Corsica, see –4595

The area notation –44 is as far as you need to go unless the subject is a government library of a more specific political subdivision. The number for the Bibliothèque Nationale will be:

027.5	governmental libraries
4	area notation for Europe
44	area notation for France
027.544	The Bibliothèque Nationale

Where would a book on an oceanographic library or architectural library be classified? The Relative Index entry "Special libraries" cites number 026. This will be the correct number for the abridged edition. The 18th edition allows for further number building by discipline (Fig. 2-22).

Fig. 2-22. Classification Schedule

026   **Libraries devoted to specific disciplines and subjects**

Class here information organizations and library departments and collections in specific fields; comprehensive works on special libraries

Use 026.0001–026.0009 for standard subdivisions

→ Add 001–999 to base number 026, e.g., medical libraries 026.61

Class special libraries not devoted to specific disciplines and subjects in 027.6

The third instruction (Fig. 2-22, page 55) says to add subject numbers 001 – 999 to the base number 026. Thus, a work on oceanographic libraries will have the following DDC number:

026	libraries devoted to special subjects
<u>551.46</u>	oceanography
026.55146	a work on oceanographic libraries (remember to move the decimal to its place after the third digit)

Using the abridged edition, the number would be 026. A work on architectural libraries will have the following DDC number:

026	libraries devoted to special subjects
<u>720</u>	architecture
026.72	a work on architectural libraries (remember to drop the zero when it is the last digit unless instructed otherwise)

Notice that under 026 there are instructions to use .0001 – .0009 for standard subdivisions. Here you can use *three* zeroes because you are instructed to do so. A periodical on special libraries will have the number 026.0005.

PROBLEMS TO SOLVE

Try to build classification numbers for the following hypothetical works:

1) a book on the Associated Press (a news service)
2) a book about books printed before 1501
3) a general collection of essays in Spanish
4) the French periodical *Paris Match*
5) the *World Book Encyclopedia*

ANSWERS TO PROBLEMS

1) 070.435 (18th edition)   070.4 (10th abridged edition)
      The Relative Index entry under "Press" leads you to the general number for journalism (070). You then go through the schedule until you arrive at the heading for specific journalistic activities (070.4). This is as far as you need go in the abridged edition, according to the listed instructions. The full edition leads you to the heading "Wire services," where you find the above number. If you first thought to look under the heading "Wire services" in the Index, then you found the correct number right away.

2) 093 (18th edition)   093 (10th abridged edition)

Again it is a matter of either looking for the right term or having to go
through a section of the schedule. If you had looked under "Incunabula" in the
Relative Index, the term for books printed before 1501, you would have found
the correct number. Looking under the more general term "Books—Rarities—
Hist. & Crit." would have given you the general number 090 for manuscripts and
book rarities. Looking through the schedule under this number, you would have
reached the correct number.

3) 086.1 (18th edition)   086 (10th abridged edition)

You need to be careful here, since the Relative Index under "Essays"
first notes numbers under the subheading "Belles-Lettres." What you want is a
number covering essays in many fields and not just in literature. Searching further,
you see the cross reference "gen. colls. see Anthologies." This heading leads you
to the correct general number, 080. Under this number is a section for specific
languages, including the language for which you are looking, with an additional
instruction to use Table 6.

4) 050 or 054.1 (18th edition)   050 or 054 (10th abridged edition)

The Relative Index entry "Periodicals" directs you to see "Serials"
("other aspects see Serials"). The entry under "Serials" has a subheading under
"publications" (050).

The schedule for the abridged edition subdivides the division into sections
for specific languages. The number for a French periodical is 054 (but you may use
the general 050 number according to instructions and arrange all general periodicals alphabetically under this number). You may use the same general number for
the 18th edition, but you may also use the class number 054. Under this number
the instruction tells you to add the language notation 41—49 from Table 6 to the
base number for periodicals (05). The summary for this table indicates that there
is a heading for Romance languages (—4), which is the area to which the French
language belongs. Under this number you indeed find French (—41). Thus, the
final number here combines 05 with —41 to become 054.1, since the decimal is
always placed after the third digit from the left.

5) 031 (18th edition)   031 (10th abridged edition)

The Relative Index under the entry "Encyclopedias" provides you with
the basic number 030 for this subject. There is a further breakdown by specific
language under this main division. *The World Book Encyclopedia* is an American
encyclopedia, so it receives the more specialized number 031 from both editions.

CHAPTER 3

CLASS 100–199
(PHILOSOPHY AND RELATED DISCIPLINES)

INTRODUCTORY NOTE

As the following outline shows, this class includes both the disciplines of philosophy and psychology. Today, of course, psychology is generally considered as a social science or even a science (in the case of clinical psychology). But in the late nineteenth century, when the original DDC outline was developed, psychology was considered as a subdivision of philosophy. The two divisions for psychology (150, psychology; 130, popular & parapsychology, occultism) have been extensively revised and made current, but their location has remained in the philosophy class. Many of the specific sections for both philosophy and psychology are cited in the "Details of the Class" in this chapter. Remember to compare these "Details" with the DDC schedules for philosophy.

The number building section includes applications of the principles of book classification as listed in Chapter 1, as well as applications of the tables for Areas (Table 2) and Racial, Ethnic, National Groups (Table 5). The problems all relate to using both the Relative Index and the schedules, and there is one example of a subject whose classification number must be determined by searching the schedule because the subject is too specific for the Relative Index.

OUTLINE OF THE CLASS

100	Philosophy and related disciplines
110	Metaphysics (Speculative philosophy)
120	Knowledge, cause, purpose, man
130	Popular psychology, parapsychology, and occultism
140	Specific philosophical viewpoints
150	Psychology
160	Logic
170	Ethics (Moral philosophy)
180	Ancient, medieval, Oriental philosophy
190	Modern Western philosophy

INTRODUCTION TO THE CLASS

The 100 class is concerned with the development and evaluation of theories and principles of reality and human nature and its existence. The ten main divisions of this class are concerned with these "relationships thru observation, speculation, reasoning, but not experimentation" (DDC, Vol. 2, p. 494).

DETAILS OF THE CLASS

The first sections, 100 to 109, cover general treatments of philosophy, with sections for works on the theory of philosophy (101), dictionaries, encyclopedias, and concordances of philosophy (103), serial publications of philosophy (105), and collections of philosophy (108). Notice that the *standard subdivisions* are included in the first three digits *before* the decimal for general works (however, a dictionary of ethics will still be 170.3).

The next division, 110–119, covers metaphysics (speculative philosophy). This includes ontology (111), which is the science of being, and subsections on existence and essence and on transcendental properties of being, with further subsections on unity, truth, goodness and evil, and beauty.

The next section is concerned with the classification of knowledge (112), which is, of course, what the DDC is all about.

The rest of the sections relate to special influences on human endeavor. Cosmology (113), the science of fundamental causes and processes, includes subsections on the origin of the universe (113.2) and the origin of life (113.8). The relation of space and matter is 114, while the relation between time and motion is 115. Time, duration, eternity is an interesting section (115); its subsection on Space-time (115.4) is used for the implications of theories of relativity. Sections 116–119 are concerned with the more abstruse aspects of this division—motion, change, evolution, matter and form, force and energy, and number and quantity.

Knowledge, cause, purpose, and man are the main subjects of the sections 120–129. Some of the important subdivisions are epistemology (121), the science of the methods, theory, origin, limit, and validity of knowledge. Number 122 covers cause and effect and the issue of chance and cause. However, the metaphysical aspects of chance (123.3) are covered in the subdivision for freedom and necessity (123).

Teleology (124) is concerned with the matter of apparent design and purpose in nature. The philosophical phases of the finite and infinite (125), consciousness and personality (126), the unconscious and subconscious (127) all lead to man and his soul, his mind, his nature, and the nature of life and death (128). The final section (129) logically covers individual aspects of man's basic inner nature—the origin and destiny of the soul, with, in the 18th edition, separate emphasis on incarnation and reincarnation and immortality.

The next sections 130–139 are devoted to popular psychology, parapsychology, and occultism. Popular psychology (131) includes areas concerned with personal well-being, happiness, and success. There are three unassigned subdivisions—132, 134, and 136. Parapsychology and occultism (133) includes such topics as apparitions, magic, witchcraft, astrology, palmistry, extrasensory perception, and spiritualism.

The next assigned number (135) covers dreams and mystic traditions. Personality analysis and improvement and graphology (the study of handwriting) are included in 137; physiognomy (the art of determining character and temperament through analysis of physical features) in 138; and phrenology (the study of the conformation of the skull to determine mental capacity) in 139.

Specific philosophical viewpoints are treated in numbers 140–149. Such well known "isms" as transcendentalism, romanticism, pragmatism, utilitarianism, materialism, liberalism, and realism are all included in this section.

The next part of the schedule, 150–159, is devoted to psychology. This is a "phoenix schedule," which was completely redeveloped in the 17th edition of DDC. The psychology division is comprehensive in its coverage. Starting with the philosophy and theory of psychology (150.1), the schedule skips 151 (which is presently unassigned) and goes on to physiological and experimental psychology (152). Within 152 are subdivisions for sensory perception, motor functions, and motivation.

Intelligence, intellectual and conscious mental processes, memory and learning, imagination, cognition (knowledge), thought and reasoning, perceptual processes, and volition (will) are treated in 153. Subconscious states and processes (depth psychology) are covered in 154. Within the scope of 154 are such areas as the subconscious, sleep, dreams, and hypnotism. (Dreams from a parapsychological point of view are classed in 135.)

Differential and genetic psychology are covered in 155. The subdivisions of 155 cover a variety of important areas in psychology, such as individual psychology, psychology as it relates to sex, children, adolescents, adults, the aged, evolution (heredity), ethnology, nations, and the influence of other factors on psychological patterns.

Comparative psychology (156) is divided into sections on animal psychology and plant psychology. Abnormal and clinical psychology (157) covers abnormal psychology, psychoses, and psychoneuroses.

The extensive field of applied psychology is covered in 158. Some of the subdivisions deal with such topics as successful living, interpersonal relations, leadership, and industrial psychology. The last section, 159, is set aside for other aspects of the field of psychology.

Logic, the science of reasoning, is assigned to 160–169. The main topics covered are induction and deduction, fallacies, syllogisms, hypotheses, argument and persuasion, and analogy.

The sections 170 to 179 cover the subject of ethics or moral philosophy. Systems and doctrines of ethics are covered in 171, while 172–179 are used for applied ethics, including the ethics of political relationships, family relationships, professional and occupational ethics, the ethics of recreation (sportsmanship, games of skill, human combat, etc.), sexual ethics, ethics of social relations, temperance and intemperance (in the use of alcohol, tobacco, and narcotics; also in other forms, such as greed), and in other applications of ethics (cruelty, courage, cowardice, respect for human life, and vices and virtues).

The historical and geographical treatment of philosophy is covered by the sections 180–199. Division 180 covers ancient, medieval and Oriental philosophy with 181 being used for Oriental (ancient, medieval, modern, and by geographic areas). Sections 182–188 are assigned to ancient Western philosophy, Greek and

Roman, and section 189 covers medieval philosophy. Division 190 covers modern Western philosophy with geographical treatment by country reserved for sections 191–199.

NUMBER BUILDING, 100–199

The examples given below illustrate the use of the 100–199 class. Remember that you should be following each step of number building in these examples in the DDC. As in the first chapter, it is not possible to give examples for every classification problem. The examples of number building in this chapter were selected to give the reader a general introduction.

Example 1

A work on the theory of relativity is an example of the need for careful analysis to be certain a work is properly classified. The Relative Index under the entry "Relativity theories" directs you to two main subject breakdowns, one for metaphysics (115.4) and one for physics (530.11) (Fig. 3-1).

Fig. 3-1. Relative Index

Relativity theories	
metaphysics	115.4
physics	530.11
spec. states of matter	**530.4**
s.a. spec. branches of physics	

The abridged edition has the same entry, but the suggested DDC numbers are 115 and 530.1, respectively.

Now it is necessary to go to the schedule and see exactly what aspects of relativity are covered in metaphysics and in physics (Fig. 3-2 below, and Fig. 3-3 on page 62).

Fig. 3-2. Classification Schedule

115	**Time, duration, eternity**
	Class here relation of time and motion
.4	**Space-time**
	Implications of theories of relativity
116	**Motion, change, evolution**
	Class relation of time and motion in 115
117	**Matter and form**
	Class relation of space and matter in 114

Fig. 3-3. Classification Schedule

530	**Physics**
	Class here matter and antimatter
	Class astrophysics in 523.01; physical chemistry in 541.3; physics of specific elements, compounds, mixtures in 546
.01 –.09	Standard subdivisions
	Class theories in 530.1, instrumentation in 530.7
.1	**Theories**
	Class applications to specific states of matter in 530.4
➤ .11	Relativity theory
	Including fourth dimension, space and time, mass-energy equivalence ($E = mc^2$)
	Class relativistic quantum mechanics in 530.12, relativistic statistical and kinetic theories in 530.13, relativistic field theories in 530.14

The 115.4 number is part of a larger subject, "Time, duration, eternity." In the abridged edition works on relativity go into 115 with a note explaining that 115 includes implications of theories of relativity. The second possible number is 530.11 (530.1 in the abridged edition), which is for relativity as one of the theories of physics (Fig. 3-3).

Now the classifier has to determine whether the work in hand deals primarily with the philosophical implications of the theories of relativity or with the scientific aspects of relativity in physics.

In Chapter 1 one of the principles of book classification said a book should be classified according to the author's intent and where it will be most useful. Section 3.42 of the Editor's Introduction to the DDC suggests that a work should be classified with the aspect of a subject receiving the most emphasis. If there is no apparent emphasis, check the schedules to see if there are any special instructions regarding interdisciplinary works; if there are none, consider classifying the work in the broader or underlying discipline—for example, science is the underlying discipline of technology. If no basic principle can be ascertained, use the class that comes first in the schedule, which in this example would be the 100 class (see DDC, Vol. 1, p. 38).

Example 2

Where would you classify a work on ghosts that haunt English castles? The primary topic is ghosts. When you check the subject "Ghosts" in the Relative Index you are given several possible classification numbers, depending on the exact aspect of ghosts covered in the work under consideration (Fig. 3-4).

Fig. 3-4. Relative Index

Ghosts	
lit. & stage trmt.	
folk lit.	
sociology	398.47
texts & lit. crit.	398.25
other aspects see	
Supernatural beings	
occultism	**133.1**
	area–455 7

Now you have to check each suggested number in the schedules until you find the one best suited to the work in hand. Remember, classify *not* from the index but from the classification schedules.

Go to 398.47 in the schedules. A subdivision of Folklore (398), this number is for ghosts and haunted places. Next check the schedules under 398.25, which turns out to be the number for ghost stories. Now, checking the last number cited in the Relative Index, we find that 133 is the number for "Parapsychology and occultism" and 133.1 is a subdivision for "Apparitions (Ghosts)" (Fig. 3-5).

Fig. 3-5. Classification Schedule

133   **Parapsychology and occultism**

For esoteric and cabalistic traditions, see 135.4

SUMMARY

133.1	**Apparitions (Ghosts)**
.3	**Divinatory arts**
.4	**Magic, witchcraft, demonology**
.5	**Mundane astrology**
.6	**Palmistry**
.7	**Frauds in occultism**
.8	**Extrasensory perception and psychokinesis**
.9	**Spiritualism**

→ .1   Apparitions (Ghosts)

.12   Haunted places

.122   Ghosts in specific types of locale

Examples: haunted graveyards, churches, forests, houses

Class ghosts in specific places regardless of type of locale in 133.129

→ .129   Ghosts in specific places

Add "Areas" notation 3–9 from Table 2 to base number 133.129

.14   Specific kinds of apparitions

Examples: poltergeists, hobgoblins, disembodied spirits

The abridged edition goes no further than 133.1. However, the full edition is more detailed. As you read down the schedule you come to 133.129, which is the number for ghosts haunting specific places (Fig. 3-5).

Now you need to determine exactly what is the emphasis of the work. Once it is determined that the book is neither folklore (398.47) nor a ghost story (398.25), the number 133.129 becomes the correct classification for a work on ghosts in English castles.

Look at 133.129 in the schedules (Fig. 3-5, page 63). Under .129 you are instructed to add " 'Areas' notation 3–9 from Table 2 to the base number 133.129" (Fig. 3-6).

Fig. 3-6. Areas (Table 2)

−42	British Isles England

Class here Great Britain, United Kingdom

For Scotland and Ireland, see −41

SUMMARY

−421	Greater London
−422	Southeastern England
−423	Southwestern England and Channel Islands
−424	Midlands of England, and Monmouth
−425	East Midlands of England
−426	Eastern England
−427	North central England
−428	Northern England and Isle of Man
−429	Wales

As you look through Table 2 you come to −4 for Europe, then −42, the area number for the British Isles, England. So the DDC number for a work on ghosts haunting English castles could be:

133	parapsychology and occultism
.1	apparitions and ghosts
.12	haunted places
.129	ghosts in specific places
4	Europe (from Table 2)
42	England (from Table 2)
133.12942	ghosts in English castles

DDC does not provide for specifying "castles" if the geographical approach is to be used. 133.122 is the number in DDC for ghosts in specific types of locale such as graveyards, churches, forests, houses, or castles (see Fig. 3-5, page 63). As 133.122 is more general than 133.12942, our first number would be preferred; however, either number is an accurate interpretation of DDC. In the abridged edition the only possible number is 133.1, which is the general number for ghosts or apparitions.

Example 3

Where would you classify a work on the ethnopsychology of Africans?
Again turn to the Relative Index and look under the entry "Psychology."
This is too broad, so look under the more specific term "Ethnopsychology,"
where you find a reference to 155.8. The abridged edition goes no further than
155.8 in the schedule. The 18th edition allows for a closer classification. As you
read down the schedule you find the number 155.84, which is for ethnopsychology of specific races (Fig. 3-7).

Fig. 3-7. Classification Schedule

155

155.82–155.84 Ethnopsychology

Class comprehensive works in 155.8

.82   Race differences

⟶ .84   Specific races

Add "Racial, Ethnic, National Groups" notation 01–99 from Table 5
to base number 155.84

.89   National psychology

Add "Areas" notation 3–9 from Table 2 to base number 155.89

Class psychology of specific races regardless of national origin in
155.84

The instructions here tell you to add the proper notation from Table 5, Racial,
Ethnic, National Groups, to the base number 155.84. The summary at the
beginning of Table 5 places Africans in −9 (Fig. 3-8).

Fig. 3-8. Racial, Ethnic, National Groups (Table 5)

−1−9 Specific racial, ethnic, national groups

SUMMARY

−1	North Americans
−2	Anglo-Saxons, British, English
−3	Nordics
−4	Modern Latins
−5	Italians, Romanians, related groups
−6	Spanish and Portuguese
−7	Other Italic peoples
−8	Greeks and related groups
−9	Other racial, ethnic, national groups

As you read down the table you find −96 for Africans. Thus, the classification
number for a book on ethnopsychology of Africans is 155.8496.

If the book above were more specialized, covering the ethnopsychology of
a national group like the Kenyans, Table 5 allows for a further subdivision by
national groups in Africa (−966−968), with instructions to add to −96 the
numbers following −6 in the Areas (Table 2) notation 66−68. The area notation

for Kenya in Table 2 is −6762. Following the instructions in Table 5 you add to the number 155.8496 the number *after* the −6 of the Kenya area number. The final number for the ethnopsychology of Kenyans is 155.8496762! We hope you never use it in a small collection, but it is a good example of how to build a long number by following simple instructions.

155	differential and genetic psychology
.8	ethnopsychology and national psychology
.84	specific races
96	Africans (from Table 5)
762	Kenyans (from −6762 in Table 2)
155.8496762	ethnopsychology of Kenyans

PROBLEMS TO SOLVE

Try to build classification numbers for the following hypothetical works:

1) a book on ethics in politics
2) a book on Chinese philosophy
3) a book on sibling rivalry
4) the collected writings of the philosopher Kant

ANSWERS TO PROBLEMS

1) 172 (18th edition)   172 (10th abridged edition)

The Relative Index entry under "Ethics" directs you to the entry "Philosophy" for various aspects of ethics. Under the entry "Politics" there is a reference to "Political relationships" in the 18th edition, but in the abridged edition a reference is made to "Ethics" and number 172. In both editions you are directed to 172. The 18th edition schedule allows a further choice of 172.1 (citizenship), 172.2 (public office), and 172.4 (international relations).

2) 181.11 (18th edition)   181 (10th abridged edition)

This is an example of a subject whose classification number must be determined by searching the schedule because the Relative Index does not lead to a specific number. The entry for "Chinese" does not lead any place, and the entry "Philosophy" simply directs you to the 100 class. This means you must search the schedules until you come to 180 for "Ancient, medieval, Oriental philosophy." Looking further down the schedule you find 181 for Oriental philosophy, with several subdivisions for specific areas, including 181.11 for Chinese and Korean philosophy. Notice that under 181.04–.09 there is a note directing the classifier to a further expansion of Chinese philosophy based on specific religions (e.g., Confucian philosophy, 181.09512, is arrived at by following the specific directions given under 181.04–.09). Another way to help find specific classification numbers if you know the main class (100, 200, etc.) is to check the "Summaries" of the 18th edition of DDC (Vol. 1, pp. 449-460).

. 3) 155.443 (18th edition)   155.4 (10th abridged edition)

Again start in the Relative Index. You may not find a specific classification number, but at least you will find a general class number. Under "Psychology" you will find only a general number, 150. Under "Siblings–psychology" you are given the number 155.443, and under "Siblings–rearing home economy" is the number 649.143. The entry "Child" gives no promising numbers. In the abridged edition these entries give you the numbers 155.4 and 649, respectively. Since the subject is rivalry and not child rearing, we will assume that the psychological aspects are the more important aspects of the subject and use 155.443 or 155.4. Remember that the contents of the book and the author's approach will be the determining factor.

4) 193 (18th edition)   193 (10th abridged edition)

The Relative Index in the 18th edition provides two specific approaches to the problem. The most likely approach is under the entry "Philosophers." Here you find a subheading "biog. & work" with the numbers 180–190. The second approach is under the type or school of philosophy–"Kantianism." This gives the subheading "indiv. phil." with numbers 180–190. The entry "Philosophy" is too broad, since you would need to look through the whole schedule. If you used this approach, however, under number 108 you would be directed to 180–190 for collections of individual philosophers.

The 10th abridged edition has only "Kantianism" as a specific entry in the index. Under the "Philosophy" entry you would have to search the schedule, and at number 108 you would find the same instructions as in the 18th edition.

Checking the schedule under 180–190 you find that you need to know the nationality of the philosopher and the historical period in which he lived. A biographical dictionary or encyclopedia will provide the information that Kant was a German philosopher who lived between 1724 and 1804. Armed with this information, you can proceed to 190 for "Modern Western philosophy" and on to section 193 for Germany and Austria.

CHAPTER 4

CLASS 200–299
(RELIGION)

INTRODUCTORY NOTE

As the "Introduction to the Class" points out, this class for religion is extensively biased toward Christianity, a bias that reflects nineteenth century American thought. Other religions are covered in the single division 290, with specific numbers for classical (i.e., Greek and/or Roman) religious mythology (292). The second example in the number building section of this chapter demonstrates the alternative possibilities of classing a non-Christian religion using the Buddhist religion as an example. This example follows directions in the DDC but would require the development of local (i.e., your own) subdivisions. The last problem is a particularly interesting one for the reader; it could have several different numbers, depending on the emphasis of the title and the purpose of the author.

OUTLINE OF THE CLASS

200	Religion
210	Natural religion
220	Bible
230	Christian doctrinal theology
240	Christian moral and devotional theology
250	Local Christian church and Christian religious orders
260	Christian social and ecclesiastical theology
270	History and geography of organized Christian church
280	Christian denominations and sects
290	Other religions and comparative religion

INTRODUCTION TO THE CLASS

As the DDC so well puts it, religion is concerned with the "beliefs, attitudes, practices of individuals and groups with respect to ultimate nature of existences and relationships within context of revelation, deity, worship" (DDC, Vol. 2, p. 526).

Most of the Religion class is devoted to the Christian religion, as is obvious from the outline of the class given above. This bias in favor of Christianity is recognized by the DDC, and the schedules provide options to give preferred treatment to any religion it may be necessary to emphasize. This preferred treatment is accomplished in the full edition by allowing the classifier to use numbers 230–280 for a religion other than Christianity and to classify the religion's scriptures in 220. If this option is used, Christianity and the Bible are classified in 298. This smaller scope for Christianity assumes that it will be of less importance when the DDC is used in a country or library where another religion is predominant.

The DDC also allows the use of sections 210, 291, or 298 for providing local emphasis and the use of shorter numbers for a specific religion. Letters or symbols may also be used for specific religions, but care must be taken to follow the instructions under centered heading 292–299 in the schedules in the unabridged edition (Fig. 4-1).

▶

Fig. 4-1. Classification Schedule

292–299 Specific religions

Arrange as below, but, if it is desired to give local emphasis and a shorter number to a specific religion, place it first by use of a letter or other symbol, e.g., Hinduism 2H0 (preceding 220), or 29H (preceding 291 or 292); add to the base number thus derived, e.g., to 2H or to 29H, the numbers following the base number for that religion in 292–299, e.g., Shivaism 2H5.13 or 29H.513

Class comprehensive works in 290

DETAILS OF THE CLASS

The first division for religion is used for the standard subdivisions (200.1– 200.9). For example, 200.3 is used for dictionaries and encyclopedias of religion and 200.6 for religious organizations.

The standard subdivisions for Christianity are covered by numbers 201 to 209. For example, 203 is used for dictionaries and encyclopedias of Christianity and 206 for Christian religious organizations.

The next division, 210, is used for "Natural religion." Natural religion is that which is developed through reason, observation of nature, and speculation instead of through revelation. The remaining numbers, 211 to 219, are concerned with God, concepts of God, the nature of God including polytheism, monotheism, pantheism and anthropomorphism, creation (including the creation of life and man), theodicy (the vindication of the justice of God in permitting the existence of evil), science and religion, good and evil, worship and prayer, man (including his nature and place in the universe and the question of his immortality), and analogy, which is belief based on inference of likeness or correspondence in functions and origins.

Division 220 covers Judaic and Christian holy scriptures—the Bible. The first section covers some general principles, such as the Bible's origins, its authenticity, the original texts, early and modern versions, interpretations, commentaries, other special aspects of the Bible, and the geography, history, and chronology of

Bible lands during Biblical times. Numbers 221 to 224 and numbers 225 to 228 cover the Old Testament and New Testament, respectively. The number 229 provides for the Apocrypha, which is the writings or statements concerning the Bible that were not found anywhere originally in Hebrew and are thus considered to be of doubtful authorship or authority.

Divisions 230 to 280 are used for Christianity. The first two of these, 230 and 240, are for Christian theology. These cover God, the Trinity, Christology, man, salvation and eschatology in sections 230 to 239, and moral and devotional theology, literature, and personal religion in sections 240 to 249.

Numbers 250 to 259 are concerned with local Christian churches and Christian religious orders. Matters relating to preaching, sermons, pastoral duties, local church government, and Roman Catholic orders are also detailed within these sections.

The numbers 260 to 269 provide for works on Christian social and ecclesiastical theology. Some important subsections provide for social theology, ecclesiology (church government and organization), days, times, and places of religious observance, public worship (including texts of liturgy), other rites and sacraments, missions, associations for religious work, religious training and instruction and organized spiritual renewal (such as revivals and retreats).

Christian church history is covered by the 270's. Specific historical periods (270.1 to 270.8) are followed by sections on special topics of church history such as persecutions and doctrinal controversies. Sections 274 to 279 provide for the geographical treatment of church history.

Christian denominations and sects are classed in numbers 280 to 289. The first section, 281, deals with primitive and Oriental churches, 282 deals with the Roman Catholic Church, and sections 283 to 289 deal with the numerous Protestant denominations.

The numbers 290 to 299 are used for non-Christian religions and for comparative religion. Remember that earlier in the chapter it was pointed out there are several options in the DDC to give greater local emphasis and shorter numbers to specific religions if this is desired. This is done by assigning the religion and its various aspects to the numbers usually used for Christianity.

Section 291 is used for comparative religion and sections 292 to 299 for religions other than Christianity. Some of the main sections include classical religions, Indic religions (such as Buddhism and Hinduism), Judaism, and Islam. Finally, 299 is used for other religions found in the Far East and Africa and for the religions of the American Indian.

NUMBER BUILDING, 200–299

The following examples will help illustrate the use of the 200–299 class.

Example 1

Where would you class a work of textual commentaries on the Ten Commandments and their relation to the code of conduct in Christianity and Judaism?

The first step is to determine the main subject of the work and the author's intent. Go back to the section on "Principles of Book Classification" in Chapter 1 and read principles 4 and 9. Also read section 3.42 in the Editor's Introduction to the DDC (DDC, Vol. 1, p. 38). Now check the entry for "Ten Commandments" in the Relative Index (Fig. 4-2).

Fig. 4-2. Relative Index

Ten
  Commandments
    Bible   **222.16**
    moral theology
      Christianity   241.52
      Judaism   296.385
    other aspects see
      Historical books (O.T.)

Here you find three possible classification numbers, depending on the nature of the work in hand.

If the book's emphasis is on textual commentaries, then 222.16 for "Bible" is a good starting point. The heading in the schedule is prefaced with instructions to "add as instructed under 222–224" (Fig. 4-3).

Fig. 4-3. Classification Schedule

222

                For Ten Commandments, see 222.16

⟶ .16   *Ten Commandments (Decalog)

           Class Ten Commandments as code of conduct in Christianity in
           241.52, in Judaism in 296.385

*Add as instructed under 222–224

Go to the centered heading "222–224 Specific parts of Old Testament" to check the instructions (Fig. 4-4).

Fig. 4-4. Classification Schedule

▶

222–224 Specific parts of Old Testament

Add to each subdivision identified by * as follows:
001–009   Standard subdivisions
01–08   General principles
                Add to 0 the numbers following
                220 in 220.1–220.8, e.g., exegesis 066
09   Geography, history, chronology
                Add to 09 the numbers following
                221.9 in 221.91–221.95, e g.,
                biography 092
Class comprehensive works in 221

The most likely place to check is the section on general principles. Checking the 220 schedule shows the number 220.7 for commentaries and 220.77 for commentaries that include the text being commented on. Following the instructions in Fig. 4-4 you arrive at the following number:

220	Bible
222	historical Books of Old Testament
.1	Pentateuch
.16	Ten Commandments
07	from 220.7 for commentaries, following the instructions under general principles to add a "0"
077	from 220.77 for commentaries with text
222.16077	textual commentaries on the Ten Commandments

If the work had a predominant emphasis on the Ten Commandments as a code of conduct in Christianity or Judaism, the correct classification number would be either 241.52 or 296.385, respectively.

The abridged edition gives the number 222 rather than 222.16077 as in our first example; for the last two examples the abridged number would be 241.5 and 296.3, respectively.

Example 2

How would a cataloger provide greater emphasis for works on Buddhism or Islam in an area where these religions were predominant?

Buddhism is a subsection (294.3) within the general section for Religions of Indic Origin (294). Islam is assigned an entire section (297). The quantity and variety of material in a library devoted to these religions may determine which of five options a cataloger would select.

A comprehensive option would be to use numbers 220 and 230 through 280 as provided in the instructions in the schedule (Fig. 4-5).

Fig. 4-5. Classification Schedule

230–280 Christianity

▶

(If it is desired to give local emphasis and more and shorter numbers to a specific religion, e.g., Buddhism, it is optional to class it here and its sources in 220; in that case class Bible and Christianity in 298)

Class comprehensive works in 200

For Bible, see 220

It is certainly possible to anticipate this comprehensive approach being used for works on Islam. In this situation 220 would be used for the sources of Islam— i.e., the Koran. It would then be necessary to take the headings within section 297 and expand them into the new divisions and sections as applicable, using a larger, more inclusive number where before a more specific number sufficed. For example, "Islamic sects and other religions" (297.8) might well be assigned an entire division, such as number 280. This then allows for a greater number of subdivisions with shorter classification numbers.

Two other options are the use of numbers 210 or 291. Specific instructions are given in the schedules on the special use of these numbers (Fig. 4-6).

Fig. 4-6. Classification Schedule

210 **Natural religion**

Religious beliefs and attitudes attained thru observation and interpretation of evidence in nature, thru speculation, thru reasoning, but not thru revelation

(If it is desired to give local emphasis and a shorter number to a specific religion, it is optional to class it here, and to add to 21 the numbers following the base number for that religion in 292–299, e.g., Hinduism 210, Mahabharata 219.23; in that case class subdivisions of natural religion in 201–209, standard subdivisions of Christianity in 200.1–200.9, standard subdivisions of religion in 200.01–200.09)

291 **Comparative religion**

(If it is desired to give local emphasis and a shorter number to a specific religion, it is optional to class it here, and to add to 291 the numbers following the base number for that religion in 292–299, e.g., Hinduism 291, Mahabharata 291.923; in that case class subdivisions of comparative religion in 290.1–290.9, standard subdivisions in 290.01–290.09)

Again, the choice is made depending on the size of the library's collection and user demand. Both options offer expansion for a greater variety of subjects for Buddhism, since it was originally only a subsection; for Islam, however, only one option (210) offers more, without any modification, than the schedule provides.

The instructions given for each option differ somewhat, so the classifier should be cautious about plunging into any optional classification (Fig. 4-6). The instructions specify what to do with the materials normally classified in the numbers. For example: (1) Numbers 220 and 230–280, Bible and Christianity, are relocated to 298. (2) For number 210 the cataloger adds to the base number 21 the numbers following the base number for the religion being substituted. Thus, Buddhism or Islam would be 210. Buddhism's sacred writings would be the base number 21 *plus* the numbers *following* the base number (294.3) from 294.382, or 82, making the number for Buddhist sacred writings 218.2. The instructions with 210 tell where to move the numbers being relocated (Fig. 4-6). The same option for Islam would yield the number 212: the base number, 21, *plus* the number (2) following the base number (297.12). (3) For number 291 the cataloger adds to this *whole* number the numbers *following* the base number for the religion being substituted. Thus, Buddhism would be 291 and its sacred writings 291.82 (291 plus the .82 following the base number 294.382). (4) Another option is to use the permanently unassigned section 298. Thus, it is possible to build a completely new section for, say, Buddhism, depending on local needs and emphasis.

(5) Finally, and potentially the most confusing, is the option of using a letter in conjunction with numbers. The instructions in the schedule are shown in Fig. 4-1, page 69.

The example for Buddhism would classify as follows:

2B0 (preceding 220)

or

29B (preceding 291 or 292);

then *add* to the *base* number

2B (dropping the 0)

or

29B

the numbers *following* the base number for the religion—Buddhism, in this example—from 292–299. Thus, the number for Buddhist sacred works using this option would be either:

2B plus the 82 from 294.3<u>82</u> (thus, 2B82)

or

29B plus the 82 from 294.3<u>82</u> (thus, 29B82).

Of course, using any of these options will lead to the development of locally specific subdivisions not listed in DDC 18.

Example 3

Another example of number building can be developed using the comparative religion section 291. Where would a cataloger classify a work on the attitude of various religions toward women?

The first step is to determine the proper class for the work. One major topic of the work is the attitude of religions, while another major topic is women. One searches in the Relative Index for the former subject, the attitude of religions.

The headings under "Religion" provide no directions for classifying the work because of its more primary interest. Looking further in the Relative Index leads to the entry "Religious," with a subheading "attitudes" and a see reference to "Social theology" for secular matters (Fig. 4-7).

Fig. 4-7. Relative Index

Religious
  architecture *see*
    Religious-purpose
    buildings
  art *see* Religion art
    representation
  association bldgs.

architecture	726.9
building	690.69

    s.a. spec. rel.
    other aspects see
      Religious-purpose
      bldgs.
  associations

Buddhism	**294.365**
Christianity	**267**
comp. rel.	291.65
Islam	297.65
Judaism	**296.67**

    s.a. other spec. rel.
➤ attitudes
  doctrines *see* Doctrinal
    theology
  secular matters *see*
    Social theology

The entry "Social theology" provides a point of departure under the subheading "Social theology—comp. rel.," which directs the user to 291.17. Actually, under the entry "Social structure—soc. theology—comp. rel." a more specific number is suggested, namely 291.17834 (Fig. 4-8).

Fig. 4-8. Classification Schedule

291

.178 34   Social structure

             Add to 291.17834 the numbers following 301.4 in 301.41 – 301.45, e.g., attitude of religions toward homosexuality 291.17834157

Scanning the schedule under 291.17 you come to 291.17834, which is the correct number for attitudes of religions toward women:

291	comparative religion
.1	relationships and attitudes of religions
.17	social theologies
.178	religious and socioeconomic problems
.1783	social problems
.17834	social structure. Following the instructions in the schedule, add to this last number the numbers *following* 301.4 in 301.41–301.45 for the subject being classified (Fig. 4-8, page 75). In the schedules at 301.41 you will see that 301.412 is used for the social role and function of women (Fig. 4-9).
12	added from 301.412 according to the instructions (Fig. 4-8) to add the number following 301.4
291.1783412	attitudes of religions toward women

Fig. 4-9. Classification Schedule

301

.41	The sexes and their relations
.411	Men
	Social role and function
.412	Women
	Social role and function
[.412 1–.412 9]	Specific aspects of women's role and function
	Numbers discontinued; class in 301.412

In the abridged edition the Relative Index has a see reference from "Religious attitudes—secular matters" to "Social theology." Under the entry "Social theology—comp. rel." the number 291.1 is given for "Relationships and attitudes of religions"; this is the correct number for the abridged edition.

PROBLEMS TO SOLVE

Try to build classification numbers for the following hypothetical works:

1) a book on religions of the American Indian
2) a history of the Society of Jesus
3) a history of the United Methodist Church in the United States
4) a book of commentaries on the Talmud
5) a book titled *The Soul of Man*

ANSWERS TO PROBLEMS

1) 299.7 (18th edition)   299 (10th abridged edition)

The Relative Index provides only peripheral help for this problem. A search under the entries "Religion" and "Religious" leads to a possible helpful subheading, "Religious practices," where there is a see reference to "Public worship." This entry, however, only leads to a note to "s.a. other spec. rel." The entry "American Indians" directs you to the term "American aboriginal," and the subheadings here lead only to a suggestion to see the entry "Primitive" for "other aspects." Under the entry "Primitive" are subheadings "religions" and "spec. rel." Here the number 299 is suggested.

The abridged edition Relative Index has an entry "Public worship—comp. rel.," which offers the number 291.3. A search of the schedule leads to 299 for "other religions."

In the full edition, a continuation of the search in the schedules under 299 leads to 299.7 for religion of North American Indians. This is the preferred number unless the book deals mainly with South American Indians.

2) 255.53   255
    or   or
    255.53009 (18th edition)   255.09 (10th abridged edition)

The Relative Index entry "Society of Jesus" directs you to the entry "Jesuits." The entry "Jesuits—rel. orders" gives the number 255.53, and checking the schedule reveals that this is the correct number. If necessary, the standard subdivision for historical treatment can be added to get the number 255.53009.

The abridged edition is a little more difficult in this case. The Relative Index has no entry under "Society of Jesus" or "Jesuits." The term "Religious orders" provides a see reference to "Religious congregations," which in turn directs the user to "Religious (members of orders)." This last entry provides no good leads. Going back to "Religious congregations," one finds a subheading for Christianity, with the number 255. A note under 255 in the schedules states that religious orders are included here. If needed, the standard subdivision for historical treatment can be added to get the number 255.09.

3) 287.673 (18th edition)   287 (10th abridged edition)

A search in the Relative Index under "United Methodist Church" provides a specific starting point, 287.6. The more general entry "Methodist Churches" gives a somewhat broader number, 287. Both these entries in the Relative Index of the full edition give the number 287, which is the correct number for that edition. The full edition allows treatment by country in 287.64–.69. The instructions in the schedule tell the cataloger to "add 'Areas' notation 4–9 from Table 2 to base number 287.6." Table 2 lists −7 for North America and −73 for the United States. Thus, the number 287.673 is the number for a history of the United Methodist Church in the United States.

4) 296.1207 (18th edition) 296.1 (10th abridged edition)

The Relative Index provides an entry under "Talmudic literature" with the number 296.12. The abridged edition provides the same entry with the number 296.1, which is the correct number for that edition. The schedule in the full edition has a section for general considerations (296.1204–296.1207). The specific number for commentaries is 296.1207.

Notice that this number (296.12) is an example of the use of more than one "0" for standard subdivisions. Thus, a book on the study and teaching of Talmudic literature would have the number 296.12007. This avoids a conflict with the number for commentaries (296.1207).

5) 128.1 (18th edition) 128 (10th abridged edition)
    or or
    233.5 233
    or or
    291.22 291.2
    or or
    297.22 296.3
    or or -
    296.32 291.2
    or
    218

A work titled *The Soul of Man* could cover several subject areas. The Relative Index provides starting points under the entries "Soul" and "Man." It is also necessary to determine whether "souls" are discussed in a metaphysical sense with 128.1 as a classification number, or as part of a religious doctrine. If it is the latter, then the religious doctrine involved must be determined.

Looking for the most *specific* number in the schedules from the two starting points suggested in the Relative Index, we find under "Soul" the heading Christianity (233.5); under "Man" we find the headings Comparative religion (291.22), Islam (297.22), Judaism (296.32), and Natural religion (218).

The abridged edition provides two numbers in the Relative Index under "Soul"—233 and 128. The entry "Man" gives the same numbers under "Christianity" and "Metaphysics." The entry for "Comparative religion" suggests 291.2, for "Judaism" 296.3, and for "Natural religion" 218.

CHAPTER 5

CLASS 300–399
(THE SOCIAL SCIENCES)

INTRODUCTORY NOTE

The majority of the disciplines making up the social sciences are covered in this very comprehensive and specific class. Psychology (150) and History (900) are both located elsewhere, as is Physical anthropology (573). The "Outline of the Class" below clearly shows the disciplines in the DDC Social Sciences. As this is a particularly long schedule, the "Details of the Class" are much longer than in previous chapters. Thus, it is even more important in this class that you compare these "Details" to the actual DDC schedules in order to have a better understanding of the material included. One division, 390, is especially worthy of careful examination. This division includes not only works on customs but particularly etiquette books (395) and folklore (398). Literary folklore is, of course, classed in literature (800's).

 ' The number building examples continue in this chapter to demonstrate how to use the Relative Index most effectively. Be sure that you are following all these examples in the actual Relative Index and schedules. The use of Table 2, Areas, is again emphasized in this section.

OUTLINE OF THE CLASS

300	The social sciences
310	Statistics
320	Political science
330	Economics
340	Law
350	Public administration
360	Social pathology and services
370	Education
380	Commerce, communications, transportation
390	Customs and folklore

INTRODUCTION TO THE CLASS

The social sciences encompass the second largest schedule by number of pages in the DDC. The social activities and social institutions covered within this class include sociology, statistics, political science, economics, law, public administration, social pathology, education, commerce, and customs and folklore.

DETAILS OF THE CLASS

The general social sciences division has only two assigned sections, 301 and 309. The first, 301, is primarily devoted to six subsections: social psychology (301.1), culture and cultural processes (301.2), ecology and community (301.3), social structure (301.4), institutions (301.5), and social conflict and accommodation (301.6).

Sections 302–308 have been unassigned since the 16th edition of the DDC. The other section of this division, 309, covers the social situation and condition of society. Here are found numbers for the historical and geographical treatment of social sciences as a discipline and for planning and assistance, these being activities related to the improvement of social conditions by governmental or private agencies.

The nine remaining divisions cover the specific social sciences described above in the Outline of the Class.

Division 310 is used for statistics. The first section, 312, covers the statistics of human population, such as vital statistics (births, deaths, illnesses), statistics on accidents and crimes of violence, statistics of marriage and divorce, statistics of physical features and measurement, and statistics of population characteristics.

Sections 311 and 313 are presently unassigned.

Sections 314 to 319 are assigned to general statistics divided by modern geographical subdivisions—continents, countries, and local subdivisions.

The next division, 320, is used for political science, the academic field concerned with human control, regulation and influence of governmental institutions, and the processes that delineate the proper relationships among men, society, the state, and other states.

The state, its theory, origin and elements, is assigned to 320.1. The role, structure, functions, and activities of government and comparative and descriptive government follow in numbers 320.2 to 320.4. The other important subjects assigned here are political theories and ideologies in 320.5 (e.g., liberalism, conservatism, collectivism, nationalism), and 320.9 for the historical and geographical treatment of the state and government.

The first section, 321, encompasses the various forms of the state by geographical distribution of power (e.g., federal states); by extent of territory governed (e.g., empires); and by the extent of popular participation (e.g., democratic, authoritarian).

The next three sections, 322–324, cover the internal relations of the state with social groups and their members (e.g., business and political groups), with residents of the state (e.g., in relation to social classes, civil rights, political rights, and citizenship) and to the electoral process.

Number 325 is used for international migration and the various aspects of immigration, emigration, and colonization. The next section, 326, is used for slavery and emancipation. Section 327 is assigned to international relations, international competition and cooperation, diplomacy, and foreign policies and relations between specific nations. The first part of number 328 is concerned with legislation and the legislative branch of government (especially its function, rules and procedures, structure and membership, and powers). The remainder of 328 (328.4 to 328.9) provides for the legislative branches of the specific jurisdictions in the modern world.

Section 329 is used for practical politics (e.g., campaign techniques) and political parties (e.g., their organization and finance). The larger part of this section (329.1 to 329.9) is used for political parties of specific countries. Political parties in the United States are covered in some detail, and there are instructions for applying the subsections used for U.S. political parties to foreign political parties.

Division 330 covers economics, which is concerned with the conditions and laws that affect the production, distribution, and consumption of material goods and the accompanying human needs and desires. 330 also covers systems and theories of economics, economic conditions in specific historical periods, and economic conditions in specific geographic areas.

The first section, 331, is assigned to labor economics. Some of the subsections here deal with the labor force and labor market (productivity, supply and demand, unemployment); conditions of employment (wages, hours, pensions, training); workers of specific age groups (children, aged); women workers; special categories of workers (migrant workers, those with physical handicaps); categories of workers by racial, ethnic, and national origin; labor by industry and occupation (managerial, industrial, public service); and labor unions and labor-management bargaining (labor union organizations, labor unions, collective bargaining, strikes).

Financial economics, 332, is another major section. The first subject covered is banks and banking, including special aspects of banking such as central banks, commercial banks, and multiple banking. Specialized banking institutions such as trust companies follow. The next subsection is for credit and loan institutions, including loan brokers and insurance companies.

The next subsection (332.4) covers the topic of money, including forms of money, monetary standards, commodity standards, and monetary policy. A short subsection (332.5) covers other mediums of exchange, such as barter.

Investment finance (including brokerage firms, securities, real estate, and investments) is covered by subsection 332.6. Credit is covered in subsection 332.7, and the next two subsections are used for the subjects of interest and discount, and counterfeiting and forgery.

Number 333, land economics, includes control of land (e.g., public and individual) and land utilization (e.g., pasture, agricultural, recreational, and mineral). 334 is devoted to cooperatives in building, housing distribution, and production, and 335 is used for socialism and its related systems. 336 is used for public finance, including reinvestment through taxation, public securities and debt, with a provision for public finance by geographical area. 337 is unassigned.

Production, the extracting and manufacture of materials and goods for use and consumption, is extensively covered in section 338. The first four subsections provide for specific industries concerned with agriculture, minerals, other extractive industries, and secondary industries such as professional services. Subsection 338.5 covers general production economics, including the aspects of costs, profit, prices, and economic fluctuations. The following subsections cover the organization of production and the structure of business organizations. Subsection 338.8 covers business combinations such as monopoly, mergers, trusts, and cartels, and subsection 338.9 is used for production programs and domestic and foreign economic policies including economic assistance and nationalization.

The final section used for economics, 339, is for macroeconomics, with subsections on income distribution and accounting, measures of national income, factors affecting national income, and economic stabilization and growth.

Numbers 340 through 349 are assigned to law. Section 340 covers the philosophy and theory of law, law reform, systems of law (primitive, ancient, Roman, medieval European, civil law, common law, Oriental law, Islamic law), and conflict of laws between two or more jurisdictions.

International law, section 341, includes subsections on treaties, sources of international law, the world community (e.g., League of Nations, United Nations), relations between states, jurisdiction and jurisdictional relations of states, disputes and conflicts between states, the law of war, and international cooperation (defense and mutual security, military installations and assistance, peace and disarmament, international economic law, social law and cultural relations, and international criminal law).

The subsequent seven sections, 342–348, are concerned with municipal law, with sections 342–345 devoted to public law.

The first section, 342, provides for constitutional and administrative law. Extensive instructions under 342.3–342.9 tell the user how to give local emphasis to this section through the Areas Table and several other options.

Section 343 is used for miscellaneous public law, which includes military and defense law, law of public property, law of public finance, tax law, regulation of industry, regulation of trade, and control of public utilities. The subsections 343.3–343.9 are used for specific geographic jurisdictions.

Social law, section 344, includes subject areas relating to labor law, social insurance, welfare, public health, public order, public works, education, educational and cultural exchanges, and culture and religion.

Criminal law, section 345, includes topics such as criminal courts, offenses, offenders, liability and guilt, criminal procedure, evidence, trials, and juvenile procedure.

Private law, section 346, includes topics such as persons and domestic relations, contracts, torts (wrongful acts that allow civil actions), property, inheritance, associations, commercial law, banking and insurance, and negotiable securities.

Civil procedure is covered by section 347. Included here are the administration of justice, courts, and court procedures relating to evidence and trials.

Section 348 is for laws (statutes), regulations, and cases. Included here are legal codes, digests of laws, reports of cases and citators. The last section for law, 349, is used for municipal law; it is an optional number.

Division 350 is assigned to public administration, the executive branch of government, and military art and science. Public administration is concerned with the "structure, internal management, activities of government agencies charged with execution of law and public policy" (DDC, Vol. 2, p. 726). Notice that the standard subdivisions in the executive branch section require a prefix of three zeroes before the number, because two zeroes are used here for subdivisions.

Topics relating to the executive have some numbers prefixed with two zeroes. These include bureaucracy (350.001), separation of powers (350.002), general considerations of the executive (350.003), executive departments and ministries (350.004), cabinet (350.005), and special commissions (350.009). Specific executive departments and ministries are given numbers prefixed with one zero (justice departments, 350.05). The subsequent subsections of 350 provide for personnel management in government, specific administrative activities (e.g., internal administration, finance, social order) and other administrative activities relating to specific areas of public life. The final subsection covers the malfunction of government, including abuse of administrative responsibility, impeachment, and conflict of interest.

Section 351 is used for general works on central governments.

Local units of government and their structure, management, and activities comprise section 352.

The next two sections, 353 and 354, cover specific national, state, and provincial governments. Section 353 is used for federal and state governments of the United States. However, if emphasis is desired for the central government of a country other than the United States, it is optional to use 353 for that government and class the United States material in another number as instructed in the schedule. Other central governments are classified in 354, where there are detailed instructions on the use of added areas notation, standard subdivisions, and building numbers for other specific aspects of government.

The next five sections, 355–359, cover military art and science. Number 355 is used for the general conduct of warfare including basic military considerations, military resources, organization, personnel, operations, training, central administration, installations, and materiel. Sections 356–359 cover specific kinds of military forces and methods of warfare: foot forces and warfare (356); mounted forces and warfare (357); armored and technical land forces and warfare, air and space forces (358); and sea forces and naval warfare (359).

Division 360 covers social pathology and social services. Social welfare (361) has subsections for casework, disaster relief, public welfare and private welfare, and community organizations devoted to social welfare. There are also provisions for historical and geographical treatment. Section 362 is devoted to social pathology and its alleviation. Here are found subject areas pertaining to physical and mental illness, mental retardation, physical handicaps, poverty, and problems of the aged, the young, and other special groups.

Other social services, in section 363, include public services and public safety, morals, public works, and public utilities. Section 364, assigned to criminology, includes subsections on criminal offenses, causes of crime and delinquency, offenders, prevention and correction of crime and delinquency, and treatment of discharged offenders. Penal institutions and such subordinate topics as prison systems, inmates, and reform of the penal system are covered by section 365.

Section 366 is devoted to fraternal and mutual assistance organizations and associations. Included here are secret and semi-secret associations and societies such as the Freemasons, Benevolent and Protective Order of Elks, Knights of Pythias, and Rosicrucians. General clubs (social clubs and study clubs) are covered in section 367.

Insurance, section 368, includes general principles of insurance and specific forms of risk. Subsections cover insurance against damage to and loss of property, against death, against illness and injury, government-sponsored insurance, liability insurance, and various other forms of casualty insurance.

Miscellaneous kinds of associations are assigned to section 369 (military, hereditary, patriotic, service, and youth organizations).

The 370 division is assigned to education. The important introductory subsections include the philosophy, theory, and principles of education (370.1) and the study and teaching of education (370.7). Some of the important topics in these subsections are educational aims, educational objectives and values, scientific principles of education, educational psychology, and education and society. Also included here are numbers for education of teachers and administrators, institutions of higher education, and educational research.

The first section, 371, is devoted to the school. It covers such aspects as teaching and teaching personnel, educational administration, methods of instruction and study, guidance and counseling, school discipline, physical plant, school health and safety, the student, and special education. The last topic, special education, is concerned with the education of students with physical and mental handicaps, delinquents, emotionally disturbed students, gifted students, and students who are exceptional because of class distinction or national, racial, or ethnic origin.

The next three sections, 372–374, cover education and schools at various levels. Section 372 is concerned with elementary education, elementary schools, and the elementary school curriculum. Section 373, secondary education, includes types of schools such as private, public, and academic and vocational schools. Section 374 is for adult education and its related areas, such as self-education, group education, and types of adult education schools.

Section 375 is set aside for the subject of curriculums. Provision is made here for general courses of study and courses of study in specific subjects.

The education of women is found in section 376. Some of the special aspects are convent education, education by level (e.g., secondary, higher), and colleges for women.

Schools and religion are covered in section 377, with subsections for religious instruction and exercises in nonsectarian schools, monastic and mission schools, and schools supported by religious groups.

Section 378 is devoted to higher education. The introductory subsections cover philosophy and theory, aims and objectives, finance, and the ownership and control of colleges and universities. Other subsections are concerned with such aspects of higher education as institutions of higher education, institutional organization and administration, faculty, types and levels of institutions, educational measurement, methods of instruction and study, discipline, academic degrees, and student financing, plus a detailed segment for geographical treatment. The last subsections, 378.4–378.9, provide for local emphasis and for the treatment of institutional publications.

Section 379 covers education and the state, including the state's role in regulation, control, and support of education at all levels.

Commerce, communications, and transportation are the subjects treated in division 380. The introductory section includes the exchange of goods and services, products of primary industries (e.g., agriculture, minerals, fishing), communication services, and transportation services.

Domestic and international trade are the subject of sections 381 and 382. The former includes commercial policy, and specific commodities and services involved in internal commerce. The latter section provides detailed breakdowns for general international economic relations, international commercial policy, commodities and services, import and export trade, tariff policy, and trade agreements.

Sections 383 and 384 cover communication services. Section 383 is used for postal communication, and 384 is used for other systems of communication, such as telegraphy, wireless communication (e.g., radio, television, satellites), and motion pictures.

Sections 385 and 386 cover transportation services, with 385 for railroad transportation and 386 for inland waterway transportation. Section 387 treats water, air, and space transportation, including seaports, ships, maritime transport, air transportation and air facilities, and space transportation.

Section 388 is used for various aspects of ground transportation, such as roads and highways, vehicular transportation, and urban transportation. The final section, 389, is devoted to metrology and standardization. The former covers the field of weights and measures and the latter pertains to the standardization of those weights and measures.

The final division of this class, 390, is concerned with customs and folklore. The introductory numbers cover the customs of specific economic and social classes. The next five sections (391–395) cover customs. Section 391, used for costume and personal appearance, has subsections for outer garments and care and adornment of the body. Customs of the life cycle and domestic life are covered by 392; included here are birth customs, rites of puberty, the home and domestic arts, courtship and betrothal, wedding and marriage, relations between sexes, and treatment of the aged.

Section 393 covers death customs—burial and mourning. Section 394 is used for general customs relating to eating, drinking, special occasions, games, official ceremonies, pageants, fairs, and chivalry.

Etiquette for specific groups, occasions, and situations is the subject of section 395. Sections 396 and 397 are unassigned.

Section 398 is assigned to folklore, its theories, its literature, and its themes using natural and physical subjects (e.g., places, time, persons, physical phenomena) and the paranatural and legendary subjects (e.g., superstitions, ogres, dragons, ghosts), and finally riddles and proverbs.

The last section, 399, is used for the customs of war and diplomacy.

NUMBER BUILDING, 300–399

Example 1

Where would a work on the immigration of Italians to the United States be classified?
The Relative Index under the entry "Immigration" lists a number of sub-headings on various aspects of immigration—criminal, legal, political, and sociological (Fig. 5-1).

Fig. 5-1. Relative Index

Immigrants *see* Ethnic groups
Immigration
    influence on crime   364.256
    law
        international   341.484
        municipal   342.082
        spec. jur.   342.3–.9
    pol. sci.   325.1
        areal trmt.   325.4–.9
———▶ sociology   301.324

So the first consideration is the emphasis of the work in hand. For our purposes here we will say the work emphasizes the social aspects of immigration, and the suggested number is 301.324 (Fig. 5-1). In the abridged edition the suggested number is 301.32, which turns out to be the complete number for this edition of the DDC. In the full DDC an explanatory statement under 301.324 indicates that this number is used for "movement of population into a specific area or country without regard to place of origin" (Fig. 5-2).

Fig. 5-2. Classification Schedule

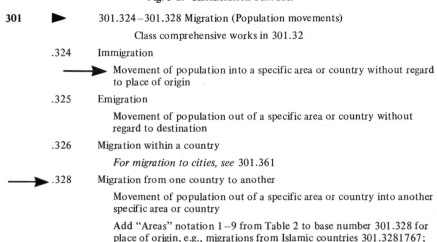

301   ▶   301.324–301.328 Migration (Population movements)
               Class comprehensive works in 301.32

    .324   Immigration

———▶ Movement of population into a specific area or country without regard to place of origin

    .325   Emigration

               Movement of population out of a specific area or country without regard to destination

    .326   Migration within a country

               For migration to cities, see 301.361

———▶ .328   Migration from one country to another

               Movement of population out of a specific area or country into another specific area or country

               Add "Areas" notation 1–9 from Table 2 to base number 301.328 for place of origin, e.g., migrations from Islamic countries 301.3281767; then add 0 and again add "Areas" notation 1–9 from Table 2 for place of entry, e.g., migration from Islamic countries to United States 301.3281767073

However, we are concerned with immigration from a specific country. An examination of the schedule shows that 301.328 is used for population movement from one country to another country. Instructions here say to "add 'Areas' notation 1–9 from Table 2 to the base number 301.328 for place of origin . . . ; then add 0 and again add 'Areas' notation 1–9 from Table 2 for place of entry . . . " (Fig. 5-2).

300	the social sciences
301	sociology
.3	ecology and community
.32	demography
.328	migration from one country to another
4	Europe –4 from Table 2
45	Italy –45 from Table 2
0	add "0" as instructed (Fig. 5-2)
7	North America –7 from Table 2
73	United States (from Table 2)
301.32845073	Italian immigration to the United States

The number for the social aspects of Italian immigration into the United States is 301.32845073. Notice that here the instructions authorize the use of the Areas Table *twice* within the same number.

Example 2

Where would you classify a work on the Liberal Democratic Party of Japan? The entry "Political parties–specific parties" in the Relative Index provides the number span 329.1–329.9. In the abridged edition the Relative Index entry "Political parties–political science" provides the number 329.

Turning to the schedule at 329.1, the cataloger finds two options for classifying political parties of specific countries (Fig. 5-3).

Fig. 5-3. Classification Schedule

▶ **329.1–329.9 Political parties of specific countries**

Arrange as below; but, if it is desired to give local emphasis and a shorter number to parties of a specific country, place them first by use of a letter or other symbol, e.g., political parties of Peru 329.P (preceding 329.1); then, if desired, arrange specific parties alphabetically as suggested at 329.9, e.g., Apra leadership 329.P A70212

Class comprehensive works in 329.02

If the classifier takes the first option, the starting point is 329.9, for political parties of other countries, to which is added the number for Japan from the Areas Table (Fig. 5-4):

Fig. 5-4. Classification Schedule

329

.9   **Political parties of other countries**

> Add "Areas" notation 3–9 from Table 2 to base number 329.9, e.g., parties of United Kingdom 329.942
>
> If desired, arrange specific parties of a specific country alphabetically, e.g., Labour Party of United Kingdom 329.942L2; then to the result add the numbers following 329 in 329.01–329.06, e.g., Labour Party leadership 329.942L20212

329.9	political parties of other countries
5	Asia-Orient-Far East (from Table 2)
52	Japan (from Table 2)
329.952	political parties in Japan

Thus the number for a Japanese political party is 329.952. This is the final number for the abridged edition. If a more specific number is desired, the instructions at 329.9 in the 18th edition allow the addition of a letter to designate the parties of a country. Thus, L could be added for the Liberal Democratic Party: 329.952L. To maintain alphabetic order a cutter number can be used for the name of each party: 329.952L6. (For a discussion of cutter author numbers, see Chapter 12.) If a further breakdown is required for a book on party leadership, the classifier is instructed at 329.9 to add to the base number 329.952 the appropriate numbers following 329 in 329.01–329.06 (Fig. 5-4).

Thus, the number for a book on the *leadership* of the Japanese Liberal Democratic Party is 329.9520212 or 329.952L60212.

329	practical politics, political parties
.9	political parties of other countries
52	number for Japan (from Table 2)
L6	a cutter number for the Liberal Party
021	party organization (taken from the range of numbers 329.01–329.06)
0212	national organizations including party leadership (taken from 329.0212)
329.952L60212	the leadership of the Japanese Liberal Democratic Party

The second option is used to give local emphasis and to provide shorter numbers (Fig. 5-3, page 87). Here the cataloger uses the number 329 followed by a letter or symbol for the country. Political parties in Japan will be 329.J. Parties can then be arranged alphabetically as instructed at 329.9. Thus, the Japanese Liberal Democratic Party would be classified 329.J L6, and a work on the party leadership 329.J L60212.

Example 3

Where would a book on the economics and speculation of gold be classified? This poses some interesting problems in determining which of the various aspects of gold should be used. Under the entry "Gold" in the Relative Index, several possible numbers are suggested:

332.4042	coins in money economics
332.452	gold standard in foreign exchange
332.4222	gold standard in relation to monetary value
338.2741	production of gold
382.174	international commerce and movement of gold
553.41	mineral aspects in economic geology

All of the above numbers are possibilities, but none relates directly to speculation in gold, as can be seen when checking the schedule. The Relative Index in the abridged edition refers the user to "Metals." The entry "Speculation" in the Relative Index (full edition) provides a number for investment economics, 332.645; the corresponding abridged edition number is 332.6. Checking the schedule shows that 332.645 is the proper number for speculation in a commodity (Fig. 5-5).

Fig. 5-5. Classification Schedule

332

.645   Speculation

Purchase of securities and commodities with intent to profit by fluctuations in price

Including buying on margin

Thus, 332.645 (332.6 in the abridged edition) is the proper number for gold speculation.

This is a good example of the need to consider possibilities other than the most obvious.

Example 4

Where would a work on the education of Black children in the United States be classified?

A search in the Relative Index under the headings "Negro," "Minority groups," "Children," and "Education" gives either no relevant number or no number specific enough for the subject. Under "Special education" the number 371.9 is provided in both the full and abridged editions. Otherwise, a search of the education schedule is required. Such a search leads to 371 for "The school," and here a "Summary" gives 371.9 for special education.

Under 371.9 another "Summary" is provided with a more specific number: 371.97 for "Students exceptional because of national, racial, ethnic origin." The abridged edition stops at 371.9. Under 371.97 in the schedule instructions are given for handling the education of special groups. Add the proper notation 01–99 from Table 5 to the base number, then add a "0" and to this the area notation 1–9 from Table 2 for the place of education (Fig. 5-6).

Fig. 5-6. Classification Schedule

371

.97   Students exceptional because of national [*formerly* 371.98], racial, ethnic origin

➤ Add "Racial, Ethnic, National Groups" notation 01–99 from Table 5 to base number 371.97, e.g., education of Jews 371.97924; then add 0 and to the result add "Areas" notation 1–9 from Table 2 for place located, e.g., education of Jews in France 371.97924044

Class study and teaching of languages at secondary and higher levels in 400

The number for education of Black children in the United States will be 371.9796073:

371	the school
.9	special education
.97	students exceptional because of national, social, ethnic origin
96	Africans and people of African descent (from Table 5)
0	add "0" as instructed at 371.97
73	area notation for United States (from Table 2)
371.9796073	the education of Black children in the United States

Example 5

Where would a work on television broadcasting by satellites be classified? A check of the entry "Television" in the Relative Index provides the number 384.55 under "Television—communication." Under "Broadcasting activities—television" a reference is given to "Television—communication." Under "Satellite systems—television" there is a reference to "Communication systems—television," which gives an engineering number, 621.3885. However, a little further on, the entry "Communications satellites—communications industry—commerce—television" provides the number 384.55456. A search of the schedule at 384.5 shows this is the number for wireless communication and 384.55 for television. Further down the schedule the number 384.5545 is given, with instructions to add to the base number 384.554 for broadcasting the numbers following 384.54 in 384.543 to 384.545 (Fig. 5-7).

Fig. 5-7. Classification Schedule

384

.554	Broadcasting
.554 3–.554 5	Economic aspects, activities, facilities
	Add to 384.554 the numbers following 384.54 in 384.543–384.545, e.g., television networks 384.55455

Checking the schedule, satellites are found at 384.5456. Following the instructions, add the 56 following 384.54 to 384.554 to get the number 384.55456, which was the number suggested in the Relative Index. This example shows how the Relative Index will occasionally develop a number as fully as the schedules.

384	telecommunication
.5	wireless communication
.55	television
.554	broadcasting
5	facilities (from 384.54<u>5</u>)
56	satellites (from 384.54<u>56</u>)
384.55456	television broadcasting by satellites

In the abridged edition the number 384.55 is given in the Relative Index under "Television communication." The entry "Broadcasting—television" refers only to "Television communication." Under "Satellites" the number referred to is an engineering number. Under "Communications—satellites—television" the number 384.55 is given, and this is the final number for the abridged edition.

PROBLEMS TO SOLVE

Try to build classification numbers for the following hypothetical works:

1) a work on the Security Council of the United Nations
2) a serial publication (periodical) on curriculums
3) a work on the foreign relations between the United States and the Soviet Union
4) a work on the strategy of naval warfare
5) a general work on the administration of police departments
6) a book titled *The Elks, History of a Club*
7) a book on the forms of social correspondence
8) a historical work on the education of women in the twentieth century
9) a work on the effect of social change on the family

ANSWERS TO PROBLEMS

1) 341.232 (18th edition)   341.23 (10th abridged edition)

The Relative Index entry under "Security Council—United Nations—internat. law" gives the number 341.232. This is verified as the correct number in the schedule. Under the heading "United-Nations—internat. law" the number 341.23 is given, which is close to the correct number. In the abridged edition the entry "United-Nations—internat. law" provides the correct number, 341.23. There is no reference to the Security Council in the abridged edition.

2) 375.0005 (18th edition)   375 (10th abridged edition)

The Relative Index provides an entry "Curriculums" and the number 375. If you looked under "Education—curriculum," you would be misled to some degree by number 375.37, which is the number for curriculums in education.

The abridged edition refers to number 375 in the Relative Index under "Curriculums." Standard subdivisions are not allowed here as instructed, so 375 is the complete number.

The full edition, however, provides for standard subdivisions using three zeroes. The standard subdivision for periodicals is —05 in Table 1; following the directions under 375, then, the number for a serial publication on curriculums is 375.0005.

3) 327.73047 (18th edition)   327.73 (10th abridged edition)

In the Relative Index the entry "Foreign relations" directs the user to "International relations." The abridged edition entry is "Foreign affairs," which also directs the user to "International relations." Under the subheading "International relations—pol. sci." both editions refer to number 327.

The abridged edition allows further subdivision only for the foreign policy of a specific country, with instructions to add area notation 3—9 from Table 2 to base number 327. If the emphasis is on U.S. policy, add —73, making the number 327.73.

The full edition provides for a more detailed number using the area notation for both countries. Add the area notation 3–9 from Table 2 to the base number 327, for 327.73. Now add a "0" for 327.730, then add the area notation 1–9 from Table 2 (for the Soviet Union, –47) to get 327.73047 for foreign relations between the United States and the Soviet Union. If the emphasis were on Soviet policy, the number would be 327.47073.

4) 359.43 (18th edition)   359.4 (10th abridged edition)

The key words here are "strategy" and "naval warfare." The Relative Index provides the number 359.43 under "Strategy—mil. sci.—naval forces." Under entries for "Naval forces—mil. sci.," "Naval science" and "Naval warfare—mil. sci." the number 359 is suggested. Under "Warfare" a more general number, 355.02, is cited. The main element here is strategy as it relates to naval warfare. Checking the schedule, 359.43 turns out to be the most specific number.

The abridged edition provides the number 359.4 in the Relative Index under "Strategy—mil. sci.—naval forces" and 359 under "Naval forces—mil. sci.," "Naval science" and "Naval warfare—mil. sci." Number 355.02 is given with "Warfare—mil. sci." The correct number is 359.4.

5) 350.74 (18th edition)   350 (10th abridged edition)

The most logical starting point is the Relative Index under "Police." Several subheadings offer possibilities, the most likely one being "Police services—pub. admin." (350.74). Checking the schedule confirms that 350.74 is correct for the administration of police departments. Notice that police administration for a central government will be classified in 351.74 and police administration for local government will be classed in 352.2.

The abridged edition provides the numbers 351.7 and 352 under the Relative Index entry "Police—pub. admin." Checking the schedule reveals that 350 is the number for general works on police administration.

6) 366.5 (18th edition)   366 (10th abridged edition)

The Relative Index provides two possible entries: "Elks (animals)—animal husbandry," 636.294; and "Elks (order)," 366.5. The word "order" in the latter entry refers to a fraternal order and not any scientific biological aspect. The book in hand is on the fraternal order of Elks. Checking the schedule shows that 366.5 is the specific number for the Benevolent and Protective Order of Elks (B.P.O.E.).

The abridged edition only refers to "Elks (animals)," so another entry must be found. There is no entry under "Elks (order)" but there is an entry "Organizations—fraternal," with reference to number 366; this is found to be the most specific number when the schedule is checked.

7) 395.4 (18th edition)   395 (10th abridged edition)

There is no entry under "Social correspondence" in the Relative Index. The term "Correspondence (communication)," however, has a reference to "Letters (correspondence)." Under "Letters (correspondence)–etiquette" is the number 395.4. The entry "Etiquette" refers only to number 395, but this poses no problem because the schedule leads to 395.4 for social correspondence.

The abridged edition, under the entries "Etiquette" and "Letters correspondence)–etiquette," provides the number 395, which is as far as this edition goes.

8) 376.904 (18th edition)   376 (10th abridged edition)

The term "Education" in the Relative Index proves too broad to find anything pertaining to the education of women. Under the entry "Women–education" is the number 376. The same results will be obtained in the abridged edition and 376 is the most specific number here.

The full edition provides for historical treatment under 376.9 and for specific historical periods by adding "the numbers following 090 in 'Standard Subdivisions' notation 0901–0904 from Table 1" to the base number 376.90. The number 376.904 then is correct for the education of women in the twentieth century, when the 4 from –0904 in Table 1 is added to the base, 376.90.

9) 301.423 (18th edition)   301.42 (10th abridged edition)

The entries "Family," "Families," and "Social" have large numbers of subheadings in the Relative Index. Since the subject is the effect of social change on the family, try to find a relevant subheading under "Family" or "Families." The entry "Family relationships–sociology" suggests the number 301.427. Under "Families–sociology," 301.42 is given. Under the entry "Social change–sociology," 301.24 is suggested. The entry "Social structure–sociology" provides another possibility at 301.4.

Checking the schedule shows that 301.24 is not the correct number. Number 301.4, however, brings the cataloger to social structure and 301.42 to marriage and the family, while 301.423 is the number for the family and social change. This shows again that the Relative Index is an *aid* in finding a DDC number; but to find the best or most specific number, it is *always necessary to classify only from the schedule.*

Using the same entries in the Relative Index in the abridged edition leads to number 301.42. Checking the schedule shows that this is the correct number.

CHAPTER 6

CLASS 400—499
(LANGUAGE)

INTRODUCTORY NOTE

European languages, like European literatures in the 800's, are given favored treatment in this class, with whole divisions for English, German, French, Italian, Spanish, Latin, and classical Greek. Most of the remaining languages of the world receive much longer numbers. Both Table 4, Individual Languages, and Table 6, Languages, are used with this class; in fact, Table 4 is used only with this class in order to give the form divisions for all languages. The form divisions in Table 4 are given with examples in Chapter 1 of this text. They include the written and spoken codes of the standard form of the language, the etymology, dictionaries, grammar, prosody, non-standard forms of the language, and standard usage of the language. Both the number-building examples and the problems in this chapter make use of Table 4, which should be carefully examined and used by the reader.

OUTLINE OF THE CLASS

400	Language
410	Linguistics
420	English and Anglo-Saxon languages
430	Germanic languages
440	Romance languages
450	Italian, Romanian, Rhaeto-Romanic languages
460	Spanish and Portuguese languages
470	Italic languages
480	Hellenic languages
490	Other languages

INTRODUCTION TO THE CLASS

The language schedule is the shortest of all the DDC's main classes. It is concerned with all forms of verbal expression and the use of words in human thought and understanding.

The emphasis in this class, as it is in religion (200) and literature (800), is on Western culture. Provision is made, however, for giving local emphasis to specific languages either by using 410 as instructed in the schedule or by using a letter or symbol preceding 420, as instructed in the schedule.

DETAILS OF THE CLASS

The first division, 400, is used for comprehensive works on language. Sections 401–409 are used for standard subdivisions such as philosophy and theory, dictionaries and encyclopedias, and study and teaching.

Division 410 is devoted to Linguistics, with sections on etymology (412), phonology (414), structural systems (415), and usage (418).

Divisions 420 to 490 are used for specific languages, with 420 to 480 devoted to Indo-European languages. All have similarly headed sections based on Table 4. For example, all have sections relating to written and spoken codes of the language, etymology, dictionaries, structural system (grammar), prosody, non-standard aspects, and standard usage (applied linguistics).

Division 420 treats the English and Anglo-Saxon languages. Division 430 is devoted to Germanic (Teutonic) languages. In division 430 provision is made for regional variations of German and for other Germanic languages such as Dutch, Afrikaans, and Scandinavian languages.

Division 440 is concerned with the French language, including such regional variations as Provençal and Catalan.

Division 450 covers Italian, Romanian, and Rhaeto-Romanic languages. Regional variations include those for continental Italy, Sicily, Sardinia, Corsica, and other areas.

Division 460 is assigned to the Spanish and Portuguese languages. The regional variations for Portuguese include the language as spoken in Brazil.

Division 470 incorporates the Italic languages (Latin) and their classical and post-classical usage.

Division 480 covers the Hellenic languages and classical and modern Greek.

Division 490 is assigned to the rest of the world's languages. Section 491 treats the East Indo-European and Celtic languages, including Indo-Iranian, Sanskrit, Indic languages, Celtic, Russian, Polish and other Slavic languages, and Baltic and other languages, such as Albanian and Armenian.

Section 492 is used for Afro-Asiatic and Semitic languages. Also covered here are ancient languages such as Assyrian and Babylonian. Other languages included are the Aramaic languages, Canaanitic languages (including Hebrew and Yiddish) and other Ethiopic and Arabic languages.

Section 493 embodies Hamitic and Chad languages and section 494 the Ural-Altaic, Paleosiberian, and Dravidian languages. The Uralic group (494.4–494.5) includes the Finnish language and Tamil language of India.

The languages of East and Southeast Asia are covered in section 495. These include Chinese, Tibetan, Japanese, Korean, Burmese, and other languages of Southeast Asia, such as Thai, Vietnamese and Cambodian.

Section 496 treats African languages. The numbers for specific languages are developed by extensive use of the language notations from Table 6.

Sections 497 and 498 are concerned with American and South American aboriginal languages. Finally, section 499 covers all other languages, including Tagalog, Indonesian, Malay, Esperanto, and Interlingua.

NUMBER BUILDING, 400–499

Example 1

What DDC number would be given to a work on the grammar of the Japanese language?

The Relative Index provides a specific number, 495.6, under the entry "Japanese language–linguistics." The schedule provides no further breakdown, but there are instructions in the full edition to add to the base number as instructed at the centered heading 420–490 (Figs. 6-1, 6-2).

Fig. 6-1. Classification Schedule

495

    .6   *Japanese

*Add to base number as instructed under 420–490

Fig. 6-2. Classification Schedule

►   **420–490 Specific languages**

Class here comprehensive works on specific languages and their literatures

Arrange as below; but, if it is desired to give local emphasis and a shorter number to a specific language, place it first by use of a letter or other symbol, e.g., Arabic language 4A0 (preceding 420), for which base number is 4A

Under each language identified by *, add to designated base number "Subdivisions of Individual Languages" notation 01–86 from Table 4

Class comprehensive works in 410

For literatures of specific languages, see 810–890

The abridged edition goes only to number 495.6, with no further breakdown. In the full edition the user is instructed to add to the base number the proper notation from Table 4, "Subdivisions of Individual Languages." Grammar, the structural system of a language, is –5 in Table 4 (Fig. 6-3).

Fig. 6-3. Subdivisions of Individual Languages (Table 4)

–5   **Structural system (Grammar) of the standard form of the language**

    Morphology and syntax

Adding –5 to the base number 495.6 yields 495.65 for a work on Japanese grammar.

495.6	Japanese
5	grammar (from Table 4)
495.65	a Japanese grammar

Example 2

What number would be given to a French language reader for use by English speaking people?

The Relative Index offers at least two possible points of entry. Under "French language–linguistics" the number 440 is provided. Under "Readers (textbooks)–appl. ling.–spec. langs." reference is made to –86 in Table 4 (Fig. 6-4).

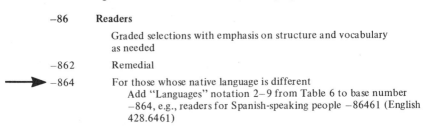

Fig. 6-4. Subdivisions of Individual Languages (Table 4)

–86	**Readers**
	Graded selections with emphasis on structure and vocabulary as needed
–862	Remedial
–864	For those whose native language is different
	Add "Languages" notation 2–9 from Table 6 to base number –864, e.g., readers for Spanish-speaking people –86461 (English 428.6461)

Keep the number –86 in mind since it may be useful in providing specificity.

From all this we conclude that the starting point will be 440. A quick search of the schedule brings the user to 448 for standard French usage or applied linguistics. This may seem to be the end of the search, but there is an asterisk by the word "French" in the schedule at 440, with instructions to add to the base number as instructed under the centered heading 420–490 (Fig. 6-2, page 97). There you are instructed to "add to designated base number 'Subdivisions of Individual Languages' notation 01–86 from Table 4." The base number for French is 44, so the number 448 can be disregarded. Table 4 shows that the number –86 is used for readers. Now we can start to build the number by adding –86 to base number 44 to get 448.6 for a reader in French. Although this may seem to be the final number, the work in question is a reader for use by English speaking students. Table 4 gives the number –864 for readers " . . . whose native language is different." Under –864 instructions say to "add 'Languages' notation 2–9 from Table 6 to base number –864" (Fig. 6-4). We now have the following number:

400	language
440	romance languages–French
44	base number for French
8	standard usage (Table 4)
8.6	standard usage readers (Table 4)
8.64	for those whose native language is different (Table 4)
21	for English speaking people (Table 6)
448.6421	a French reader for English speaking people

The abridged edition provides entry points under "French language—linguistics," which gives number 440, and under "Readers (textbooks)—appl. ling.—spec. langs." and language subdivision −86. Again the division heading at 440 has an asterisk. The instructions say to use base number 44 and to add to this the appropriate notation from Table 4, which is −86 for readers. The final number here will be 448.6.

PROBLEMS TO SOLVE

Try to build classification numbers for the following hypothetical works:

1) a work on language for the deaf
2) an English language dictionary
3) a monograph on the Basque language
4) an English-Russian dictionary

ANSWERS TO PROBLEMS

1) 419 (18th edition)   419 (10th abridged edition)

Again the initial problem is to find a starting point in the Relative Index. The most logical term is "Sign language." Under this the subheading "Manual alphabet" gives the number 419. The term "Manual alphabet language" has a cross reference to "Sign language." Under the entry "Deaf mute language" is a reference to "Sign language." Thus, 419 is the correct number; this is verified by checking the schedule.

The abridged edition also refers to number 419 under "Manual alphabet language" and "Sign language—manual alphabet." Here, too, 419 is the correct number.

2) 423 (18th edition)   423 (10th abridged edition)

The Relative Index entry "Dictionaries—linguistics—spec. lang.—standard forms" refers to Table 4 for subdivisions of individual languages. This is not too helpful. Under "English language—linguistics" a more usable number, 420, is cited. The abridged edition has similar entries and similar references.

Going through the schedule under 420 leads to 423—in both editions of DDC—for dictionaries of standard English.

  3) 499.92 (18th edition)   499 (10th abridged edition)

The entry under "Basque language—linguistics" in the Relative Index gives the number 499.92. The same entry in the abridged edition gives the number 499.

The schedule gives only the number 499, with no other subsections and no Basque language is listed. However, the instructions say to "add 'Languages' notation 99 from Table 6 to base number 4." Turning to Table 6 and searching the –99 number the cataloger finds that –9992 is used for the Basque language. Adding this to base number 4 as instructed creates 499.92 for a work on the Basque language.

The abridged edition does not have the Table 6 option and stops with number 499.

  4) 491.7321 (18th edition)   491.73 (10th abridged edition)

  The Relative Index gives the number 491.7 for Russian linguistics, and this is also indicated as the base number for Russian in the schedules. Since the Russian language is asterisked in the schedules, you should follow the directions under 420–490 (Fig. 6-2, page 97). These directions send you to Table 4, where the digit 3, meaning dictionaries, is added to the base number, along with the digits for the English language, 21. Russian is the language that is classed first, since it is the lesser known language in this country. In the abridged edition, Table 4 has no provision for indicating a second language.

CHAPTER 7

CLASS 500–599
(PURE SCIENCES)

INTRODUCTORY NOTE

Six separate disciplines in science receive one division each in the development of this class. As the following outline shows, these are mathematics (510), astronomy (520), physics (530), chemistry (540), geology (550), and paleontology or the study of fossils (560). The remaining major scientific discipline, biology, is covered by the last three divisions—life sciences (570), botany (580), and zoology (590). It is important to recognize that this entire class is devoted to pure science; applied science, being classed as technology, is in the next class (600's). A good scientific dictionary or glossary will be most helpful for understanding the many scientific terms used in this schedule. The lengthy "Details of the Class" section of this chapter should be carefully studied and compared to the schedule. The student should use a scientific dictionary to look up terms that are not clear.

The examples and problems in this chapter show how important number building is in this class and how extensively this synthetic device may be applied. Here you must be exact in regard to the division you are using and the meaning of the terminology. After consulting the Relative Index, always try to determine which division (e.g., mathematics, astronomy, or physics) is most appropriate to the material being classed before locating a specific number in the schedules. The need for this type of precision may be clearly seen in the first example in the number building section. You will need all your care and precision in order to arrive at the correct solution of the last two problems.

OUTLINE OF THE CLASS

500	Pure sciences
510	Mathematics
520	Astronomy and allied sciences
530	Physics
540	Chemistry and allied sciences
550	Sciences of the earth and other worlds
560	Paleontology
570	Life sciences
580	Botanical sciences
590	Zoological sciences

INTRODUCTION TO THE CLASS

This class, the third longest schedule in the DDC, is devoted to the pure sciences. Included here are mathematics, astronomy and allied sciences, physics, chemistry, sciences of the earth and other worlds, paleontology, life sciences, botanical sciences, and zoological sciences.

The division for mathematics, 510, is one of the two "phoenix" schedules in the 18th edition of DDC, having been completely revised with little or no reference to earlier editions of the DDC.

DETAILS OF THE CLASS

Comprehensive works on the major areas of the pure and applied sciences are covered by the numbers 500.1 to 500.9. The numbers 501 to 509 are used for the standard subdivisions.

The first division, 510, is for mathematics. The first section, 511, covers general mathematical concepts, such as inductive and intuitive mathematics, symbolic logic, approximations and expansions, theory and construction graphs, combinatorial analysis, numerical analysis, and mathematical models.

Algebra is the subject of section 512. Some of the subtopics of algebra within the section are groups, fields, rings, linear algebra, number theory, and pedagogical algebra for secondary school and college.

Section 513, used for arithmetic, covers arithmetic operations, arithmetic and geometric operations, digital representation, non-weighted systems, and special purpose mathematics (e.g., business arithmetic).

Section 514 is concerned with topology and its three main areas—algebraic topology, topology of spaces, and analytic topologies.

Analysis, the study of functions and limits, is the topic of section 515. The main areas of concern are generalities (e.g., properties of functions, operations on functions, sequences and series, equations and functions, and inequalities), differential calculus and equations, integral calculus and equations, special functions, other analytic methods, functional analysis, and the functions of real and complex variables.

Geometry comprises section 516. Again there is a subsection for generalities of the subject and major subsections for Euclidian geometry and analytic geometries (with subsections for plane and solid geometry and trigonometry).

Sections 517 and 518 are currently unassigned.

Section 519 covers probabilities and applied mathematics. These subjects include game theories, applied numerical analysis, statistical mathematics, and programming.

Division 520 is assigned to astronomy and its allied sciences. The first section, 521, is devoted to theoretical astronomy and celestial mechanics including such topics as orbits; theory of planets, stars, and galaxies; theory of satellites, meteors, and comets; and eclipses.

Practical and spherical astronomy is in section 522. Here are found subdivisions on observatories, optical telescopes, other astronomical instruments, special methods of observations, and spherical astronomy. Section 523, descriptive astronomy, is the largest in this division; it incorporates astrophysics, the universe, the solar system, the moon, the individual planets of this solar system, meteors, comets, our sun and the stars, and star systems.

Section 524 is presently unassigned. Section 525 is used for the earth in relation to astronomical geography (e.g., orbit, seasons, tides).

Mathematical geography is assigned to section 526. Geodetic surveying, geodetic and positional astronomy, gravity determinations, map drawing, and surveying make up the subtopics of this section.

Celestial navigation and its various aspects (latitude, longitude, fixes, and direction and course) are covered in section 527.

Ephemerides (nautical almanacs) are covered in section 528 and section 529 is devoted to chronology (time) and its aspects of sidereal and solar day, intervals of time, and calendars.

Division 530 is used for physics. Basic theories of physics are covered first: relativity theory, quantum theory, statistical and kinetic theories and field and wave theories. These are followed by numbers for states of matter, instrumentation and physical units, dimensions, and constants.

Section 531 is used for mechanics, with subsections for dynamics, statics, mechanics of solids, mass and gravity, energy, and simple machines. Sections 532 and 533 cover the mechanics of fluids and gases, respectively. Some of the special topics here are hydromechanics, hydrostatics, vacuums, aeromechanics and kinetic theory of gases.

Sound and related vibrations are covered by section 534. Some of the important subsections are devoted to the generation, propagation, characteristics, measurement, analysis, and synthesis of sound and vibrations.

Visible light (optics) and its theories, physical aspects, transmission, absorption, emission, dispersion, and diffraction are found in section 535. Also in this section are subsections for light beams, color, and special developments in the physics of light.

Section 536 covers the subject of heat. Subsections are devoted to heat theories, its transmission and radiation, effects of heat on matter, temperature, heat measurement, calorimetry, and thermodynamics.

Section 537 is concerned with electricity and electronics, with subsections on theories, electrostatics, electronics (including radio and microwave electronics), electrodynamics, and thermoelectricity.

Section 538 covers magnetism, with subsections on magnets and magnetic induction, magnetic properties and phenomena, magnetohydrodynamics, and geomagnetism.

The final section, 539, is used for modern physics. Some of the subtopics here are structure of matter, radiations, molecular physics, atomic and nuclear physics (including particles, X, gamma, and cosmic rays, and nuclei), nuclear structure, and radioactivity.

One of the largest divisions of this class, 540, is devoted to chemistry and its allied sciences. The first eight sections, 540–547, pertain specifically to chemistry and the last two to allied sciences.

The first section, 541, is used for theoretical and physical chemistry. The former includes molecular and atomic structure and quantum chemistry. The latter covers photochemistry, thermochemistry and thermodynamics, electro- and magnetochemistry, radiochemistry, and chemical reactions and synthesis.

Chemical laboratories, apparatus, and equipment are provided for in section 542.

The next three sections, 543—545, are devoted to analytical chemistry. The first, 543, is used for general analysis; 544 for qualitative analysis; and 545 for quantitative analysis.

Section 546 is used for inorganic chemistry—the chemistry of elements, inorganic compounds, and mixtures. Notice the comprehensive table of terms (page 923 in the Schedules) whose assigned numbers are to be added to specific elements covered in 546.2 to 546.7. The first two subsections cover hydrogen and hydrogen compounds, and compounds and mixtures of metals. Subsections 546.4 to 546.7 cover various groups of elements such as rare earth elements, the titanium, chromium and manganese groups, the iron series, the copper group (including gold and silver), the zinc, boron and carbon groups, and the groups of non-metals (nitrogen, oxygen, halogen, and rare gases). The final subsection deals with the periods of the periodic table of elements according to their atomic number.

The last main section on chemistry is 547, organic chemistry. The first subsections include the general groupings of compounds including the hydro-carbons, nitrogen, sulfur, phosphorus, and silicon. The primary subsections consist of the physical, theoretical, and analytical aspects of organic chemistry, including a subsection on synthesis and named reactions. The next three subsections, 547.4 to 547.6, cover aliphatic, cyclic, and aromatic compounds, followed by two sub-sections on macromolecular and related compounds such as alkaloids, steroids, hormones, vitamins, proteins, enzymes, carbohydrates, and the fossil substances of coal tar, petroleum, polymers, man-made fibers, and dyes and pigments.

Section 548 is used for the field of crystallography and its chemical, physical, and structural aspects. Included here too is optical crystallography.

The field of mineralogy is incorporated in section 549. Mineralogy is con-cerned with the distribution, description, and identification of naturally occurring minerals and their compounds.

Division 550 is used for geologic sciences of this planet (earth) and other worlds. A lengthy section, 551, is devoted to physical and dynamic geology. Included here are geologic structure, volcanic and seismic phenomena, surface processes of ice and water, geomorphology, meteorology (including climatology and weather), and historical geology.

Section 552 pertains to rocks and petrology (e.g., igneous, volcanic, meta-morphic, and sedimentary rocks). Section 553 covers economic geology, which is concerned with the occurrence and distribution of those materials (metals, coal, gems, water, gases, etc.) that have economic value. Subsections cover the formation and structure of deposits and the occurrence and distribution of specific materials. Sections 554 to 559 are used for regional geology or geology of specific areas—continents, countries, localities.

Paleontology and paleozoology comprise the 560 division. The first sub-sections cover the philosophy, theory, historical and geographical treatment of this division. The initial section, 561, deals with paleobotany, with subsections on fossil seed plants, fossil flowering plants, fossil seedless plants and fossil moss plants. The remaining sections cover specific animals and groups of animals: fossil invertebrates, 562; fossil Protozoa, Parazoa, and Metazoa, 563; fossil Mollusca and molluscoidea, 564; other fossil invertebrates (e.g., worms, Crustacea, Arachnida, and insects), 565;

fossil vertebrates, 566; fossil Anamnia and fossil fishes, 567; fossil reptiles and birds, 568; and fossil mammals, 569.

Division 570 deals with the life sciences. The first section, 571, is unassigned. Section 572 covers human races, including their origins, physical characteristics, specific races, and geographical distribution of races. Section 573 is assigned to physical anthropology, which includes organic evolution and genetics of man, prehistoric man, and physical characteristics of men.

Section 574 is assigned to biology. Its major subsection, 574.1, covers physiology, the processes and activities of life and living organisms. Some of the subjects included here are circulation, respiration, reproduction, biophysics, and biochemistry. The science of diseases, pathology, is an important subsection, and other subsections deal with development and maturation, anatomy and morphology, ecology, economic biology, tissue, cellular and molecular biology, and geographical treatment of biology.

The subsequent five sections, 575–579, are concerned with special biological fields and techniques. The first of these, 575, deals with organic evolution and genetics, including numbers for the basic theories of evolution. Section 576 covers microbes and the general principles of microbiology. Section 577 deals with the general nature of life, section 578 with microscopy in biology, and section 579 with biological specimens.

The botanical sciences are assigned to division 580. The first section, 581, is concerned with the general aspects of botany, including such areas as the physiology and pathology of plants, plant development and maturation, plant anatomy and morphology, ecology of plants, economic botany, tissue, cellular, and molecular botany, and general geographical treatment.

The remaining eight sections, 582–589, are used for specific plants and groups of plants. Seed-bearing plants (Spermatophyta) are assigned to 582, flowering plants (Angiospermae), including the grasses, are provided for in 583 and 584; naked-seed plants (Gymnospermae) are in 585; seedless plants (Cryptogamia) are in 586; vascular cryptogams (Pteridophyta), including ferns and club mosses, in 587; Bryophyta, the true mosses, in 588; and Thallophyta, including lichens, fungi, and algae, in 589.

The science class is completed with division 590, zoological sciences. The general aspects of this field are covered in section 591; included here are physiology, pathology, development and maturation, anatomy and morphology, ecology, economic aspects, tissue, cellular, and molecular zoology, and general geographical treatment.

Specific animals and groups of animals are covered in the eight subsequent sections, 592–599.

Sections 592 to 595 cover the invertebrates. Section 592 is devoted to general topics, section 593 covers Protozoa, Parazoa, and Metazoa (i.e., sponges, corals, jellyfish, starfish, sea urchins); section 594 covers the Mollusca and molluscoidae (e.g., clams, oysters, snails, octopuses); and section 595 is used for other invertebrates such as worms, Arthropoda, Crustacea, Arachnida and Insecta.

The final four sections are devoted to Chordata, the vertebrates.

The general principles of the field are covered by section 596. Section 597 covers the Anamnia, or fishes and amphibians (e.g., lampreys, sharks, sturgeons, eels, catfishes, sea horses, salmon, tunas, frogs, and salamanders).

Reptiles and birds are assigned to section 598. The first subsection, 598.1, is concerned with reptiles (e.g., lizards, snakes, turtles, crocodiles). The remaining subsections, 598.2 to 598.9, cover the Aves, or birds. General treatment of the subject is handled in 598.2, and the remaining subsections are for specific orders of birds.

The final section of the zoology division, 599, is for Mammalia, or mammals. Starting with general principles, other subsections cover the following mammalian orders: the Monotremata (e.g., platypuses), Marsupialia (e.g., kangaroos, opossums), Unguiculata (e.g., aardvarks, anteaters, armadillos, sloths, rabbits, beavers, squirrels, mice, rats, porcupines, hedgehogs, moles, shrews, lemurs), Chiroptera (e.g., bats), Cetacea and Sirenia (e.g., whales, dolphins, dugongs), Paenungulata (e.g., elephants), Mesaxonia, Paraxonia, and Ferungulata (e.g., horses, zebras, tapirs, rhinoceroses, hippopotamuses, pigs, caribou, deer, giraffes, antelopes, cattle, goats, oxen, sheep, camels, llamas, mongooses, hyenas, cats, dogs, wolves, pandas, raccoons, bears, otters, skunks, seals, walruses, and elephant seals), Primates (e.g., monkeys, apes, gibbons, chimpanzees, and gorillas) and finally, the Hominidae, otherwise known as man.

NUMBER BUILDING, 500–599

Example 1

Where would a work on binary system be classified? Here the cataloger faces some interesting classification possibilities. The Relative Index suggests four possibilities. Under the entry "Binary" there are four headings, one with a number and three with see references (Fig. 7-1).

Fig. 7-1. Relative Index

```
Binary
    invariants algebra see Invariant
        theory algebra
    numeration system                    513.52
    s.a. spec. appls.
    salts see Simple salts
    stars see Visual binary stars
```

At this point it becomes necessary to check the work in hand to see exactly what aspect of "binary" is discussed.

If the binary system has to do with an arithmetic numeration system and digital representations, then 513.52 is the correct DDC number.

If the work is about star systems, then the reference in the Relative Index to "Visual binary stars" leads to two numbers: 523.841 for description of binary stars and 521.5841 for the theory of binary stars. The former number is used for binary and multiple stars. The latter number, used for the theoretical aspects of binary star systems, is built as follows:

520		astronomy
521		theoretical astronomy and celestial mechanics
	.5	theory of planets, stars, galaxies
	.58	theory of stars and galaxies
	41	as instructed at .589—.585 (star systems and aggregations), add to 521.58 the numbers following 523.8 in 523.84—523.85. Thus, the 41 from 523.841, for binary and multiple stars, is added to 521.58.
521.5841		the theory of binary star systems

If the work in hand is about binary salts, then you look under "Simple salts" as instructed in the Relative Index (Fig. 7-1). Under "Simple salts metals–inorganic" the number 546.342 is cited (Fig. 7-2).

Fig. 7-2. Classification Schedule

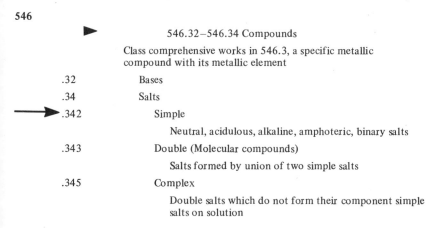

546

546.32–546.34 Compounds

Class comprehensive works in 546.3, a specific metallic compound with its metallic element

.32		Bases
.34		Salts
.342		Simple
		Neutral, acidulous, alkaline, amphoteric, binary salts
.343		Double (Molecular compounds)
		Salts formed by union of two simple salts
.345		Complex
		Double salts which do not form their component simple salts on solution

Checking the schedule shows that this number is correct for binary salts as one aspect of simple salts (Fig. 7-2).

If the work in hand is on the binary system in algebra, then check the reference in the Relative Index to "Invariant theory algebra," 512.944, which is a subsection of "Theory of equations" (Fig. 7-3).

Fig. 7-3. Classification Schedule

512	Theory of equations
	Equations and systems of equations, radical theory
.942	Specific types and systems of equations
	Polynomial, quadratic, cubic, quartic, mixt
.943	Matrices and determinants
.944	Quantics (Theory of forms) and algebraic invariant theory

In the schedule, however, no mention is made of the word binary, so the Relative Index is the authority here.

The abridged edition has no entry for "Binary" in the Relative Index, so more effort is needed to determine a starting point. A search of the schedule leads to Arithmetic and number 513, where binary is mentioned in the terms covered by section 513. If the cataloger knew the subject was theory of equations (in which case the word binary would probably not be used in the title), then 512.9 would be used.

In astronomy, the abridged edition uses 521 for "specific theories and their application to celestial bodies and kinds of bodies" (Abridged DDC, p. 213); number 523.8, used for stars, specifically mentions binary stars. In the Relative Index the entries are "Stars–astronomy–description" and "Stars–astronomy–theory."

Under "Salts" there are three subheadings but none relate to binary salts. Under "Metals–chemistry–inorganic" the number 546 is cited. Salts are inorganic, so the number 546 is used for inorganic salts.

As shown here, the abridged edition requires somewhat more searching than the full edition, and it is necessary to search the schedules directly to get some idea of where to classify the materials.

Example 2

Where would a book on the San Diego, California, Zoo be classified? The Relative Index has no entry for "Zoo," but there is one for "Zoos–animal husbandry for," which gives number 636.08899. This number, however, is not for a comprehensive work on a zoo but for works on the maintenance of zoological animals. Under "Zoological" is the subheading "gardens." "Zoological gardens" is a more academic term for a zoo, and the number cited here is 590.744. In the schedule there are instructions for adding Areas notation from Table 2 to the base number (Fig. 7-4).

Fig. 7-4. Classification Schedule

590	**Zoological sciences**	
	For paleozoology, see 560	
.7	**Study and teaching**	
.74	Exhibits	
.742	Museums	
	Add "Areas" notation 1–9 from Table 2 to base number 590.742	
➤ .744	Zoological gardens	
	Add "Areas" notation 1–9 from Table 2 to base number 590.744	

The number for the San Diego Zoo is:

590	zoological sciences
.744	zoological gardens
794	California (from Table 2)
7949	southern counties (from Table 2)
79498	San Diego County (from Table 2)

590.74479498   zoological gardens in San Diego, California

In the abridged edition the only related entry in the Relative Index is "Zoological sciences," and number 590 is cited. For this edition of DDC, 590 would be the most logical place to classify zoos.

Example 3

Where would a work on the molecular structure of uranium be classified?

The Relative Index has an entry under "Uranium—chemistry—inorganic" and cites number 546.431. In the schedule there are number building instructions under 546.431 to "add as instructed under 546." Under number 546 the number 4 is used for theoretical chemistry, which includes molecular structure (Fig. 7-5).

Fig. 7-5. Classification Schedule

546   Inorganic chemistry

Chemistry of elements, of inorganic compounds and mixtures

Class here physical and theoretical chemistry [*both formerly* 541], analytical chemistry [*formerly* 543—545], physics of specific elements, compounds, mixtures, groupings; comprehensive works on inorganic and organic chemistry of specific elements, compounds, mixtures, groupings

Add to each subdivision identified by * as follows:
- 1   The element
- 2   Compounds
- 22   Acids and bases
- 24   Salts
- 25   Complex compounds
- 3   Molecular and colloidal mixtures
- 4   Theoretical chemistry
    - Of element, compounds, mixtures
    - Add to 4 the numbers following 541.2 in 541.22—541.28, e.g., molecular structure 42
- 5   Physical chemistry
    - Of element, compounds, mixtures
    - Add to 5 the numbers following 541.3 in 541.34—541.39, e.g., radiochemistry 58
- 6   Analytical chemistry
    - Of element, compounds, mixtures
- 64   Qualitative methods
- 65   Quantitative methods

For organic chemistry, see 547

Following the instructions under 4, add to the base number (546.431) the number 4 and the numbers following 541.2 in 541.22–541.28 (Fig. 7-5); 541.22 turns out to be the number for molecular structure, so the last 2 is added to the 4 for 42. The following number is thus built:

540		chemistry and allied sciences
546		inorganic chemistry
	.4	group 3B
	.43	uranium, neptunium, plutonium
	.431	uranium
	4	theoretical chemistry (from the table under 546)
	42	molecular structure (from 541.2̲2̲, as instructed under 546)
546.43142		molecular structure of uranium

The abridged edition's Relative Index under "Uranium" has a see reference to "Metals" and under "Metals–chemistry–inorganic" cites 546. Under "Molecular structure–chemistry," the number 541 is cited. Under 541 are instructions to class the chemistry of specific inorganic elements in 546. Remember that it is the molecular structure of a *specific* element we are concerned with, and not the general aspects of molecular structure. Thus, 546 is the correct number for the abridged edition.

PROBLEMS TO SOLVE

Try to build classification numbers for the following hypothetical works:

1) a book on college algebra
2) a book on periodic law in chemistry
3) a book on nuclear fusion
4) a book on continental drift
5) a book on the ecology of the ocean
6) a book on palms as a useful plant to man
7) a book on making economic products from palms
8) a book on the behavior of ants in their communities

Editor's note: The last two problems may seem to the reader to be quite difficult. Actually, they are not difficult, but they are complex. If you have difficulty, simply analyze the solutions for all the necessary steps.

ANSWERS TO PROBLEMS

1) 512.9 (18th edition)   512.9 (10th abridged edition)

Both editions of DDC have Relative Index entries for "Algebra," citing number 512, but there is no specific reference to college level algebra. The "Summary" under 512 in the schedule (full edition) provides a clue, listing subsection .9 for "pedagogical algebra." But, unless the cataloger realizes that "pedagogical algebra" has to do with the teaching, learning, and instruction of algebra, it is necessary to check the entire 512 schedule. Under 512.9 is a scope note instructing the cataloger to classify college algebra here. A search of the schedule at 512 in the abridged edition also leads to 512.9, which is used for college algebra.

2) 541.901 (18th edition)   541 (10th abridged edition)

The Relative Index is particularly helpful in providing guidance. Periodic law has nothing to do with law, which is classed in 340. The Relative Index entry "Periodic law—theoretical chem." cites number 541.901. The abridged edition has the same index entry and cites number 541.

It should be noted that a work solely on the periodic table of elements (arranged according to periodic law) would classify in 546.8 in the full edition or 546 in the abridged edition. The Relative Index entry for both editions is "Periodic table—chemistry."

3) 539.764 (18th edition)   539.7 (10th abridged edition)

There are several entries in the Relative Index that could pertain to nuclear fusion, though there is no entry under nuclear fusion itself.

First, "Nuclear reactions—physics" provides number 539.75, and in the abridged edition "Nuclear physics" provides number 539.7. Second, "Reaction—cross sections—nuclear" gives a reference to "Nuclear reactions." This entry is not in the abridged edition. Third, under "Thermonuclear reactions" there is a reference to "Fusion—nuclear." This entry too is not in the abridged edition. And, finally, the entry "Fusion—nuclear physics" cites number 539.764. The abridged edition entry is "Fusion—nuclear physics," with number 539.7.

Upon checking the schedule 539.764 and 539.7 are found to be the correct numbers for the full and abridged edition, respectively.

4) 551.41 (18th edition)   551.4 (10th abridged edition)

The Relative Index has no entry for continental drift, nor does the term "drifts" appear in the Index with this connotation. Under "Continents—shelves" there is a reference to "Continents—geomorphology," which cites the number 551.41. In the schedule the main subsection geomorphology is 551.4, and the scope note says that this number includes the "creation and modification of topographic land and water features." The instructions under 551.41–.44 direct the user to "add to 551.4 the numbers following 14 in 'Areas' notation 141–144 from Table 2."

In the Areas Table, −141 is assigned to continents, so the final 1 in −141 is added to 551.4 to get 551.41, which is the correct number for continental drift.

The Relative Index in the abridged edition has an entry "Continents—geomorphology," with number 551.4. A check of the schedule provides the information that this number includes the "origin, development, transformation of topograph features, e.g. continents . . . "

5) 574.52636 (18th edition)   574.5 (10th abridged edition)

The entry "Ocean" in the Relative Index provides no useful terms. The term "Ecology—life sci." is used in both editions of DDC and cites the number 574.5. This number is correct for the abridged edition, but it can be more specific for the unabridged edition. Checking the schedule under 574.5 leads to 574.52636 for ecology of salt water, which, of course, includes oceans. Again, remember not to accept the first number referred to in the Index; always check the schedule for the most specific number.

6) 584.50461 (18th edition)   584 (10th abridged edition)

The Relative Index has a reference from "Palm—families" to "Palmales," which provides the number 584.5 under "Palmales—botany." In the schedule, 584.5 has instructions to see the centered heading 582–589 and add the appropriate numbers as instructed. The standard subdivisions do not provide a specific number. Following the instructions for 04, general principles, one finds the number 581.6 for economic botany and 581.61 for "plants beneficial to man's interests." The instructions say to add to 04 the numbers following 581 in 581.1 to 581.8, so the final number will be:

584.5	Palmales
04	general principles
6	economic botany (from 581.<u>6</u>)
<u>61</u>	plants beneficial to man's interest (from 581.<u>61</u> as instructed)
584.50461	benefits of palms to man

The abridged edition has no entry for either palms or Palmales, so it is necessary to go directly to the schedule at division 580 for botanical sciences. There, however, it is necessary to know which family of plants include palms. A search in the work at hand or in a botanical dictionary or encyclopedia will provide the information that palms belong to the botanical subclass monocotyledons. The final number then is 584.

7) 338.1749745 (18th edition)   338.1 (10th abridged edition)

This problem provides an interesting exercise in using three different classes to build a number. The main subject is economic aspects of palms. Under "Palms" the Relative Index offers no help, but the entry "Palmaceous fruits—prod. econ." cites number 338.17461—.17462. The term "Production—economics—gen. wks." provides the number 338, a further clue to the economics number needed.

A search of the economics schedule at 338.17 (specific products) does not reveal 338.17461—.17462 as suggested in the Relative Index. However, there are instructions to "add to 338.17 the numbers following 63 in 633–638. Remember that 63 stands for agriculture and related technologies. A search of the schedule at 633–638 leads to 634.6 for tropical and subtropical tree fruits, including palmaceous fruits. But the subject of the book encompasses more than fruits.

Under 634.9, for forestry, there is a subsection 634.97 for specific kinds of trees. Now it is necessary to ascertain what family a palm belongs to. A botanical dictionary or encyclopedia provides the information that palms are monocotyledons, which are classed in 634.974.

Now following the instructions under 338.17 to add the numbers following 63 you get 338.174974. However, under 634.974 there are instructions to "add to 634.974 the numbers following 584 in 584.1–584.9. These are the numbers for monocotyledons in the botanic division. Here subsection 584.5 is used for Palmales (palms). So the final 5 in 584.5 is added to make the number for a work on economic products of palms 338.1749745.

The abridged edition has no entry in the Relative Index for "Palms," but under "Production–economics," reference is made to 338. A search of the schedule shows that 338.1 is used for production economics in agriculture. No further breakdown is necessary for the abridged edition.

    8) 595.79604524 (18th edition)   595.7 (10th abridged edition)

The term "Behavior–animals–ecology" in the Relative Index provides the number 591.5 and a note to see also specific animals. Under "Communities–ecology–life sci." is a reference to "Synecology–life sci."; its number is 574.524. Under the specific term "Ants" there is a reference to see "Formicidae." Under "Formicidae–zoology," the number 595.796 is cited.

The abridged edition also has a reference from "Behavior–animals–ecology" to see specific animals. Under "Communities–ecology" there is a reference to see "Ecology." Under "Ecology–life sci.–animals" there is the number 591.5. There is no entry for "Ants" or "Formicidae"; however, under "Insects–zoology" is the number 595.7, which is correct for the abridged edition.

In the full edition the logical starting point is 595.796 for ants (Formicidae). Here you are instructed at the bottom of the page to add as instructed under the centered heading 592–599. Under 592–599 are instructions for adding numbers for specific aspects of the subject. The 04 number for "general principles" provides the possibility for further specificity. Therefore, to 595.796 add 04, and to 04 the numbers following 591 in 591.1–591.8. The subject is on behavior in communities. A search of 591.1 to 591.8 brings one to 591.52–.57 which includes environments (e.g., communities). At this point are instructions to add to 591.5 the numbers following 574.5 in 574.52–574.57. 574.524 is for synecology including ecology of communities. Adding the −24 from this number to 591.5 results in the number 591.524. Following the original instructions at 592–599 add the numbers following 591 (thus, .524) to 595.79604, which results in the number 595.79604524:

595.796	Formicidae (ants)
04	general principles (from centered heading 592–599)
5	ecology (according to the instructions to add the numbers following 591 in 591.1–591.8)
52	specific relationships and environments
4	synecology, the ecology of communities (according to instructions to add the numbers following 574.5 in 574.52–574.57; the number for synecology is 574.52<u>4</u>)
595.79604524	behavior of ants in their communities

CHAPTER 8

CLASS 600–699
(TECHNOLOGY–APPLIED SCIENCES)

INTRODUCTORY NOTE

Of all the classes in DDC the order of the divisions in the 600's may be the most confusing. The natural order that can be seen in most of the classes is not readily apparent here, so the order of these divisions must be memorized. And just as in the preceding class (500's), the cataloger must be sure of the division in which material should be classed before fully developing the number (problem 3 in this chapter is an excellent example of the importance of this). Many of the divisions are quite long and need to be treated almost as separate classes. Further it must be noted that many practical as well as technical works will be classed here; for example, both cook books and medical treatises go in this class as do typing manuals and works on laser technology. The breadth of the 600's is clearly demonstrated in the "Details of the Class." Again it is necessary to warn the reader to consult specialized dictionaries when the terminology is not familiar.

OUTLINE OF THE CLASS

600	Technology (Applied sciences)
610	Medical sciences
620	Engineering and allied operations
630	Agriculture and related technologies
640	Domestic arts and sciences
650	Managerial services
660	Chemical and related technologies
670	Manufactures
680	Miscellaneous manufactures
690	Buildings

INTRODUCTION TO THE CLASS

This class, the longest in the DDC, encompasses the fields of medicine, engineering, agriculture, home economics, managerial services, chemical technology, manufacturing technology, and building trades.

DETAILS OF THE CLASS

The sections 600 to 609 are used for the standard subdivisions with the addition of section 604 for general technologies (including technical drawing, waste technology, and hazardous materials technology).

The first main division, 610—619, is devoted to the medical sciences. Number 610 is used for medical organizations, medical personnel, study and teaching, and nursing practice. Section 611 is assigned to human anatomy, cytology, and tissue biology. Some of the important subsections cover anatomic embryology, cytology, tissue biology, and gross anatomy.

Section 612 covers human physiology. Important subsections include human chemical and physical phenomena (i.e., biophysics and biochemistry), control mechanisms, the physiology of specific activities such as work and sports, specific functions of systems and organs, reproduction, development and maturation, motor functions and integument, and neurophysiology and sensory physiology.

Section 613 covers general and personal hygiene, with subsections for hygiene by sex and by age groups. Other subsections cover hygiene in natural environments, hygiene for establishing and maintaining health, hygiene in artificial environments and special topics such as industrial and military hygiene, physical fitness, addictions, and birth control and sex hygiene.

The field of public health is covered in section 614. The first subsection is concerned with public health personnel and certification and registration of personnel. Some important topics in the subsections include adulteration and contamination of drugs and food; incidence, distribution, and control of disease (and especially of specific diseases, including mental illness); disposal of the dead; environmental sanitation (including the effects of air pollution, wastes, soil, water, and noise on public areas); and a final subsection on safety and first aid.

Section 615 covers pharmacology and therapeutics. The first subsections cover drugs and groups of drugs (i.e., synthetic, vegetable, animal), practical pharmacy and therapeutics (i.e., homeopathy, osteopathy, chiropractic) and methods of medication. The section is completed with subsections on pharmacodynamics, which is concerned with the physiological and therapeutic effects of drugs; physical and other therapies including massage, phototherapy, music therapy, radio therapy, electrotherapy, and mental therapy; and toxicology, the study of poisons and poisoning.

Section 616, which is lengthy, is used for the "causes (etiology), effects, diagnoses, prognoses, treatment" of diseases. Treated first are general topics such as medical microbiology, pathology, and psychosomatic medicine. Subsections 616.1 to 616.8 are concerned with diseases of the various systems of the body—cardiovascular system, respiratory system, digestive system, blood-forming system, lymphatic and endocrine systems, integument, hair, nails, urogenital system, musculoskeletal system, and nervous system. The last subsection, 616.9, includes all other diseases such as eruptive fevers, bacterial and viral diseases, parasitic diseases, allergies, and cancer.

Surgery and related topics are assigned to section 617. After covering such general topics as personnel, general surgery, and diagnoses and prognoses, the remaining subsections (617.1 to 617.9) are used for specific types of surgery, classified as follows: wounds and injuries, results of injuries (e.g., shock, infection), orthopedic surgery, surgical operations by systems, regional surgery, dentistry, ophthalmology, otology and audiology, and surgical techniques and specialties (e.g., plastic surgery, anesthesiology, military surgery).

Section 618 covers gynecology, obstetrics, pediatrics, and geriatrics. The first field deals with diseases and disorders of women, the second with diseases and disorders of pregnancy, and the last two fields are for diseases and disorders of infants and children and the aged, respectively.

The final section for medicine, 619, is used for experimental medicine and the use of laboratory animals.

Division 620 encompasses engineering and its related fields. After a subsection on general concepts, it proceeds to a major subsection on engineering mechanics, 620.1. Included here are statics, dynamics, solid mechanics, fluid mechanics, gas mechanics, and engineering materials (e.g., wood, cement, glass, metals, soils, plastics, and adhesives). Other general aspects of engineering covered here are sound and related vibrations (620.2), mechanical vibrations (620.3), miscellaneous general engineering technologies (620.4), systems engineering (620.7), and biotechnology–environmental engineering (620.8).

Section 621 is used for applied physics. The first subsections encompass fluid power technology and hydraulic power technology. A lengthy subsection, 621.3, includes electrical, electronic and electromagnetic engineering. Some of the topics are power generation and transmission, illumination and lighting, applied optics, laser technology, communication engineering, radio and radar engineering, telephony, television, and other communication devices.

Other important subsections include heat engineering and various types of motors and engines (621.4), pneumatic, vacuum and low-temperature technology (621.5), fans, flowers, and pumps (621.6), factory operations engineering, including assembly line technology (621.7), machine engineering (621.8), and tools and fabricating equipment (621.9).

Section 622 is concerned with mining engineering and specific aspects of mining such as prospecting, exploration, subsurface mining, other types of mining, mining of specific minerals, mine environment and technology, ore processing, and mine health and safety.

The next section, 623, covers military and nautical engineering. Some of the specialized topics here are fortifications, demolition operations, engineering of defense (e.g., against invasion, against biological and nuclear warfare), ordnance, ballistics and gunnery, military transportation, and nautical engineering and seamanship.

Civil engineering is assigned to section 624. The primary topics here are structural engineering (e.g., foundations, loads, stresses, strains) and the engineering of bridges.

Section 625 is used for railroad and highway engineering. Some of the topics here are rail bed construction, rolling stock, and highway construction and maintenance. Section 626 is unassigned.

Hydraulic engineering is the topic of section 627. This field of engineering is concerned with the utilization and control of water. Subsections cover inland waterways, subsurface waters, harbors, ports, flood control, land reclamation, and dams and reservoirs.

The next section, 628, is used for sanitary and municipal engineering. Some of the important subtopics include water supply, sewerage treatment and disposal, public sanitation, industrial and rural sanitation, and finally a subsection on fire-fighting, lighting, and extermination of insects and rodents.

The final section of this division, 629, covers all other branches of engineering, including transportation engineering, health and safety engineering, aerospace engineering, motor land vehicles, air-cushion engineering, astronautics, and automatic control engineering.

Division 630 is devoted to agriculture and related technologies. Section 631 covers general agricultural techniques, apparatus, equipment, and materials. The more important subsections include agricultural structures, agricultural machinery, soil and soil conservation, cultivation and harvesting, soil improvement, irrigation, water conservation, and fertilizers and soil conditioners.

The following section, 632, is used for plant injuries, plant diseases, and pests. Some specific topics include environmental injuries, bacterial and fungal diseases, pests harmful to plants, viral and rickettsial diseases, and pest control.

Sections 633 to 635 cover the production of specific crops. Number 633 is used for field crops such as cereal grains, forage crops, legumes, root and tuber crops, fiber crops, sugar and starch plants, alkaloidal crops (e.g., tobacco, tea, coffee, cocoa) and other plants grown for industrial processing. Number 634 covers orchards, fruits, and forestry. And section 635 is assigned to horticulture—raising garden crops and ornamental plants. Subsections cover edible roots, tubers, and bulbs (e.g., potatoes and onions), edible leaves, flowers, and stems (e.g., cabbage, cauliflower, spinach, celery), edible fruits and seeds (e.g., melons, squashes, beans, corn), aromatic and sweet herbs, and mushrooms and truffles. A final subsection covers flowers and ornamental plants.

Animal husbandry is assigned to section 636. The section begins with coverage of general materials relating to animal production, maintenance, and training. The following subsections are devoted to specific animals (e.g., horses, sheep, cattle, poultry, dogs).

Dairy products and their related technologies comprise section 637. Subsections cover milk, butter and cheese production, manufacture of frozen desserts, and egg production.

Section 638, for insect culture, includes subsections on apiculture (honeybees), silkworms, resin- and dye-producing insects, and other insects raised for specific purposes.

The last section, 639, is devoted to non-domesticated animals and plants. Covered here are hunting and trapping, commercial fishing, whaling, and sealing, the culture of cold-blooded vertebrates, the culture of mollusks and crustaceans (e.g., oysters and lobsters), the culture of other invertebrates (e.g., worms) and the conservation of biological resources.

Division 640 treats domestic arts and sciences, also known as home economics. The first topics covered include household finances, study and teaching, and consumer education. Section 641, food and drink, includes applied nutrition, alcoholic beverages, foods and foodstuffs, preservation of food, cookery, and cooking processes and techniques.

Section 642 provides for food and meal service, including table service and decor. Section 643 covers the home, household equipment, and improvement and remodeling of the home. Section 644 is used for household utilities such as heating, lighting, air conditioning, and water supply. Household furnishings are assigned to section 645, while section 646 includes sewing, clothing, and personal grooming. Section 647 is assigned to public households and their employees. Public households include apartments, hotels, public eating and drinking establishments, and religious and educational households. Household sanitation, including laundering, housekeeping, pest control and eradication, and storage are the subjects of section 648. The final section, 649, is used for child rearing and home nursing. Included are aspects of child rearing by age and sex, children of specific classes, exceptional children, feeding, clothing, manners and habits, and moral, religious, and character training.

Division 650 is assigned to managerial services. The first topics covered are success in business, financial success, and personal improvement. Office services, section 651, covers office equipment and supplies, office organization, office practice, and information management (e.g., records management, communication, and data processing). The last subsection, 651.9, covers office services in specific kinds of enterprises.

Section 652 treats the processes of written communication including penmanship and typewriting. Section 653 is used for shorthand and basic shorthand systems.

Sections 654–656 are currently unassigned.

The next active section, 657, is used for accounting. Special topics included here are bookkeeping, financial reporting, specific fields of accounting (e.g., auditing, tax), kinds of accounting (e.g., public, private), accounting for specific phases of activities, accounting for enterprises in specific kinds of activities (e.g., welfare, finance and real estate, government, public utilities) and finally accounting for specific kinds of organizations (e.g., partnerships, corporations, cooperatives).

Section 658, a lengthy one, covers general management, which the DDC defines as "the science and art of conducting organized enterprises, projects, activities. Planning, organizing, financing, staffing, directing, coordinating, reporting, [and] other functions common to all types of enterprises" (DDC, Vol. 2, p. 1270). Examples of the topics covered here are organization and finance, plant management, personnel management, general principles of management, management of production, management of materials (including their procurement, transportation, and storage), management of distribution (i.e., marketing), which includes sales and salesmanship, and finally a subsection on the management of specific kinds of enterprises.

The last section in the division, 659, covers advertising and public relations. Subsections provide for the use of specific media in advertising and public relations, and advertising and public relations for specific organizations, products, and services.

One of the largest divisions of the 600 class is 660, which is used for chemical and related technologies. The introductory subsections provide for general works on chemical engineering, industrial biology, and industrial stoichiometry (the application of the laws of definite proportions and of the conservation of matter and energy to chemical activity). The first section, 661, deals with the technology of industrial chemicals. This includes the production of chemicals for use in production of other products. Some types of chemicals covered here are compounds, non-metallic elements, acids, bases, and salts, ammonium salts, sulfur and nitrogen salts, and organic chemicals (e.g., petroleum, hydrocarbons).

Section 662 covers the technology of explosives, fuels, and related products, such as fireworks, detonators, matches, fuels (coal, wood, synthetic fuels), coke and charcoal, and non-fuel carbons (e.g., graphite).

Section 663 is used for beverage technology. Included are the making of alcoholic beverages, wine and wine making, brewed and malted beverages, distilled liquors and non-alcoholic beverages—carbonated drainks, coffee and tea.

Food technology is the subject of section 664. Here the concern is the manufacture of food products, raw materials, processes, additives, quality controls, by-products, and packaging. The rest of the section covers specific foods and food groups—sugars and sirups, starches, fats and oils, food salts, flavoring aids, special purpose foods, grains, seeds, fruits and vegetables, and meats.

Section 665 is concerned with the technology of industrial oils, fats, waxes, and gases. The subsection for waxes provides for both vegetable and animal waxes. Other important subsections cover animal and vegetable fats and oils, mineral oils and waxes, petroleum refining, and natural and manufactured industrial gases.

Section 666 provides for ceramic and allied technologies. Included here are the technologies relating to glass and glassmaking, enameling and enamels, pottery, porcelain, earthenware and stoneware, clay products, synthetic and artificial minerals and stones (e.g., synthetic diamonds, concrete blocks) and masonry adhesives (e.g., gypsum, plastics, Portland cement).

Section 667 is assigned to cleaning, color, and related technologies. Included here are cleaning and bleaching, dyes and pigments, dyeing and printing, inks, printing inks, paints, varnishes, and coatings.

The technology of other organic products is provided for in section 668. Some "other organic products" are surface-active materials (e.g., soaps, detergents), glycerin, adhesives, plastics, perfumes and cosmetics, and agricultural chemicals (including fertilizers and pesticides).

The last section, 669, is concerned with metallurgy, which is the production of metals from their ores. The first subsection covers the various methods of ore extraction followed by subsections on specific metals and groups of metals, metallurgical furnaces, and physical and chemical metallurgy.

Division 670 is assigned to manufactures, the "planning, design, [and] fabrication of products" (DDC, Vol. 2, p. 1318). The first three sections, 671–673, are used for metal manufactures, including foundry practice, forming of metals, finishing metals, and the manufacture of specific metals.

Section 674 is used for technologies relating to lumber, cork, and wood use. The topics assigned to this section are structure, properties, and types of lumber, sawmill operations, lumber storage, production of finished lumber, grading lumber, and cork technology.

The next section, 675, is assigned to leather and fur processing and the manufacture of imitation leather.

Pulp and paper technology is the subject of section 676. Besides a subsection on wood pulp processing, subsections are devoted to pulp products (e.g., paper) and papers made from man-made fibers.

Section 677, used for textiles, includes the "production of fibers [and] manufacture of fabrics and cordage" (DDC, Vol. 2, p. 1327). The introductory subsections cover equipment used in textile manufacturing, and these are followed by subsections on specific textiles. The last subsection is for cordage, which includes ropes, twines, and strings.

Section 678 deals with elastomers and elastomer products, including rubber and rubber products, latexes, and natural and synthetic elastomers.

The final section, 679, is used for the manufacture of products of other specific materials. The three subsections cover keratinous and dentinal materials (e.g., feathers, ivory), fibers and bristles, and tobacco (e.g., cigars, cigarettes).

Division 680 is used for miscellaneous manufactures, including their "planning, design, [and] fabrication of final products." Section 681 is concerned with the manufacture of precision instruments (e.g., computers, clocks), testing and measuring instruments, optical instruments, printing and duplicating equipment, other scientific and technical instruments and machinery, and musical instruments.

Section 682 is used for small forge work, or blacksmithing. Section 683 covers hardware (e.g., locksmithing, household appliances) and section 684 is for furnishings and home workshops (e.g., woodworking, furniture, fabric furnishings). The following section, 685, deals with leather, fur goods, and such related manufactures as fur coats, footwear, gloves, and luggage.

Section 686 is assigned to printing and related activities. The first subsections cover the invention of printing, its historical development, and the development of alphabets and typography. The last two subsections deal with bookbinding and photo duplication processes, including xerography.

Section 687 is assigned to the manufacture of clothing for men, women, and children. All types of clothing—outer and under garments, hosiery, sweaters, and headgear—are treated here.

The last section, 688, is used for other manufactured products not covered in earlier sections. Some of these products are models, costume jewelry, smoking supplies, and recreational equipment. Section 689 is currently unassigned.

Division 690, the last one in this class, covers buildings. All phases of building are classified here including the "planning, analysis, engineering design, construction, maintenance, repairs, destruction of habitable structures and their utilities" (DDC, Vol. 2, p. 1345). The first subsections cover general materials on building, with numbers for works on specific types of buildings.

Section 691 incorporates the "selection, preservation, [and] construction properties" (DDC, Vol. 2, p. 1346) of building materials including timber, natural stones, concretes, ceramic materials, glass, metals, and plastics. A short section, 692, is used for auxiliary construction practices such as plans, drawings, construction specifications, cost estimating, and contracting.

Section 693 is concerned with construction using specific materials and for specific purposes. Some of the materials are natural stone, bricks, tiles, terra cotta, concrete, plaster and stucco, and metals. Two sections, 693.8 and 693.9, cover resistant construction (fireproof, pest resistant, shock resistant) and construction in other materials, respectively.

Wood construction and carpentry are the subjects of section 694. The first subsection is concerned with the planning and design of wood construction. Other subsections cover rough carpentry, or framing, and finish carpentry, or joinery.

Section 695 covers roofing and the various roofing materials including wood, slate, concrete and tile, metal, and textiles.

Section 696 covers utilities, with emphasis on plumbing and hot-water supply. Section 697 covers heating, ventilating, and air conditioning. Subsections provide for various aspects of heating and air-conditioning design, installation and maintenance practices, and central heating systems. The last assigned section, 698, is used for detail finishing. The topics assigned here include painting, calcimining and whitewashing, finishing woodwork, glazing, paperhanging, and floor coverings. Section 699 is currently unassigned.

NUMBER BUILDING, 600–699

Example 1

Where would you classify a work on the physical effects of marijuana?

The Relative Index provides a good example here of how a topic can be classified several different ways. The entry "Marijuana" provides two "see" references—the first to "Indian hemp" for agricultural and economic aspects and the second to "Narcotics" for narcotic aspects.

A search of the entries under "Narcotics" provides only two possible classification numbers: 616.863 for "Narcotics addiction—gen. med." and 614.58 for "Narcotics addiction—pub. health." Checking the schedule reveals that neither of these numbers applies to the subject here.

The entry "Indian hemp" covers agricultural aspects and provides a seemingly tenuous "see" reference to "Hemp" for other aspects, with a reference under "Hemp" to "Urticales." Under "Urticales" there are two leads—one to 583.962 under botanical aspects and one to 615.323962 for medical aspects.

Another possible entry is "Drugs" where the number 615.1 is suggested; under "Drugs—pharmacology," 615.1 is again suggested.

A search of the schedules starting at 615.1 leads to 615.3 for organic drugs and 615.323–.327 for drugs derived from specific plants (Fig. 8-1, page 122).

Fig. 8-1. Classification Schedule

▶ **615.2-615.3 Specific drugs and groups of drugs**

Pharmaceutical chemistry, preservation, general therapeutics

Class comprehensive works in 615.1

.2 **Inorganic drugs**

Add to 615.2 the numbers following 546 in 546.2-546.7, e.g., calomel 615.2663

If preferred, arrange specific inorganic drugs alphabetically

.3 **Organic drugs**

Arrange by kind and source as below; but, if preferred, arrange specific organic drugs alphabetically

.31 Synthetic drugs

Add to 615.31 the numbers following 547.0 in 547.01-547.08, e.g., sulfonamides 615.3167

Class synthetic vitamins in 615.328

.32 Drugs of vegetable origin

Class enzymes of vegetable origin in 615.35

.321 Pharmacognosy

Crude drugs and simples, alkaloids, herbals

For drugs derived from specific plants, see 615.323-615.327

➡ .323-.327 Drugs derived from specific plants

Add to 615.32 the numbers following 58 in 583-587, e.g., belladonna 615.32379

For drugs derived from thallophytes, see 615.329

There are instructions here to add to the base number 615.32 the numbers following 58 in 583-587. Checking the 583-587 schedule reveals that it is necessary to identify the specific plant or plant family that includes marijuana. The number 615.323962 found in the Relative Index under "Urticales-med. aspects" is a possible clue. The 3962 here may be a clue since it is from 583.962, according to the instructions in Fig. 8-1.

Another way to identify the plant family is to look under "Cannabis" if you happen to remember that this is the scientific name for the marijuana plant or if you have found this information in a scientific or botanical encyclopedia. The Relative Index cites two "see" references, from "Cannabiaceae" to "Urticales" and from "Cannabis sativa" to "Hemp." It is necessary to check the schedule to verify the correct number. The search will be in the sections 583-587. With the "clues" already given (i.e., Urticales, 583.962, and its medical aspects and general pharmacological aspects, 615.323962) turn to number 583.962 which is indeed the correct number for the Cannabiadeae family, to which marijuana belongs.

The number building thus proceeds as follows:

600	applied sciences
615	pharmacology and therapeutics
.3	organic drugs
.32	drugs of vegetable origin
3	following instructions at .323–.327, add the number following 58 in 583–587. 583 is the base number for dicotyledones
39	the Apetalae (from 583.9)
396	the Balanopsidales and Urticales (from 583.96)
3962	the Urticales (583.962), which include the Cannabiaceae and the Cannabis sativa (marijuana). Following instructions at 615.323–.327, add the numbers after 58 in 583–587 (i.e., 583.962) to 615.32.
615.323962	the physical effects of marijuana

The abridged edition has a see reference from "Marijuana" to "Narcotics," which leads to a general number for drug addiction. Under the entry "Drugs– pharmacology" the number 615 is cited. This is the most specific number for the abridged edition.

Example 2

Where would you classify a report on agricultural irrigation in the Sahel? This particular problem involves greater analysis than most of the other problems presented.

The first problem is to identify the term Sahel. If you had the report in hand (as it would be in a "real" cataloging situation), the term would undoubtedly be defined in the report. We have no book in hand, so a research problem is presented. The term is not in the Relative Index. It is probably a geographic location, and a search in a major encyclopedia identifies the Sahel as a region of semi-arid land stretching through Central Africa just south of the Sahara Desert.

The primary subject is irrigation–specifically, irrigation for agriculture. The entry in the Relative Index under "Irrigation–agriculture" cites number 631.7. The entries "Agricultural" and "Agriculture" provide no entries for irrigation. The entry "Irrigation-farming–crop prod." gives number 631.587, but upon check- ing the schedule it does not seem appropriate.

Checking 631.7 in the schedule shows it to be the proper base number for agricultural irrigation. Now it is necessary to subdivide further by area and physiographic feature. Refer to the Areas Table (Table 2). If the work is a *comprehensive* one on deserts in general, you use the standard subdivision –091 for geographical treatment by areas, regions, and places in general in Table 1 and then add the area number. Here, however, we are concerned with a specific region and a desert. A search of Table 2 brings one to the centered heading −3−9 (Fig. 8-2).

Fig. 8-2. Areas (Table 2)

▶   −3−9 **Specific continents, countries, localities; extraterrestrial worlds**

Class here specific instances of the subject

If desired, add to each number as follows:

009   Regional treatment

Add to 009 the numbers following −1 in −11−19 of this table, e.g., Torrid Zone of Asia −50093, rivers of England −42009693, Italian-speaking regions of Switzerland −4940097551, cities of ancient Greece −38009732

An alternative treatment is shown under −1

01−09   Historical periods

Add to base number the historical period numbers in corresponding subdivisions of 930−990, using one 0 in all cases, e.g., Tudor England −4205, Tudor Berkshire −422905, United States during administration of Dwight D. Eisenhower −730921

Class comprehensive works in "Standard Subdivisions" notation 09 from Table 1; areas, regions, places not limited by continent, country, locality in −1; persons regardless of area, region, place in −2

Here the instructions refer to −1 for areas, regions, and places in general. Under −1 in Table 2 you are given more instructions for specific geographic breakdown (Fig. 8-3).

Fig. 8-3. Areas (Table 2)

−1   **Areas, regions, places in general**

Not limited by continent, country, locality

If desired, add to each number as follows:

03−09   Treatment by continent, country, locality

Add 0 to base number and then add "Areas" notation 3−9 from this table, e.g., Torrid Zone of Asia −1305, rivers of England −1693042, Italian-speaking regions of Switzerland −175510494, cities of ancient Greece −1732038

You can first identify the physiographic feature—a desert—then provide an area number for the specific locality. As you search the −1 schedule you find −154 for deserts and desert vegetation. Adding −154 to the base number 631.7 produces 631.7154 for agricultural irrigation in deserts. (If this were a general work on desert irrigation, −09 would be interposed between 631.7 and −154 for 631.709154.) Now you look for an area number for the specific geographical region.

The instructions under −1 in Table 2 (Fig. 8-3) instruct you to add a "0" to the base number before adding the area number. Now you have 631.71540, to which may be added the area number for the Sahel.

The Sahel includes sections of the African countries of Senegal, Mali, Upper Volta, Niger, Chad, and the Sudan. This is, in fact, a large semi-arid area immediately south of the Sahara Desert. Area number −66 covers West Africa and four of the countries above, and it includes the Sahara Desert. Area number −67 covers Central Africa, one of the countries named (Chad), and Africa *south* of the Sahara. While it is tempting to use −66, that number is not correct; −67 is the correct number according to the schedule (Fig. 8-4).

Fig. 8-4. Areas (Table 2)

−67   **Central Africa and offshore islands   East Africa**

       Class here Negro Africa, Black Africa, Africa south of the Sahara

       Class each specific country of Negro Africa, of Black Africa, of Africa south of the Sahara not provided for here with the subject, e.g., Nigeria −669

The result of our number building exercise is:

630		agriculture and related technologies
631		general agricultural techniques, apparatus, equipment and materials
	.7	irrigation and water conservation
	154	the three digits (−154) from Table 2 for deserts
	0	added as instructed under −1 in Table 2
	6	the area number for Africa
	67	the area number for Africa south of the Sahara
631.7154067		agricultural irrigation in the Sahel

The abridged edition's Relative Index refers to 631.7 under "Irrigation–agriculture." Here you are allowed to use the standard subdivision −09 from Table 1. To −09 you are instructed to add from "areas" notation −1 in Table 2. The "areas" notation for deserts is −15, so the number using the abridged edition is 631.70915.

Example 3

Where would one classify a manual for the restoration of a 1932 Ford coupe? This problem presents an example of using an indirect entry in the Relative Index to arrive at a suitable location in the schedule.

The entry for "Manuals" has no references associated with motor vehicles, but only refers to standard subdivision –0202. The entry "Restoration" also makes no reference to motor vehicles. The entry "Cars" has a reference to see specific kinds, e.g., automobiles. There are entries for both "Automobile" and "Automobiles," but neither has a direct reference to automobile restoration. The entry "Automobiles–engineering–tech. & mf." seems to be the best possible subject entry; number 629.2 is cited here.

If you consider a restoration a repair, then the entry "Repairs and repairing–automobiles–technology" offers the best suggested number, 629.287–.288. Checking the schedule shows that 629.287–.288 is the correct number sequence to build on.

The abridged edition has no direct entries for automobile restoration. The entry "Cars" has a see reference to "Automobiles," and the entry "Automobiles–engineering" cites number 629.2. The entry "Repairs and repairing" provides no help. Checking the schedule at 629.2 leads to 629.28 for maintenance and repair of automobiles. This is the correct number for the abridged edition.

In the full edition the number 629.288 is used for maintenance and repairs by owners, and a note verifies that this is the number in which to class restoration of automobiles (Fig. 8-5).

Fig. 8-5. Classification Schedule

629

.287   Maintenance and repairs

Add to 629.287 the numbers following 629.22 in 629.222–629.229, e.g., repair of motorcycles 629.28775

Subarrange each type by trade name of vehicle; but, if preferred, arrange all vehicles regardless of type alphabetically by trade name

Class maintenance and repair of specific parts in 629.24–629.27

For maintenance and repairs by vehicle owners, see 629.288

.288   Maintenance and repairs by vehicle owners

Class here restoration, conversion

Add to 629.288 the numbers following 629.22 in 629.222–629.229, e.g., maintenance of private cars 629.28822

Subarrange each type by trade name of vehicle; but, if preferred, arrange all vehicles regardless of type alphabetically by trade name

A second note gives instructions to "add to 629.288 the numbers following 629.22 in 629.222–629.229." Number 629.222 is used for passenger automobiles and 629.2222 for private transportation. The number built now would be 629.28822, the –22 coming from 629.2222, as instructed above (Fig. 8-5). Instructions under 629.2222 say to arrange alphabetically by the name of the car. This can be interpreted two ways–to arrange alphabetically by type (i.e., sports cars) or to arrange alphabetically by trade name (i.e., Ford). The latter interpretation is verified by the note under 629.288, which says to arrange each type (i.e., private cars) by trade name. Now the letter F, for Ford, is added, building

629.28822F. It is possible to stop here. If desired, however, the standard sub-division for a manual (–0202) can be added to build the following number:

620	engineering and allied operations
629	other branches of engineering
.2	motor land vehicles and cycles
.28	tests, operation, maintenance, repairs
.288	maintenance and repairs by vehicle owners and restoration
2	passenger automobiles (from the numbers following 629.22 in 629.222
2	private transportation (from 629.2222)
F	for the trade name of the car (i.e., Ford)
02	standard subdivision for miscellany from Table 1
0202	standard subdivision for manuals from Table 1
629.28822F0202	a manual on the restoration of a 1932 Ford coupe

Example 4

Where would a work on the techniques of dyeing cotton fabrics be classified?

The key word here is cotton, since it is the most specific term. Secondary terms are dyeing and fabrics. The Relative Index provides an excellent starting point under "Cotton–textiles–dyeing," and the suggested number is 667.321. The entry "Dyeing–clothing–technology" cites number 667.3, while the entry "Fabrics" only refers to "Textiles." The entry "Dyeing–clothing–comm. proc." cites number 667.

Checking the schedule shows that 667 is the general number for cleaning, color, and related technologies, including dyeing. In the abridged edition 667 would be the correct number, though, if desired, the standard subdivision for techniques (–028) could be added, to build number 667.028.

Searching the 667 schedule in the full edition for 667.321, the number suggested for dyeing cotton textiles, reveals that there is no such number in the schedule. There is 667.31–.35, however, for dyeing specific textiles (Fig. 8-6).

Fig. 8-6. Classification Schedule

667

.3	**Dyeing and printing**
	For dyes, see 667.25–667.26
.31–.35	Dyeing specific textiles
	Add to 667.3 the numbers following 677 in 677.1–677.5, e.g., dyeing nylon 667.3473

The instructions here say to add to the base number 667.3 "the numbers following 677 in 677.1–677.5." It is now obvious that the number suggested in the Relative Index was a "built" number and not one specifically listed in the schedule.
This emphasizes again the necessity of cataloging from the schedule and not from
the Relative Index. Under 677, cotton is found in 677.21. Following the instructions to add the numbers following 677 to 667.3 gives 667.321 as the number for
dyeing cotton. Remember, however, that you want the number for dyeing cotton
fabrics.

An asterisk by cotton at 677.21 refers to instructions at the bottom of the
page to add as instructed under 677.1–677.5, which is a centered heading for
textiles (Fig. 8-7).

Fig. 8-7. Classification Schedule

►   **677.1–677.5 Textiles of specific composition**

Add to each subdivision identified by * the numbers following 677.028 in 677.0282–677.0287, e.g., linen fabrics
677.1164

Class comprehensive works in 677, special-process fabrics
regardless of composition in 677.6

.1	**Textiles of bast fibers**
.11	*Flax
.12	Hemp
.13	Jute
.15	Ramie
.18	Coir
.2	**Textiles of seed-hair fibers**
.21	*Cotton
.23	Kapok

The instructions say to add the numbers following 677.028 in 677.0282–.0287.
These numbers turn out to be assigned to generalities associated with textiles.
Checking the schedule gives 677.02864 for fabrics. As instructed, you add the
numbers following 677.028 in 677.02864 to the number 667.321 for
667.32164.

Since the subject of the work covers *techniques*, should the standard subdivision –0028 be added? The answer is no. The instructions under standard subdivisions at 677.001–.009 say to class techniques in 677.028. Also, the Editor's
Introduction to the DDC states "that the classifier should not add standard subdivisions when they are redundant, e.g., if the number already means technique,
it is unnecessary for him to add standard subdivision 028 Techniques, apparatus,
equipment, materials" (DDC, Vol. 1, p. 34). Thus, the final number will be:

660	chemical and related technologies
667	cleaning, color, and related technologies
.3	dyeing and printing
21	cotton (from 677.21 as instructed)
64	fabrics (from 677.02864 as instructed)
667.32164	techniques of dyeing cotton fabrics

Example 5

Where would you classify a book of drafting diagrams for an automobile gas turbine engine?

Again it is necessary to determine the best place in the schedule to look for a number. From the information above the main subject of the work is drafting—not as a method but as a subject, in that one is working with specific kinds of drafting diagrams. The specific subject of the drafting diagrams is gas-turbine engines for use in automobiles.

The Relative Index provides several possibilities. The entry "Drafting (drawing) procedures—tech. drawing—spec. subj." cites number 604.26. The entry for "Diagrams—spec. subj." refers only to standard subdivision −0223. The entry "Gas turbine engines—tech. & mf.—land vehicles—parts and systems" refers to number 629.252−.258. The entry for "Engines" has a reference to see "Power plants." The entry "Power plants—automobiles—tech. & mf." cites number 629.25. The entry "Automobiles—engineering—drawing" cites number 604.26292.

The abridged edition index has several relevant entries. "Drafting—tech. drawing" cites number 604.2, while "Diagrams" provides the standard subdivision −022. "Turbine steam engines—stationary—tech. and mf." refers to number 621.1, and the entry "Turbines—tech. and mf." refers to 621.4. Under the entry "Automobiles" the only relevant entry is "Automobiles—engineering," number 629.2.

Checking the schedules in the full edition shows that 629.25 is too broad and that 629.252−.258 refers to parts and auxiliary systems of internal combustion engines. Look back to numbers 629.2503−.2506, for different types of internal combustion engines. Although our main subject is drafting, we are concerned with drafting for a specific type of engine. Once we decide on a base number, we have an idea of how to proceed with the number building. Checking the number suggested for "Drafting" (604.2) leads to 604.26, which is used for drafting specific subjects (Fig. 8-8).

Fig. 8-8. Classification Schedule

604

→ .26   Drafting specific subjects

        Add to 604.26 the numbers following 6 in 610−690, e.g., aeronautical drafting 604.262913

Directions are given at 604.26 to add the numbers following 6 in 610–690. Since the subject is automobile engines, go to number 629.2 for motor land vehicles and cycles. Add to 604.26 the numbers following 6 in 629.2, to build number 604.26292. This, you will recall, was the number given in the Relative Index under the entry "Automobiles–engineering–drawing."

Now to the number 604.26292 we need to add a number for a specific type of power plant–the gas turbine. Number 629.25 is the general number for automobile power plants, and numbers 629.2501 to 629.2509 are used for specific types of engines. Gas turbines are an internal combustion engine so some place in numbers 629.2503–.2506 will be the place to develop the number. At this point, however, add 50 (from 629.2503) to get 604.2629250. Remember that you previously added to 604.26 all the numbers after 6 in 629.2. The instructions at 629.2503–629.2506 say to add to the base number 629.250 the numbers following 621.43 in 621.433–621.436; gas turbines are at 621.433, so you add the last 3, building 604.26292503. The number is built as follows:

604	general technologies
.2	technical drawing
.26	drafting specific subjects
292	motor land vehicles (from 629.2, as instructed)
5	power plants (from 629.25, as instructed)
0	add 0 to form base number (from 629.2503–.2506)
3	gas turbine engines (from 629.2503, developed from 621.433 as instructed)
604.26292503	drafting diagrams for automobile gas-turbine engines

Since the work consists mostly of diagrams, the standard subdivision for diagrams, –0223, could be added if required: 604.262925030223. This, however, is an extremely long number that would be used only in the largest collections.

The abridged edition stops at 604.2 for technical drawing. The standard sub-division for diagrams, –022, could be added to build 604.2022.

PROBLEMS TO SOLVE

Try to build classification numbers for the following hypothetical works:

1) a work on the prevention of heart disease
2) a general work on recycling waste materials
3) a. a work on properties of laminated wood for engineering purposes
   b. a work on the production of plywood and wood laminates
   c. a work on uses of plywood in building construction
4) a work on the care and training of dogs as pets
5) a cookbook on Mexican cooking
6) a work on basic shorthand practice for medical work using the Gregg system

7) a work on techniques of glass blowing for making scientific apparatus
8) a dictionary of terms used in furniture making

ANSWERS TO PROBLEMS

1) 616.1205 (18th edition)   616.1 (10th abridged edition)

The Relative Index entry "Heart" provides a subdivision "Heart diseases— gen. wks.," with number 616.12. The abridged edition entry is the same, and the suggested number is 616.1. For the abridged edition this is as far as you can go. The full edition, however, allows for further subdivision as instructed under the centered heading 616.1–616.9, where a list of specific aspects of diseases and treatments is listed. The number –05 is used for preventive measures. When this is added to the base number, it produces 616.1205 for a work on prevention of heart disease. Notice that standard subdivisions use two zeroes: 001–009. Thus, a periodical on prevention of heart disease would be: 616.12005.

2) 604.6 (18th edition)   604.6 (10th abridged edition)

There is no entry for "Recycling" in the Relative Index. Under "Waste" there are references to "Photography" and "Pollution." The latter entry relates to water-supply engineering. The term "Wastes—technology" provides number 604.6 and "Wastes—utilization—prod. management" provides number 658.567. Checking the schedule at 658.567 shows that it treats waste as an aspect of production management. The number 604.6 has a note in the schedule that included here are "methods and equipment for salvaging and utilizing waste materials." This is the correct number (provided that the recycling is not done by the manufactures).

The abridged edition entry "Wastes—technology" cites the same number, 604.6, which is also correct for this edition.

3) a. 620.12 (18th edition)   a. 620.1 (10th abridged edition)
    b. 674.834   b. 674
    c. 694   c. 694

The Relative Index provides four main entries for these subjects: "Plywood," "Wood," "Laminates," and "Sandwich." The term "Plywood" gives a specific entry under "Plywood—mf. tech.," with number 674.834.

Checking the schedule at 674.834 confirms this number is correct for a work on the production of plywood. If the work covered other types of wood laminates, the more general number 674.83 could be used. (The number 674.835 would be used only in cases where special types of plywood or sandwich panels are being considered.)

Under the entries "Wood—bldg. construction," "Wood—eng. materials," and "Wood products—manufacturing—technology" are numbers 694, 620.12 and 674.8, respectively. The entry "Laminates—wood—mf. tech." gives number 674.835. Thus, under "Wood" and its subdivisions possible numbers are found for each work. The term "Sandwich panels—bldg. construction" cites number 693.92.

Checking the schedule at 694 reveals there is no more specific number for wood construction that includes plywood. In fact, under 693.92, for sandwich panels, a note says to class such panels made of a specific substance with the subject–e.g., wood 694. Thus, 694 is correct for a work on the use of plywood in building construction. The number 620.12 for "Wood–eng. materials" proves to be correct for the properties of laminated wood for engineering purposes.

In the abridged edition there is no entry for "Plywood" or "Sandwich" (in relation to wood). Under "Laminates–wood–mf. tech.," number 674 is given. Under "Wood–bldg. construction" and "Wood–eng. materials" numbers 694 and 620.1 are cited. These numbers are the most specific ones for the works being classified: production of plywood, 674; uses of plywood in building construction, 694; and properties of plywood for engineering purposes, 620.1.

4) 636.70887 (18th edition)   636.7 (10th abridged edition)

The Relative Index provides several starting points under "Dogs." "Dogs–animal husbandry" in the full edition and "Dogs–domestic animals" in the abridged edition refer to number 636.7. For the abridged edition this number turns out to be the most specific number.

The full edition provides for further subdivision under 636.701–.708 for general principles. Here instructions direct one to add to number 636.70 the numbers following 636.0 in 636.01–636.08. The number 636.0887 is used for training of animals as pets. Adding 887 to 636.70 builds number 636.70887 for the care and training of dogs.

5) 641.5972 (18th edition)   641.5 (10th abridged edition)

There is no Relative Index entry for "Cookbooks" in either edition. There is, however, an entry under "Cookery" in both editions and a suggested number, 641.5. For the abridged edition this is the correct number; it covers cookbooks regardless of geographic environment.

The full edition provides number 641.59 for cookery of specific geographic environments through the addition of "areas" notation 3–9 in Table 2. To base number 641.59, add "areas" notation –72 for Mexico. A book on Mexican cookery will have the number 641.5972.

6) 653.4270428 (18th edition)   653 (10th abridged edition)

The two terms to look for in the Relative Index are "Shorthand" and "Gregg." The term "Shorthand" is used in both editions, and number 653 is given. Only the 18th edition has an entry for "Gregg–shorthand systems" with the more specific number 653.427. Checking the schedule in the full edition reveals that an even more specific number for basic shorthand practice is given, 653.427042, with instructions to add the numbers following 653.1 in 653.13 to 653.18 for specific aspects. At 653.18 is a heading for specific uses of shorthand, and medical uses is one example given. The number built will be 653.4270428. The abridged edition uses 653.

7) 666.122 (18th edition)   666 (10th abridged edition)

The entry "Glass" is the most logical place to begin searching in the Relative Index. Under "Scientific" there is no subdivision for apparatus. The most likely entry seems to be "Glass–manufacturing–technology" and number 666.1. The abridged edition has an entry "Glass–manufacturing," number 666, which turns out to be the most specific number for this edition.

In the full edition a note under 666.1 gives instructions to use 666.12 for glass techniques, apparatus, equipment, and materials. Here a centered heading cites numbers 666.122–666.129 for specific glassmaking operations. Checking the schedule shows that 666.122 is used for glass blowing. No further breakdown is allowed for glass blowing for scientific apparatus, so 666.122 is the correct number.

8) 684.1003 (18th edition)   684.103 (10th abridged edition)

There are numerous entries under "Furniture" in the Relative Indexes of both editions. The most promising possibility is the entry "Furniture–manufacturing–technology," number 684.1. The abridged edition also gives 684.1 under the entry "Furniture–manufacturing."

Checking the schedule shows that 684.1 is the correct general number for furniture. The full edition uses .001–.009 for the standard subdivisions. The standard subdivision (Table 1) for a dictionary is –03 (or –003, in this case) so the number will be 684.1003. For the abridged edition, add –03 (the standard subdivision for dictionaries) to 684.1, giving 684.103. The double "0" is not required here.

CHAPTER 9

CLASS 700–799
(THE ARTS)

INTRODUCTORY NOTE

The majority of the divisions in this class are devoted to the visual arts (710–770); however, the last two divisions must be examined separately. Division 780 is assigned to music, and theater, dance, sports, and recreation are grouped in the last division, 790. This last division must be considered in detail because of the diversity of material located there. Study both the "Details of the Class" and the schedules for this division with deliberate care and note the many popular subjects classed here.

The number building examples in this chapter demonstrate the use of three auxiliary tables—Areas (Table 2), Racial, Ethnic, National Groups (Table 5), and Individual Literatures (Table 3). The use of Table 3 shows the close relationship between theater (792) in this class and drama in the literature class (800). In fact, theater may be considered as applied drama, just as technology is applied science.

OUTLINE OF THE CLASS

700	The arts
710	Civic and landscape art
720	Architecture
730	Plastic arts, Sculpture
740	Drawing, and decorative and minor arts
750	Painting and paintings
760	Graphic arts, Prints
770	Photography and photographs
780	Music
790	Recreational and performing arts

INTRODUCTION TO THE CLASS

The 700 class comprises the fourth longest schedule in the DDC. The concern in this main class is with the theory, development, and application of the fine arts. One division, 790, is used for the performing arts and recreation and sports.

The subjects and disciplines in this main class are diverse, ranging from landscape architecture to goalkeeping in soccer. Because of this diversity it is particularly important to become familiar with the whole class before attempting to build numbers.

DETAILS OF THE CLASS

The generalities of the fine and decorative arts are assigned to numbers 701 to 709. The philosophy and theory of these fields and their appreciative aspects, inherent features (e.g., composition, color, form, style, perspective, decorative value) and methodology are provided for in 701. Section 702 is used for miscellany and techniques and equipment, while dictionaries, encyclopedias, and concordances are covered by section 703.

Section 704 is set aside for general special aspects of the class. This concept is explained in the Editor's Introduction as the "subdivision of a topic according to a characteristic which has general applicability to other subdivisions of the topic which are based on different characteristics" (DDC, Vol. 1, p. 31). Two special areas here are persons occupied with art (using the "Persons" notations from Table 7) and iconography (visual representations relating to a specific topic) and general collections of writings. Some of the subsections for iconography cover the human figure, architectural subjects, mythology and legend, and religion and religious symbolism.

Sections 705 to 707 cover serial publications, organizations, and study and teaching, respectively. Section 708 covers art galleries, museums, and private collections of art; emphasis is on geographical treatment, using the "Areas" notation from Table 2. (The reader will recall the use of 069 for general museums in the first class of DDC.) The last section of this division, 709, is reserved for the historical and geographical treatment of the arts. There are provisions for art during specific periods of time from primitive peoples to the present. Two subsections are used for geographical coverage and for artists regardless of geographical location.

Civic and landscape art is assigned to division 710. The initial section, 711, encompasses area planning and civic art and the related procedural, social, and economic problems. Section 712 is used for landscape design or landscape architecture and its basic principles, professional practice, technical procedures, and application to specific kinds of land (e.g., public and private parks and grounds, institutional grounds). Section 713 is devoted solely to landscape design of trafficways.

The specific elements in landscape design are assigned to sections 714–717. These sections respectively cover water features, woody plants, herbaceous plants, and the relationship of structures to landscape design. The two final sections, 718 and 719, cover the design of cemeteries, and natural landscapes such as public parks and wildlife reserves.

The discipline of architecture is covered by division 720. The first section covers general works and architectural drawing, and it provides for the historical and geographical treatment of the field. Section 721 deals with architectural construction and structural elements such as foundations, walls, columns, arches, roofs, and floors. The next three sections, 722 to 724, cover various architectural schools and styles and provide geographical and chronological treatments.

Specific types of structures are assigned to sections 725 to 728. Section 725 is used for public structures (e.g., government buildings, commercial buildings, recreation buildings); section 726 is used for buildings for religious purposes; section 727 is used for buildings for educational and research purposes (e.g., schools, colleges, museums, and libraries); and section 728 is used for residential or domestic buildings (e.g., low-cost housing, multiple dwellings, urban housing, suburban housing, and other special purpose housing).

The last section in this division, 729, covers design and decoration of structures. Subsections deal with special topics, such as design in planes (vertical and horizontal), design of structural elements (e.g., walls, arches, roofs, doors) and decoration in specific mediums (e.g., paint, relief, veneer, mosaic, and glass). A final subsection covers built-in ecclesiastical furniture.

Division 730 is assigned to the plastic arts and sculpture. The first section covers generalities of the field of sculpture, including a subsection on the historical and geographical treatment of sculpture. Section 731, concerned with the processes and representation of sculpture, includes materials, apparatus, techniques, style, sculpture in the round, and iconography. The next four sections are assigned to specific styles and schools of sculpture—primitive, ancient and Oriental in 732; Greek, Etruscan, and Roman in 733; medieval in 734; and modern in 735.

The last four sections, 736 to 739, cover the other plastic arts. Section 736 covers carving and carvings in various materials—semi-precious stones, stone, ivory, ornamental fans, and other materials such as ice and paper. Section 737 covers numismatics (coins) and sigillography, which is the art of engraved seals, and signets. Section 738 covers ceramic arts. The first subsection is used for techniques, apparatus, equipment, and materials, and subsequent subsections are devoted to ceramic products in various materials—porcelain, earthenware, and stoneware. Other subsections are used for specialized ceramic products—enameling, mosaic ornaments, and ornamental bricks and tiles. The last section, 739, which is fairly long, deals with art metalwork. After subsections for general materials, subsections cover metalwork in specific metals; the final subsection is assigned to metalwork involving arms and armor.

The next division, 740, covers drawing and the decorative and minor arts. The first three sections are devoted to drawing. Section 741 covers the general aspects of drawing and drawings, including a subsection for the critical appraisal of drawings and biographies of artists. Some other topics in this section are the techniques, equipment, and materials for drawing; cartoons, caricatures and comics; commercial art drawing; silhouettes; and collections of drawings with emphasis on specific periods and places.

Section 742 is assigned to the theory, principles, and methods relating to perspective. Section 743 covers drawing and drawings by subject. The main topics covered here encompass general works on drawing and the drawing of the human figure, drawing animal life and plant life, and collections of drawings by subject. Section 744 is currently unassigned.

The decorative and minor arts, including folk art, are covered in section 745. Subsections deal with antiques, industrial art and design, design and decoration, handicrafts, lettering, illumination, and heraldic design, decorative coloring, and panoramas, cycloramas, and dioramas. A final subsection is used for other decorative arts, with emphasis on floral arts and floral arrangements.

Textile arts and handicrafts are found in section 746. A point to note is the special "table of precedence," listing those subjects whose number should be used in the case of a work encompassing more than one subject listed within the section. Some of the subsections here cover spinning and weaving, laces, pictures, hangings, and tapestries, needlework and handwork, beadwork, printing, painting, and dyeing, and rugs and carpets. A final subsection is used for other textile arts such as furniture covers, bedclothing, and towels.

Section 747 is used for interior decorating. The first subsection is used for historical and geographic treatment. The following subsections are concerned with the decoration of specific elements such as ceilings, walls, doors, windows, and floors. Other subsections cover decorating with draperies, upholstery, and carpets. Two subsections are concerned with decorating specific rooms in residences and specific types of buildings. The last subsection deals with specific decorations (such as lighting) and decorating for specific occasions (such as parties and weddings).

Glass and its decorative qualities are assigned to section 748. Some of the special aspects covered here are glassware, stained, painted, leaded, and mosaic glass and its historical and geographical aspects. Two subsections deal with methods of decoration and with specific articles (e.g., mirrors, paperweights).

The concluding section, 749, is used for furniture and home accessories. After a subsection on the historical and geographical treatment of furniture, the following subsections cover specific kinds of furniture, built-in furniture, ornamental woodwork in furniture, heating and lighting fixtures, and picture frames.

Division 750 is used for painting and paintings. The subsections in 750 cover the philosophy and theory of painting and give an optional number for painters. Section 751, used for processes and forms, essentially covers the techniques, equipment, and materials of painting. Also here are numbers for the reproduction, copying, care, preservation, and restoration of paintings. A final subsection covers specific forms of painting such as murals, panoramas, scene painting, and miniatures.

Section 752, with no subdivisions, is used for color. The next four sections, 753–756, cover iconography, the "development, description, critical appraisal, [and] collections of works regardless of form." Section 757 is used for human figures and their parts in relation to attire, types of persons, and specific groups and situations. Section 758 deals with other subjects such as landscapes, animals, still life, industrial subjects, and architectural subjects. The concluding section, 759, is used for the historical and geographic aspects of painting, which are especially important areas. The initial subsections cover the history of painting from primitive to modern times, while the final subsections provide for a detailed geographical treatment.

The 760 division is assigned to the graphic arts, print making, and prints. The subsections at 760 cover the generalities of the field including the philosophy and theory of prints and print making. Sections 761 to 767 cover topics relating to print making. The various print making processes covered include relief processes, lithographic processes, chromolithography and serigraphy, metal engraving, mezzotinting, etching, and dry print. Section 768 is unassigned. The final section, 769, covers prints, print collecting, print care and preservation, and prints by subject, including paper money and postage stamps. The last subsection provides for the historical and geographical treatment of print making, prints, and print makers.

Division 770 is devoted to photography and photographs. The first subsections cover the philosophy and theory of photography, photography as a profession and hobby, its techniques, darkroom practice, and historical, geographical, and biographical treatment. Section 771 deals with photographic apparatus, equipment, and materials, including laboratories and darkrooms. The next three sections, 772 to 774, cover special photographic processes—metallic salt processes, pigment processes, and holography. Sections 775 to 777 are currently unassigned. Specific fields of photography are treated in section 778. Some of the fields covered are photographic projection, motion pictures and television photography, trick photography, and photography of specific subjects. The last section, 779, is used for collections of photographs.

Music is assigned to division 780. Covered in the first subsections are generalities, philosophy and esthetics, organizations, study and teaching, performances, collections, miniature scores, and historical, geographic, and biographical treatment.

Section 781 is used for the general principles of music and theory of music, which is not classed in 780.1. Some of the topics here are scientific principles, harmony, melody and counterpoint, musical forms (e.g., sonata, dance, jazz), composition and performance of music of ethnic and national origin, and other topics such as musical instruments, bibliographies, and thematic catalogs. Section 782 is concerned with dramatic music and musical drama. After subsections on generalities, the two main subsections cover opera and theater music. Included in the latter are film, radio, and television music. The last subsection covers all other forms of dramatic music, including music for the ballet.

The next section, 783, is a rather lengthy one devoted to sacred music. The first subsections cover generalities and music for specific religious groups. The next nine subdivisions, 783.1 to 783.9, are used for specific kinds of sacred music (e.g., instrumental, liturgical, oratorios, songs), for types of performing groups (e.g., choirs and vocal groups), and for hymns.

The next six sections, 784 to 789, are assigned to individual mediums of musical expression. Preceding section 784 is a special table of precedence with instructions for classifying a work covering two or more mediums of expression. Section 784 covers voice and vocal music, including choruses, choral works, songs for one to nine parts (e.g., solos, duets, trios, nonets), folksongs, songs for specific groups or subjects, and a subsection for other kinds of songs such as national airs and ethnic and cultural songs. The last two subsections cover collections of vocal music and voice training and performance.

Sections 785 to 789 cover materials on musical instruments and instrumental music. The first section is used for instrumental ensembles such as orchestras, bands, and chamber ensembles. After this introductory material subsequent subsections cover specific kinds of music such as symphonies, band music, concertos, chamber music, and suites. Also included in 785 are numbers for dance music and jazz. Sections 786 to 789 cover specific musical instruments and their music. The first, 786, covers keyboard instruments (e.g., piano, organ). Section 787 deals with string instruments and their music. Some examples of instruments here are the harp, guitar, banjo, and viola. All other plectral instruments are also classified here. Section 788 covers the wind instruments and their music (e.g., trumpet, French horn, flute, and bassoon); all other wind and reed instruments are also found here. The final section, 789, is assigned the percussion, mechanical, and electrical musical instruments. Included here are such instruments as drums, cymbals, bells, carillons, and the music box. The last subsection, 789.9, is used for electronic instruments, music recording, and critical appraisal of recordings. Concrete music (musique concrète) is included at 789.98.

The last division in the 700 class, 790, is used for recreational and performing arts. This first section, devoted to generalities of recreation, include subsections on recreational activities for individuals and specific groups by age levels and sex.

Public performances "other than musical, sport and game" are found in 791. Here are found numbers for amusement parks, traveling shows, circuses, motion pictures, radio, and television, and minor performing arts.

Theater presentations are assigned to section 792. Covered here are the specific types of presentations including techniques, equipment, and materials. Some special topics are make-up, costuming, and settings. There is also provision for historical and geographical treatment. The final subsections cover specific kinds of dramatic performances including tragedy, comedy, pantomime, vaudeville, and ballet.

Section 793 is used for indoor games and amusements, including parties, dancing, games of all kinds, and magic. Section 794 is assigned to indoor games of skill such as chess, checkers, bowling, and indoor ball games (e.g., pool and billiards). Games of chance are assigned to number 795. After a subsection on the theory of games of chance, there are numbers for specific games such as craps and other dice games, card games (e.g., poker, bridge, rummy) and other games of chance including baccarat and blackjack.

Athletic and outdoor sports and games are assigned to section 796, which is one of the lengthiest in the schedule. Following the numbers for generalities, philosophy and theory, and coaching are nine subsections that provide for all types of sports and games. The first two, 796.1 and 796.2, deal with miscellaneous games (e.g., leapfrog, hide and seek) and miscellaneous games requiring equipment (e.g., roller skating, horseshoes). The next subsection is devoted to ball games in specific categories, such as basketball, volleyball, golf, football, soccer, and tennis. For each sport numbers are available to classify specific aspects. Athletic exercises and gymnastics are in 796.4, which also accounts for track and field athletics and specific field events. The next subsection, 796.5, is assigned to outdoor life and its various activities such as walking, camping, and exploring. The next two subsections are for cycling and driving motor vehicles, respectively. The two final subsections, 796.8 and 796.9, cover combat sports (e.g., wrestling, judo, boxing) and ice and snow sports (e.g., ice skating, skiing).

Aquatic sports and air sports are covered in section 797. The aquatic sports include boating, water skiing, swimming and diving, and water games. Air sports, an area becoming ever more popular, covers motor driven aircraft, gliders, and parachuting, with its adjunct, skydiving. Equestrian sports and animal racing are found in 798. Here provision is made for all aspects of horsemanship and horse racing, including gambling, driving and coaching, and racing animals other than horses (e.g., dogs).

The final section, 799, is used for fishing, hunting, and shooting. Notice that these subjects are separated from outdoor life and camping (796.5), with which they are often associated. The introductory subsections cover the techniques and equipment of fishing in fresh water and salt water and fishing for specific kinds of fish. The subsection on hunting provides for the technique and equipment of hunting, including provisions for various categories of firearms. The following subdivisions are concerned with the general aspects of hunting game and hunting specific kinds of animals, while the last subsection is concerned with shooting in general with guns (e.g., skeet shooting) and with bows and arrows (archery).

NUMBER BUILDING, 700–799

Example 1

What number would be assigned to a work on goldsmithing in Renaissance Italy?

The key word to consider is goldsmithing, which is the primary subject. The other limiting aspects of the work, "Renaissance" and "Italy," narrow the scope chronologically and geographically. The Relative Index has entries for all three key words. Under "Goldsmithing—arts—decorative" there is a reference to 739.22. The entry for "Italy" provides only an area notation, —45, and under "Renaissance art—design and decoration—specific places" the number cited is 745.449.

Checking the suggested numbers in the schedule shows that 739.22 is the correct one for goldsmithing. Now one needs to see if a more specific number can be built for historical or geographical treatment. Searching the schedule leads to 739.227, for historical or geographical treatment. For the work here the geographical treatment is deemed more important, so we will build our number from 739.2271–.2279 (Fig. 9-1).

Fig. 9-1. Classification Schedule

739

.227	Historical and geographical treatment
.227 01–.227 04	Historical periods

                         Add to 739.2270 the numbers following 090 in "Standard Subdivisions" notation 0901–0904 from Table 1, e.g., goldsmithing in 15th century 739.227024

→ .227 1–.227 9   Geographical treatment

                         Add "Areas" notation 1–9 from Table 2 to base number 739.227, e.g., goldsmiths 739.2272

                         If preferred, class goldsmiths in 739.22092

The instructions at 739.2271–.2279 say to "add 'Areas' notation 1–9 from Table 2 to base number 739.227." Go to Table 2, keeping in mind that this work is limited both geographically (Italy) and chronologically (Renaissance). The instructions in Table 2 at 3–9 allow two alternatives—geographical treatment by region or a combination historical geographic treatment (Fig. 9-2).

Fig. 9-2. Areas (Table 2)

►   **–3–9 Specific continents, countries, localities; extraterrestrial worlds**

Class here specific instances of the subject ·

If desired, add to each number as follows:

    009   Regional treatment

                   Add to 009 the numbers following –1 in –11–19 of this table, e.g., Torrid Zone of Asia –50093, rivers of England –42009693, Italian-speaking regions of Switzerland –4940097551, cities of ancient Greece –38009732

                   An alternative treatment is shown under –1

    01–09   Historical periods

⟶   Add to base number the historical period numbers in corresponding subdivisions of 930–990, using one 0 in all cases, e.g., Tudor England –4205, Tudor Berkshire –422905, United States during administration of Dwight D. Eisenhower –730921

The second alternative allows the addition of notations for historical periods to the base number for areas. The specific instructions allow the addition "to base number the *historical period numbers in corresponding subdivisions* of 930–990, using one 0 in all cases" (Fig. 9-2). In the 930–990 range you will drop the first 9 and add all subsequent digits.

In this case the historical period number is 945.05. The number for Italy in the 900 class is 9<u>45</u>. Remember that the entry "Italy" in the Relative Index cited area notation –<u>45</u> (this is another mnemonic feature of the DDC). A check of the

1000 sections summary table in Volume 1 (pp. 451ff.) would also help locate Italy in the 900 class. History of Italy during the Renaissance (1300-1494) is found in the schedule at 945.05.

Following the instructions in the schedule at 739.227, add the area notation for Italy, −45, from Table 2 (or the −45 from 945, dropping the first digit). To this number, 739.22745, add the notation for the historical time period, −05, from 945.05 for Renaissance Italy. Our final number is 739.2274505. It is built as follows:

730		plastic arts and sculpture
739		art metalwork
.2		work in precious metals
.22		goldsmithing
.227		historical and geographical treatment (.2271–.2779, geographical treatment)
	45	area notation for Italy from Table 2 or schedule
	05	from 945.05 in the schedule for Renaissance Italy
739.2274505		goldsmithing in Renaissance Italy

The abridged edition's entry under "Goldsmithing–arts–decorative" cites number 739.2. The entry for "Renaissance" cites only a number for "Europe history," 940.2. The entry for "Italy" provides only an area notation, −45.

Under 739.2 in the abridged edition no specific provision is made for historical or geographical treatment. If more specialized treatment is considered necessary, the standard subdivisions and area notations can be used in this edition. At the standard subdivision −09 for historical and geographical treatment, there are instructions to add the "Areas notation 3–9 from Table 2 to base number −09." Add −09 to 739.2 for 739.209. Now add the area notation −45 for Italy to build 739.20945. There are no provisions in this edition for further number building for specific historical periods.

It is interesting to note that the abridged edition and the full edition have different approaches to this particular problem. The full edition number, 739.2274505 was built using the area notation and subsections within the 900 class in the schedule. The abridged edition's number, 739.20945, was built using a standard subdivision and an area notation. Beyond the basic number, 739.2, the only similarity is the −45 for Italy. These numbers present evidence that the two editions of the DDC should not be used interchangeably; a library should use only one edition at a time. Shifting to the full edition will usually require some reclassification in areas where distinct conflicts exist in methods of number building.

Example 2

What is the most specific number for a work on folk songs of West Africa? The subject matter here is straightforward. The primary subject is songs, with the restrictive term "folk" and the geographic limit of West Africa. The

Relative Index provides the following entries and numbers: "Songs–music–general works–secular," number 784; "Folk–songs–music," number 784.4; and "West Africa," with area notation −66 from Table 2.

The number 784 for songs turns out to be the general number for voice and vocal music. Number 784.4, cited under "Folk songs," is a more specific number. However, the directions at 784.4 suggest that numbers 784.75−784.76 be used for songs of specific ethnic and cultural groups (Fig. 9-3).

Fig. 9-3. Classification Schedule

784

.4   *Folk songs

          Class national airs, songs, hymns in 784.71, songs of specific ethnic and
          cultural groups in 784.75−784.76 ◀———

Now check the sequence 784.75−.76 to see if it is correct for the work being classified (Fig. 9-4).

Fig. 9-4. Classification Schedule

784

▶   784.75−784.76 Songs of specific ethnic and cultural groups

               Class comprehensive works in 784.7

.75   Songs of ethnic and cultural groups in United States and Canada

               (If it is desired to give local emphasis and a shorter number to songs of
               ethnic and cultural groups of a specific country, it is optional to class
               them here; in that case class songs of ethnic and cultural groups in
               United States and Canada in 784.76)

.751   Amerindians

.752   Gipsies

.755   Anglo-Americans and Celtic-Americans

.756   *Negroes

               Examples: minstrel and plantation songs, spirituals

———▶ .76   Songs of ethnic and national groups in other countries

               Add "Racial, Ethnic, National Groups" notation 01−99 from Table 5
               to base number 784.76

Number 784.76 is the correct base number for songs of ethnic and national groups in other countries. The instructions say to add to the base number the notations 01−99 from Table 5 for Racial, Ethnic, and National Groups (Fig. 9-4).

The summary at the beginning of Table 5 places Africans in −9, and the summary table at −9 in Table 5 places Africans in −96 (Fig. 9-5).

Fig. 9-5. Racial, Ethnic, National Groups (Table 5)

−9   Other racial, ethnic, national groups

SUMMARY

−91   Other Indo-European peoples
−92   Semites
−93   North Africans
−94   Peoples of North and West Asian origin or
        situation, and Dravidians
−95   Peoples of East and Southeast Asia
−96   Africans
−97   American aborigines
−98   South American aborigines
−99   Other peoples

"Africans," −96, is too broad so the table must be searched for a more specific number for West Africa. Notation −966−968 is found to be used for national groups in Africa (Fig. 9-6).

Fig. 9-6. Racial, Ethnic, National Groups (Table 5)

−966−968   National groups in Africa

> Add to −96 the numbers following 6 in "Areas" notation 66−68 from Table 2, e.g., Nigerians −9669, South Africans −968

> Class nationals of specific ethnolinguistic groups in −961−963

> *For South African Anglo-Saxons, see* −28; *Afrikaners*, −3936

To see if further number building is possible for West Africa, follow the directions at −966−968 (Fig. 9-6). There you are told to "Add to −96 the numbers following 6 in 'Areas' notation 66−68 from Table 2." In Table 2, −66 is used for West Africa. Following the instructions in Table 5, add the numbers *following* 6 in Table 2 to −96 in Table 5. Thus, add the second 6 from −66 to −96, to build −966. Add this to the base number 784.76 to build 784.76966. The number building is developed as follows:

780		music
784		voice and vocal music
	.7	other kinds of song
	6	songs of ethnic and national groups in other countries
	96	Africans and people of African descent (from Table 5)
	6	the second 6 from −66 for West Africa in Table 2, added as instructed
784.76966		folk songs of West Africa

The Relative Index to the abridged edition has the following entries and numbers: "Songs–music–secular," 784; "Folk songs–music," 784.4; and "West Africa," area –66.

Checking the schedules shows that 784.4 is the best starting point. A note in the schedule, however, says to class songs of specific ethnic and cultural groups in 784.7. At 784.7 no specific provision is made for geographic subdivision, so the correct number for this edition is 784.7. It is, of course, possible to use the standard subdivision –09 and add an area notation to the standard subdivision. However, users of the abridged edition might not want such a long number.

Example 3

Where would a book on the stage treatment of love, in comedy, be classified? This is a bit tricky because the book refers not only to the kind of performance, but to its treatment of a specific subject.

The number given for "Theater" in the index is 792. This, however, is too broad. Under "Love–lit. & stage trmt.," the index refers the reader to "Life cycle," which has the following number under stage treatment: 792.0909354; however, this number does not reflect the stage treatment of love in comedy. Under "Comedy– stage performance" the number 792.2 is provided. This is the correct base number for the work. An asterisk, however, refers to a note that says to "add as instructed under 792.1–792.8" (Fig. 9-7).

Fig. 9-7. Classification Schedule

▶

792.1–792.8 Specific kinds of dramatic performance

Add to each subdivision identified by * as follows:
    01–09   Standard subdivisions
                Apply the extended meanings of 792.01–792.09

Class comprehensive works in 792, specific productions of specific kinds in 792.9

.1   *Tragedy and serious drama*

        Class here historical, Passion, morality, miracle plays

.2   *Comedy and melodrama*

The instructions at 792.1–792.8 say to add the standard subdivisions and their extended meanings. These are found in the schedule from 792.01 to 792.09. A search of this span of numbers leads to 792.0909, which is an extended meaning in this part of the schedule for standard subdivision –09 (Fig. 9-8).

Fig. 9-8. Classification Schedule

792

    .090 9   Special aspects

                Add to 792.0909 the numbers following 080 in "Subdivisions of Individual Literatures" notation 0801–0803 from Table 3, e.g., treatment of sex in the theater 792.0909353

This is, of course, the basis for the index entry 729.0909354.

As Fig. 9-8 shows, there are instructions to add "the numbers following 080 in 'Subdivisions of Individual Literatures' notation 0801–0803 from Table 3." A search of the suggested numbers in Table 3 leads to 080354 for life cycle, including love. Now, following the instructions, add the numbers following 080 in 080354 to .0909 to build .0909354. This number is added to the base number for comedy, 792.2, to build 792.20909354. The number building is developed as follows:

790	recreational and performing arts
792	theater
.2	comedy and melodrama
09	historical and geographical treatment
09	special aspects, an extended meaning of standard subdivisions
354	life cycle, including love, from Table 3 as instructed (the 354 is from 080354 in Table 3, following instructions to use the numbers following 080)
792.20909354	the stage treatment in comedy of love

The abridged edition also provides number 792 for "Theater" and 792.2 under "Comedy–stage performance." Checking the schedule shows that 792.2 is the most specific number required.

Example 4

Where would a collection of photographs on aeronautical subjects be classified?

The emphasis in this work is on photography as an art form and only secondarily on aeronautics. Under "Photographs–arts" and "Photography–arts" number 770 is cited. The index entry "Aeronautics–technology" refers to 629.13, which may be of use later for building on to a base number.

There is no summary in the schedule at 770, so it is necessary to go through the schedule to see if a more specific number is available. At 770.92 there is a note to class collections of works in 779 (Fig. 9-9).

Fig. 9-9. Classification Schedule

779   **Collections of photographs**

Class here collections of *works of individual photographers*

Add to 779 the numbers following 704.94 in 704.942–704.949, e.g., photographs of children 779.25

Instructions here say to add to 779 the numbers following 704.94 in 704.942–.949. Looking through the schedule at 704.942, it is seen that these numbers pertain to general subjects of art works. Aeronautics is not specifically listed. However, the last number, 704.949, is used for other specific subjects (Fig. 9-10).

Fig. 9-10. Classification Schedule

704

.949   Other specific subjects

Add 001–999 to base number 704.949, e.g., industrial subjects
704.9496

To 704.949 the instructions allow the addition from the schedules of 001–999 to the base number. This is where the number for aeronautics, 629.13 can be used. Add this to 704.949 to build 704.94962913. Now, following the instructions at 779, add to 779 the numbers following 704.94, to build 779.962913. The number building sequence is as follows:

770	photography and photographs
779	collections of photographs
.9	from 704.949 as instructed in the schedule
62913	for aeronautics, added as instructed at 704.949 in the schedule
779.962913	a collection of photographs on aeronautical subjects as an art form

The abridged edition has entries for "Photographs–arts" and "Photography–arts," and both cite number 770. Under "Aeronautics," number 629.13 is given. Searching the 770 schedule leads to 779 for collections of photographs. No provisions are made here for a more specific number for collections on a particular subject. Therefore, 779 is the correct number for this edition.

PROBLEMS TO SOLVE

Try to build classification numbers for the following hypothetical works:

1) a work on Renoir's impressionism
2) a work on commemorative stamps of the United States
3) a work on Kerman rugs and their designs
4) a general work on stamp collecting
5) a work on the Russian art museum, the Hermitage
6) a work on the architecture of public library buildings in the United States

ANSWERS TO PROBLEMS

1) 759.4 (18th edition)   759.4 (10th abridged edition)

The work in hand would probably provide the information that impressionism is a style of painting and that Renoir was a major impressionist and a French painter. If necessary, an encyclopedia or art reference work will provide this information, which must be known before the work can be classified.

The Relative Index under "Impressionism–painting–specific places" cites number 759.1–.9. Under "Painters (arts)–biography and work" the same number span is given. The schedule shows that numbers 759.1–.9 are used for geographical treatment of painting. A scope note says to "class here *individual painters* regardless of process, form, subject." A *general* work on impressionism would be classed in 759.05.

It has already been established that Renoir was a French painter, so the numbers 759.2–.8, for modern European countries, will be used. There are instructions here to add to base number 759 the numbers *following* 4 in "Areas" notation 42–48 from Table 2. The "Areas" notation for France is –44. Adding the second 4 to 759 gives 759.4 for Renoir. [**Editor's note**: Period could be indicated by using the standard subdivision –09 with its chronological expansion, to give –09034 for the nineteenth century. This would result in the number 759.409034.]

The abridged edition's Relative Index has no entry for either "Impressionism" or "Painters." Under "Painting–arts" and "Paintings–arts" there is a reference to number 750. This is only a general number, so it is necessary to read through the schedule until you find numbers 759.1–.9 for historical and geographical treatment. There a note says to class individual painters, regardless of process, form, or subject, in this number span. The numbers for modern Europe are 759.2–.8, and the instructions say to add the numbers following 4 in "Areas" notation 42–48 from Table 2. France is –44̲ in Table 2, so the second 4 is added to base number 759 to build 759.4.

2) 769.56973 (18th edition)   769 (10th abridged edition)

The topic of the work is concerned with a specific type of stamp— commemoratives of the United States. The Relative Index provides two likely possibilities—"Commemorative stamps–philately" (number 769.563) and "Postage stamps–arts" (number 769.56). The general term "Philately" cites number 769.56.

The schedule shows that 769.563 is a general number used for stamps commemorating persons and events. The stamps of a specific country are involved, however; if that is an overriding factor in order to place together all books on a specific country's stamps, then look further in the schedule for a geographical treatment. At 769.5691–.5699 provision is made for geographic treatment. Here instructions say to add "Areas" notation 1–9 from Table 2 to base number 769.569. The "Areas" notation for the United States is –73. Adding –73 to the base number 769.569 builds 769.56973 for commemorative stamps of the United States. [**Editor's note**: This number does not specifically indicate commemorative stamps, but it is geographically more specific than 769.563 could be.]

In the Relative Index of the abridged edition there is no entry for "Commemorative." The entry "Postage stamps–arts" refers to number 769, and the entry "Philately" also refers to number 769. This is the most specific number for the abridged edition, since there is no provision for historical or geographical treatment.

3) 746.75582 (18th edition)   746.7 (10th abridged edition)

The Relative Index entry for "Rugs–textile arts" is the most promising starting point, because rug design is more applicable to art than rug manufacturing. The number given is 746.7.

Next it is necessary to determine the meaning and relationship of the term Kerman to rugs. Is it a place, a manufacturer or a process? The Relative Index provides a possible answer. An entry for "Kerman Iran" provides the area notation –5582. This means that Kerman can refer to a particular type of rug made in a specific area of Iran.

The schedule confirms that 746.7 is the correct number for rugs, and a further division, 746.75, covers rugs woven with pile. A span of numbers for Oriental rugs, 746.751–.759, is also provided. The instructions under 746.751–.758 say to add area notation 51–58 from Table 2 to the base number 746.7. Iran is found at notation –55, and the Kerman area at –5582. Add –5582 to base number 746.7 for 746.75582.

The abridged edition entry under "Rugs–textile art" cites number 746.7. No further subdivision is provided for in the schedule, so this is the correct number for this edition.

4) 769.56075 (18th edition)   769.075 (10th abridged edition)

Problem 2 concerned commemorative stamps of the United States. Now we are concerned with finding the DDC number for a general work on stamp collecting.

The Relative Index entries for "Postage stamps–arts" and "Postage stamps–postal communication" seem like good possibilities. Number 769.56 is cited with the former entry, and checking the schedule shows that this number is for general philately. The latter entry cites number 383.23, which is not applicable since it is used for the economic aspects in relation to rates and costs.

The schedule at 769.56 does not mention stamp collecting or make any reference to another number. A search in the Relative Index under "Collecting" provides a possible solution. "Collecting–specific objects" cites standard subdivision –075. A check of Table 1 shows this standard subdivision can be added as required to an appropriate number from the schedule to indicate the collecting of the object. Thus, a general work on stamp collecting will be classified in number 769.56075.

A similar number building sequence is used in the abridged edition; the difference is that the Relative Index entry "Postage stamps–arts" gives number 769 for the base number. To 769 the standard subdivision –075 is added to build 769.075, which is correct for this edition.

5) 708.745 (18th edition)   708 (10th abridged edition)

A reading of this hypothetical work would undoubtedly describe the Hermitage as one of the world's great art museums located in Leningrad, Russia.

Interestingly, the Relative Index entries for "Museum" and "Museums" have no reference to art. The entry "Art—museum buildings" does not mention specific museums. Under the entry "Galleries—arts" the number 708 is given. Checking the schedule confirms this is the correct number to use for art galleries and museums. A geographical treatment is provided for in numbers 708.1–.9, and numbers 708.2–.8 are used for modern European countries. The instructions say to add to base number 708 the numbers following 4 in "Areas" notation 42–48 from Table 2. A quick check in the Relative Index under "Leningrad, RSFSR" provides the area notation –4745. This is confirmed in Table 2. Adding the numbers following 4 to base number 708 builds number 708.745.

In the abridged edition there is also a lack of references to the base number for art galleries under "Art—museum buildings" and "Museums." Only under "Galleries—arts" is number 708 provided. The schedule shows that this is the correct number for art galleries. The provision for geographical subdivision has been discontinued, so 708 is the most specific number for this edition.

6) 727.82473 (18th edition)   727

                                        or

                              727.0973 (10th abridged edition)

The Relative Index provides several leads under keyword entries. Under "Architecture" there is nothing specific for library buildings. The entry "Architectural design" provides a note to see also specific kinds of buildings. Under "Buildings" there is also a note to see specific kinds—e.g., library buildings. Under "Library buildings—architecture" number 727.8 is given. Remember that we are interested in public library architecture. The entry "Public libraries—buildings—architecture" gives a more specific number, 727.824.

The schedule provides number 727.82 for general libraries, with instructions to add to this base number the numbers following 027 in 027.1–027.8. In the schedule we find 027.4 is used for public libraries. However, we have a work on public libraries in the United States, and instructions at 027.42 direct the user to class public libraries treated geographically in 027.43–027.49. At 027.43–.49 the instructions say to add "Areas" notation 3–9 from Table 2 to base number 027.4. In Table 2, –73 is the area notation for the United States. Add –73 to 027.4 to build 027.473. Now, in accordance with the instructions at 727.82 to add the numbers following 027, add the 473 from 027.473 to base number 727.82, building 727.82473.

The abridged edition's Relative Index provides several entries under the terms "Architectural" and "Architecture." The subdivisions under these terms refer to the 720's, but there are no references for specific types of buildings. Under "Library buildings—architecture" number 727 is cited. Turning to 727 in the schedule we find it is the most specific available number. If desired, a geographic notation could be added using the standing subdivision –09 from Table 1 and an area notation from Table 2. To 727 add –09 for geographical treatment and –73, the area notation for the United States, to build 727.0973.

CHAPTER 10

CLASS 800–899
(LITERATURE)

INTRODUCTORY NOTE

The divisions of the 800's and their order follow that of the 400's and Table 6, Languages. The only exception to this is the separate assignment of 810 to American literature and 820 to British literature. As we have already stated, the result of assigning whole divisions to major European languages (English, German, French, Italian, etc.) is that other languages have much longer base numbers. Besides studying the "Details of the Class" and the schedules for this class, it is important to review Table 3, Individual Literatures, which gives the subdivisions for individual literary forms, as shown in Chapter 1 of this text.

The approach of the number building section of this chapter is different from the approach used in the other chapters. Here, long DDC numbers are carefully analyzed to demonstrate how they were built. This approach is most appropriate in this class because of the many different possible subdivisions and elements represented in each number. These elements include the base number for the language, a possible number for literary form (poetry or drama, for example), a possible number for the time or period of the work, a number for collections or history and criticism, and, finally, a number for specific themes. Example 1 in the number building section contains all these elements. In either building or analyzing a number in this class it is essential to know what the base number is. It may be only one digit long or it may have several digits.

OUTLINE OF THE CLASS

800	Literature (Belles-lettres)
810	American literature in English
820	English and Anglo-Saxon literatures
830	Literatures of Germanic languages
840	Literatures of Romance languages
850	Italian, Romanian, and Rhaeto-Romanic literatures
860	Spanish and Portuguese literatures
870	Literatures of Italic languages (Latin)
880	Literatures of Hellenic languages
890	Literatures of other languages

INTRODUCTION TO THE CLASS

This class is used for both works of literature and works about literature. The literary forms included here are poetry, drama, fiction, essays, speeches, letters, satire and humor, and quotations and epigrams.

Although the 800's are a comparatively short schedule, they can nonetheless be complex in their application. This complexity is attested to in the two-page Table of Examples at the end of the 800 schedule, which is meant to serve as a guide to number building in the literature class. In addition, this class relies heavily on Tables 3 and 6, as discussed in Chapter 1.

The introductory materials at 800 in the schedule provide the classifier with general directions and a table of precedence to follow for works that combine or treat two or more literary forms. The example provided with the table (822 for English poetic drama) shows that the work is classed in the number for English drama rather than English poetry because dramatic form precedes poetic form in the table of precedence.

This class has special provisions to "give preferred treatment to, or make available more and shorter numbers for the classification of, literature of any specific language that it is desired to emphasize" (DDC, Vol. 2, p. 1483). Full instructions for these provisions appear at numbers 800, 810–890, 820, 840, 860, and 869. Briefly, there are three main options for classifying a literature that is not given full treatment elsewhere in the schedule. The first is to class the literature in division 810. The second is to place specific literature to be emphasized before 810 by using a letter symbol. And the third, in cases where two or more countries use the same language, is either to use initial letters to identify separate countries or to use "the special number designated for literatures of those countries which are *not* preferred" (DDC, Vol. 2, p. 1483).

DETAILS OF THE CLASS

The first section, 801, is used for the philosophy and theory of literature. Two important subsections are assigned to the value, influence, and effect of literature, and the nature of literature. The latter subsection also covers psychology, esthetics, and criticism as they are applied to literature. The subdivision for criticism, 801.95, is further subdivided (801.951–801.957 for the criticism of specific literary forms). The next six sections, 802–807, are used as the standard subdivisions of the class except for section 804, which is currently unassigned.

Section 808, a lengthy one, is used for rhetoric and collections of literature. Some of the special topics covered by the initial subsections are authorship, editorial techniques, composition in various languages and types of literature (e.g., professional, technical, children's). The next seven subsections, 808.1–808.7, cover rhetoric for specific forms of literature—poetry, drama, fiction, essays, speech, letters, and satire and humor. The final subsection, 808.8, is used for collections from more than one literature. Provisions are made at 808.8 for building numbers for collections from specific periods, collections emphasizing specific qualities (e.g., idealism, romanticism), collections with specific elements (e.g., narrative, plot) and collections with specific themes and subjects (e.g., law, places, times, life cycles, philosophic concepts). Subsections 808.81–808.88 are used for collections of specific forms of literature—poetry, drama, fiction, essays, speeches, letters, satire and humor, and special collections on miscellaneous topics.

The last section, 809, provides for works on the history, description, and criticism of more than one literature. The first seven subsections, 809.1–809.7, cover literature in specific forms. Subsection 809.8 covers "literature for and by specific kinds of persons" (e.g., age groups, sex, occupation). A table of precedence here provides instructions for classifying collections covering several different kinds of persons. The final subsection, 809.9, is used for collections of literature with specific features, qualities, or elements. Number building instructions allow the use of the entire schedule to account for any topic or discipline.

The following nine divisions, 810–890, are assigned to the literatures of specific languages. When classifying works of literature keep in mind two basic principles: 1) A work of literature is classed in the language in which originally written. For example, if a work being classified is in English, but was translated from the *original* French, it will be classified with French literature. 2) A work of literature written in a dialect of a basic language is classed with the basic language. For example, a work written in cockney—a dialect used in London—would be classified with English literature.

The first division, 810, is assigned to American literature written in English. Special provisions are made for English language literature of the Western Hemisphere and Hawaii. Instructions allow the literatures of specific countries to be distinguished by the use of letters before the DDC number (for example, Canadian literature, C810, or Brazilian literature, originally in English, B810). Period tables for chronological treatment are given for Canada and the United States. Each of the following eight sections, 811–818, covers a specific form of American literature: 811, poetry; 812, drama; 813, fiction; 814, essays; 815, speeches; 816, letters; 817, satire and humor; and 818, miscellaneous writings. The last section, 819, is for literatures not requiring local emphasis. For example, if a library emphasizes United States literature, then Canadian literature or other Western Hemisphere literatures can be classed here. And if a library wants to emphasize Canadian literature, then United States literature can be classed here.

Division 820 is assigned to the literatures of English and Anglo-Saxon languages. As in the previous division the literatures of specific countries may be distinguished by using letters before the DDC number (for example, Irish literature, Ir820; Australian literature, A820; Indian literature, In820). Period tables for English literature written in Asian countries, Australia, Great Britain, Ireland, New Zealand, and South Africa are provided.

Section 821 is used for English poetry. The following section, 822, is assigned to English drama, with two subsections, 822.3 and 822.33, devoted respectively to the Elizabethan period and to William Shakespeare. For William Shakespeare there is a special table of book numbers that can be used to arrange works both by and about Shakespeare. The table can also be modified and used to help arrange the works of any other author. As with the divisions for other literatures, the next six sections respectively cover specific forms of literature: 823, fiction; 824, essays; 825, speeches; 826, letters; 827, satire and humor; and 828, miscellaneous writings. It is optional to class the English language literatures of non-American countries in 828. For example, if a library emphasizes British literature, then Australian or other literatures can be classified here. And, if a library chooses to emphasize Australian literature, then British literature may be classed here. The concluding section, 829, is assigned to Anglo-Saxon (Old English), with special subsections for poetry and for three individual works of literature—Caedmon, Beowulf, and Cynewulf.

The literatures of the Germanic languages, including German literature, are found in division 830. There is a period table for use with German literature. The first eight sections cover the same topics in the same order as the earlier two divisions: 831, poetry; 832, drama; 833, fiction; 834, essays; 835, speeches; 836, letters; 837, satire and humor; and 838, miscellaneous writings. The last section, 839, is used for the literatures of all other Germanic languages. Some examples of these other Germanic languages are Yiddish, Low German languages (e.g., Dutch, Flemish, Afrikaans), Scandinavian languages (Swedish, Danish, Norwegian), and East Germanic languages (e.g., Gothic, Vandalic).

Division 840 deals with the literatures of the Romance languages, with emphasis on French literature. There are three special period tables to use with the literatures written in French in Belgium, Canada, and France. The next eight sections, 841—848, are assigned respectively to poetry, drama, fiction, essays, speeches, letters, satire and humor, and miscellaneous writings. Section 848 is used for literatures of specific countries. For example, a library emphasizing French literature can classify French-Canadian literature here. And, if a library chooses to emphasize French-Canadian literature, then French literature can be classified here. The last section, 849, is used for Provençal and Catalan. For each of these literatures there is a period table.

The literatures of Italian, Romanian, and Rhaeto-Romanic languages are covered in division 850. There is a special period table to use with Italian literature. The next eight sections, 851—858 (for Italian literature), again cover the major literary forms: 851, poetry, 852, drama; 853, fiction; 854, essays; 855, speeches; 856, letters; 857, satire and humor; and 858, miscellaneous writings. Finally, section 859 is assigned to Romanian and Rhaeto-Romanic literatures, with a period table for Romanian literature.

The 860 division includes the literatures of the Spanish and Portuguese languages. There are period tables for literature in Spanish written in American countries and in Spain. Sections 861—868 for Spanish literature are each assigned to a literary form: 861, poetry; 862, drama; 863, fiction; 864, essays; 865, speeches; 866, letters; 867, satire and humor; and 868, miscellaneous writings. Section 868 has a subsection that allows the option of classifying literatures of individual countries there. And, there is an option to use the other sections for other literatures and to classify Spanish literature here. Section 869 is used for Portuguese-language literatures, with period tables for both Brazil and Portugal.

The next division, 870, is assigned to the literatures of Italic languages and Latin. There is a period table to use with Latin literature. The structure of the sections here differs from that of the other divisions, but it is similar to division 880. The next eight sections cover specific forms of Latin literature: 871, poetry; 872, poetry and drama; 873, epic poetry and fiction; 874, lyric poetry; 875, speeches; 876, letters; 877, satire and humor; and 878, miscellaneous writings. Section 879 is used for other Italic languages such as Venetic, Aequian and Sabine.

Division 880 is used for the Hellenic languages and classical and modern Greek literature. There is a period table for classical Greek literature. Sections 881—888 are used for the literary forms of classical Greek literature. The specific literary forms are: 881, poetry; 882, dramatic poetry and drama; 883, epic poetry and fiction; 884, lyric poetry; 885, speeches; 886, letters; 887, satire and humor; and 888, miscellaneous writings. The concluding section, 889, used for modern Greek literature, includes a period table.

The last division of this class, 890, is used for the literatures of other languages. Many of the languages in this division are assigned period tables. Section 891 is assigned to East Indo-European and Celtic languages. Some examples of these languages are Sanskrit, Iranian languages, Celtic languages, Russian, and Czech. Section 892 is used for Afro-Asiatic languages such as Assyrian, Aramaic languages, Hebrew, and Arabic. Section 893 treats Hamitic and Chad languages, examples of which are Coptic and Hausa. Section 894 includes Ural-Altaic languages such as Turkish, Finnish, and Estonian; Paleosiberian languages such as Ainu; and the Dravidian languages. Section 895 includes the languages of East and Southeast Asia, including Chinese, Japanese, Korean, and Burmese. Section 896 is used for African languages. The languages of American and South American aboriginals (Indians) are covered in sections 897 and 898. The last section, 899, is used for all other languages some of the more important and interesting being Tagalog, Bahasa Indonesia, and Esperanto.

NUMBER BUILDING, 800–899

In addition to providing number building examples like those given in earlier chapters, we will also take several DDC numbers like the ones given in the Table of Examples at the end of the 800 schedule and follow the steps necessary for building them. This approach may prove helpful for the literature class.

Example 1

Where would a collection of late 20th century Italian drama about marriage be classified?

For this example we will start with the DDC number, 852.914080354, and trace the steps needed to build it. The Relative Index entry "Italian language– literature" provides number 850, and it is easy to find 852 in the schedule, for Italian drama. A period table for Italian literature gives notation –914 for later 20th century (Fig. 10-1, page 156).

Fig. 10-1. Classification Schedule

Base number for Italian: 85

PERIOD TABLE FOR ITALIAN

1   Early period to 1375
2   Period of classical learning, 1375–1492
3   Age of Leo X, 1492–1542
4   Later 16th century, 1542–1585
5   Period of decline, 1585–1748
6   Period of renovation, 1748–1814
7   Early 19th century, 1814–1859
8   Later 19th century, 1859–1900
9   1900–
91   20th century
912   Early, 1900–1945
914   Later, 1945–

This notation is added to base number 852 to build 852.914. This is the *general* number for Italian drama in the late 20th century. In the schedule there are instructions to add to the base number as instructed under 810–890. The base number for Italian drama is 852. At 810–890 there are directions to add to the base number the appropriate notation from numbers 01–89 from Table 3, "Subdivisions of Individual Literatures."

In Table 3 the notation –0803 is used for collections dealing with specific themes and subjects. The specific topic of the collection here is marriage, and at notation –080354 there is provision for the life cycle and marriage. This is added to the base number for late 20th century Italian drama, 852.914, to build 852.914080354. The elements of this number building example are:

850	Italian literature
852	Italian drama
.9	from period table, 1900–
.91	from period table, 20th century
.914	from period table, Later, 1945–
08	collections (from Table 3 as instructed)
03	collections dealing with specific themes and subjects
5	humanity and human existence
54	life cycle, including marriage
852.914080354	collection of late 20th century Italian drama about marriage

In the abridged edition the Relative Index entry "Italian language–literature" cites number 850, and again the schedule shows that 852 is used for Italian drama. There are instructions to go to the centered heading 810–890 for instructions on number building. At 810–890 there are instructions to add from notations 01–809 in Table 3. In Table 3 notation –08 is used for collections. This is added to the base number for Italian drama, to build number 852.08, which is the correct number for this edition.

Example 2

What classification number would be assigned to a collection of drama from several literatures with marriage as a theme?

In this example, the number 808.829354 is correct. Again, we will trace the steps in building this number. The Relative Index entry "Collections" has a reference to see special kinds, but this is really of little help. The entry "Literature" also provides no help. The entry "Literary themes—gen. wks.—collections" is a good possibility; it cites number 808.803. The entry "Marriage—lit. & stage trmt." has a reference to "Life cycle," which gives several possible numbers (Fig. 10-2).

Fig. 10-2. Relative Index

```
Life
   after death see Future
         state of man
   biology                            577
   civil right pol. sci.              323.43
   creation see Life origin
   cycle
      customs                         392
      lit. trmt.
         folk lit.
            sociology                 398.354
            texts & lit. crit.        398.27
         gen. wks.
            collections               808.803 54  ◄——————
            hist. & crit.             809.933 54
         spec. lits.
            collections          lit. sub.–080 354
            hist. & crit.        lit. sub. –093 54
         stage trmt.                  792.090 935 4
            s.a. spec. mediums e.g.
            Television
```

Checking the schedule one finds that 808.803 is the number for collections from more than one literature dealing with specific themes and subjects. Remember, however, that we are dealing with a collection of a specific *form* of literature—drama. The centered heading 808.81—808.88 provides for collections of literature in specific form (Fig. 10-3).

Fig. 10-3. Classification Schedule

808.81—808.88 Collections in specific forms

Number 808.82 is used for collections of drama and 808.829 is used for drama displaying specific features. Instructions are given for further subdivision (Fig. 10-4).

Fig. 10-4. Classification Schedule

808

> .829   Drama displaying specific features
>
>> Add to 808.829 the numbers following 808.80 in 808.801–808.803, e.g., drama about Abraham Lincoln 808.829351
>>
>> Class drama of specific mediums, scopes, kinds regardless of feature in 808.822–808.825

The instructions say to "add to 808.829 the numbers following 808.80 in 808.801–808.803." In the range of numbers from 808.801 to 808.803, which cover specific themes in literature, it is found that 808.80354 covers the life cycle and includes marriage. (Remember that the previous example arrived at the life cycle notation in Table 3.) Following the instructions, add the numbers *after* 808.80 in 808.80354 to 808.829 to build 808.829354. The number building developed as follows:

808	collections of literature
.8	collections from more than one literature
.82	collections of drama
.829	collections of drama displaying specific features
.8293	from 808.803 for collections dealing with specific themes
35	from 808.8035 for humanity and human existence
354	from 808.80354 for life cycle
808.829354	a collection of drama from more than one literature with marriage as a theme

The abridged edition's index has an entry "Drama—gen. wks.—collections," which provides number 808.82. The number 808.82 is not specifically cited in the schedule. There is, however, a span of numbers 808.81–808.87 for collections from more than one literature in specific forms. The instructions tell the classifier to "add to 808.8 the numbers following 808 in 808.1–808.7." Number 808.2 is for drama, so add the numbers after 808 in 808.2 to 808.8, thus building 808.82 for collections of drama. This is the most specific number for this edition.

Example 3

To continue the theme of marriage, where would one classify a work on the history of dramatic literature of the nineteenth century dealing with marriage? The number for this work is 809.29354034. It is built as follows. The Relative Index entries for "Marriage," "Literary themes—gen. wks." and "Life cycle" provide little help. Under "Drama—gen. wks.—hist. & crit." a more specific number is provided: 809.2. The number 809.2 is not listed in the schedule; however, there is a number span 809.1—.7 with directions for building numbers for specific forms of literature (Fig. 10-5).

Fig. 10-5. Classification Schedule

809

.1–.7　　Literature in specific forms

　　　　　　Add to 809 the numbers following 808.8 in 808.81–808.87, e.g., history, description, critical appraisal of science fiction 809.3876

The directions say to "add to 809 the numbers following 808.8 in 808.81–808.87." Number 808.82 is used for drama, and adding the numbers following 808.8 to 809 builds the number 809.2, cited in the index.

There are two additional problems to consider: the historical limitation of the nineteenth century and the specific theme of marriage. At 809.1–809.7 there are directions to add to 809 the numbers following 808.8 in 808.81–808.87. At 808.829 we find the number for drama displaying specific features (Fig. 10-4). Instructions at 808.829 say to "add to 808.829 the numbers following 808.80 in 808.801–808.803." Number 808.80354 is used for the life cycle, including marriage. Adding the numbers following 808.80 in 808.80354 to 808.829 builds 808.829354. Now add to 809, as instructed, the numbers following 808.8 in 808.829354 to build 809.29354.

Now we need to deal with the chronological or historical period, the nineteenth century. At the centered heading 808.81–808.88 there are instructions to "add to 0 the numbers following 090 in 'Standard Subdivisions' notation 0901–0904 from Table 1" (Fig. 10-6).

Fig. 10-6. Classification Schedule

▶　　　808.81–808.88 Collections in specific forms

Add to each subdivision identified by * as follows:
001–009　　Standard subdivisions
01–04　　Historical periods
　　　　　　Add to 0 the numbers following 090 in "Standard Subdivisions" notation 0901–0904 from Table 1, e.g., 18th century 033

In Table 1, –09034 is used for the nineteenth century. Thus the 34 from 09034 is added to 0, for notation 034, which is then added to 809.29354 to build 809.29354034. (Or the –034 could have been added to 808.<u>829354</u> building 808.829354034, and then added to 809.) The number building developed as follows:

809	history, description, critical appraisal of more than one literature
.2	history of drama (from 808.8<u>2</u> as instructed at 809.1–.7)
.29	drama displaying specific features (from 808.8<u>29</u>)
3	collections of drama dealing with specific themes (from 808.80<u>3</u>)
54	life cycle, including marriage (from 808.803<u>54</u>, as instructed)
0	the prefix for the notation for the historical period, as instructed at 808.81–.88
3	from –090<u>3</u> for the modern period (from Table 1)
34	from 090<u>34</u> for the 19th century (from Table 1)
809.29354034	a work on the history of dramatic literature of the 19th century on the theme of marriage

In the abridged edition the Relative Index entry for "Literature" cites a general number, 800. Under "Drama—gen. wks.—hist. & crit." there is a more specific number, 809.2. In the schedule there is no number 809.2, but a span of numbers 809.1–.7 with directions for building number 809.2. To 809 the instructions say to "add the numbers following 808 in 808.1–808.7." Number 808.2 is for drama, and adding the 2 from 808.2 to 809 builds 809.2 for drama. There is no provision for further subdivision, so this is the most specific number for this edition.

PROBLEMS TO SOLVE

Try to build classification numbers for works on the following subjects:

1) a collection of Tagalog poetry relating to farm life
2) history of idealism in American fiction
3) a work on old Icelandic sagas
4) a critical appraisal of Shakespeare's comedy *All's Well That Ends Well* (there are two possible arrangements)
5) a collection of literary writings on miscellaneous topics by Italian-American scientists

ANSWERS TO PROBLEMS

1) 899.21110080355 (18th edition)   899
                                            or
                                 899.108 (10th abridged edition)

The Relative Index has an excellent starting point under "Tagalog language–literature," with number 899.211. The schedule shows that this indeed is the base number for Tagalog, which is a Filipino language. The asterisk at 899.211 refers to directions under the centered heading 810–890, and the fifth instruction there directs the classifier to use the appropriate notation from Table 3.

There is no specific number for Tagalog poetry, as there is in the major literatures. We want to see if notations are available for poetry collections on farm life. In Table 3 notation –1 is used for poetry. Searching Table 3 reveals that notation –10080355 is used for everyday life, including occupations (Fig. 10-7, page 162).

Fig. 10-7. Subdivisions of Individual Literatures (Table 3)

–100 803 54	Life cycle
	Birth, love, marriage, death
–100 803 55	Everyday life
	Examples: food, dwellings, occupations, recreation

This notation is added to the base number 899.211, to build 899.21110080355, a long but easily built number (the thirteen-digit number is built in only two steps).

In the abridged edition the Relative Index entry "Tagalog language–literature" provides number 899. No provision is made for further subdivision. If desired, the notation –108 from Table 3 (for collections of poetry by more than one author) could be used to build 899.108.

2) 813.00913 (18th edition)   813.09 (10th abridged edition)

There are no entries in the Relative Index specific enough to provide a substantive lead to the schedule. Entries for "American literature," "Fiction," and "Idealism" are either non-existent or too general. Thus it is necessary to go to the 800 schedule and search until you find 813 for fiction in American literature. There are instructions at 810 to follow the instructions at the centered heading 810–890 to build a number. At 810–890 are instructions to use Table 3 for further subdivision.

In Table 3 the notation –3 is assigned to fiction. At –3001–3009 there are instructions to "add to –300 the numbers following –100 in –1001–1009." The work here is a history, so go to notation –1009 for history, description, and critical appraisal. Searching the table leads to notation –100913, for "Idealism." Now, following the instructions add to base number 81 (from 813) –300 for 813.00, then add the numbers following –100 in –100913 to 813.00 for 813.00913. This is the number for a history of idealism in American fiction.

In the abridged edition there are no direct leads in the Relative Index. In the schedule 813 is used for American fiction, and there are instructions to go to Table 3, where notation −09 is used for history. No further number building is required, so 813.09 is the correct number for this edition.

3) 839.6103 (18th edition)   839.6 (10th abridged edition)

In the Relative Index "Icelandic language–literature" provides number 839.69. There is no provision there, however, for old Icelandic sagas. The entry "Old Icelandic" refers to "Old Norse" and there is also a reference to "West Scandinavian languages." Under "West Scandinavian languages–literatures" number 839.6 is cited. This is the correct number for Old Icelandic. At 839.6 there are instructions to add from Table 3 as directed at 810–890.

If it was not already known, an encyclopedia would show that Old Icelandic sagas are for the most part considered epic poetry. [**Editor's note**: *Oxford Companion to English Literature* describes them as "narrative compositions in prose"; thus, 839.6303 is also possible.] In Table 3, notation −1 is used for poetry and the notations −102 to −108 for specific kinds of poetry. Notation −103 is used for epic poetry; when this is added to base number 839.6, it builds number 839.6103 for Old Icelandic sagas.

In the abridged edition the Relative Index entry "Icelandic language–literature" provides number 839.6. In the schedule, however, there is no number 839.6. This number, however is correct. The number 839.6 can be entered in the schedule for the abridged edition so that future works will also be assigned the number. In this case the number is accepted from the Relative Index.

4) 822.33   822.3 (10th abridged edition)
   or
   822.33<u>02</u> (18th edition)

There are two possible ways to classify a critical appraisal of Shakespeare's comedy *All's Well That Ends Well*. Under the entry "Shakespeare–William–English drama" number 822.33 is provided. The schedule shows this is the correct number for Shakespeare. It is unnecessary to add to the number. The notation −09 for history, description, and critical appraisal in Table 3 notes that single authors should use notations −1−8. Under notation −2 for drama, notation −21−29 is used for drama of specific periods, with a note to "class in each period without further subdivision description, critical appraisal, biography, single and collected works of single authors regardless of medium, scope or kind of drama." However, the first 3 in 822.33 already stands for a specific historical period (1558-1625). To add anything to this to indicate an historical period would be redundant and therefore unnecessary (i.e., 822.33<u>23</u> would be incorrect since the first <u>3</u> and the <u>23</u> both refer to the same historical period). So 822.33 is the correct number.

The alternative to 822.33 is to use the suggested book numbers in the table found in the schedule at 822.33. The play *All's Well That Ends Well* is assigned notation <u>O</u>1−2 (notice that the O is a *letter, not a digit*). The instructions say to use the second number for critical appraisal. Thus the number here will be 822.33<u>O</u>2.

The abridged edition has an index entry "Shakespeare—William—English drama," which cites number 822.3. Upon checking the schedule this number proves to be the most specific one available.

5) 808.89925 (18th edition)   808.8 (10th abridged edition)

The Relative Index does not really have any useful direct entries, though "Written communication—rhetoric" provides number 808. A search of the schedule brings one to number 808 for rhetoric and collections.

Searching section 808 leads to 808.89 for literary collections for and by specific kinds of persons. Before proceeding it is necessary to check the table of precedence at 808.89 (Fig. 10-8).

Fig. 10-8. Classification Schedule

808

.89   Collections for and by specific kinds of persons

Observe the following table of precedence, e.g., collections for or by American Roman Catholic children 808.899282
  Persons of specific age groups
  Persons of specific sexes
  Persons of specific occupations and interests
  Persons of specific racial, ethnic, national groups
  Persons resident in specific continents, countries, localities
  Persons resident in specific regions

Class literature in specific forms for and by specific kinds of persons in 808.81–808.88, literature displaying specific features for and by specific kinds of persons in 808.801–808.803

It is necessary to see whether precedence is given to an ethnic group, people from a specific country, or an occupational group. The occupational group is listed first, so the number is built on this basis. The span of numbers for persons in specific occupations is 808.899209–.899279. Instructions here direct the classifier to "add 'Persons' notation 09–79 from Table 7 to base number 808.8992." In Table 7 notation –5 is assigned to persons occupied with pure sciences. This is added to the base number 808.8992 to build number 808.89925.

In the abridged edition the best place to start is the 800 schedule. Section 808 is used for literary collections and 808.8 for collections from more than one literature. Looking further in the schedule it is found that a specific number for collections for and by specific kinds of persons (808.89) has been discontinued and there are directions to class these works in 808.8.

CHAPTER 11

CLASS 900–999
(GENERAL GEOGRAPHY AND HISTORY
AND THEIR AUXILIARIES)

INTRODUCTORY NOTE

This class is closely related to the Areas Table (Table 2). In fact, the last seven divisions, 930–990, have a parallel expansion to −3–9 of Table 2. Similarly, division 910 for geography and travel uses Table 2 for specific expansion. The history of specific geographic areas is covered by 930–990. General history may be classed in the 900–909 division. Historical works in which geography and/or travel is the dominant theme are classed in division 910. Division 920 is for biography that is not classed elsewhere. Example 2 in the number building section shows *five* different possible methods of classing biography. The use of Table 2 for geographic areas is the major thrust in both the examples and the problems in this chapter. The reader should review Table 2 as well as our previous discussion of it in Chapter 1.

OUTLINE OF THE CLASS

900   General geography and history

910   General geography, Travel

920   General biography, genealogy, and insignia

930   General history of the ancient world

940   General history of Europe

950   General history of Asia

960   General history of Africa

970   General history of North America

980   General history of South America

990   General history of other areas

INTRODUCTION TO THE CLASS

There have been several changes in this class effective January 1, 1975. Since that date, the DDC numbers assigned by the Library of Congress have reflected the revisions. Mention will be made of these changes at the appropriate places in the "Details of the Class" section. When working on the problems later in this chapter, however, we will use the DDC numbers in the printed schedules in order to avoid any confusion. The printed schedules of the 19th edition of the DDC will reflect these changes.

DETAILS OF THE CLASS

The first section, 900, is used for general works on history. Section 901 is assigned to the philosophy and theory of general history, and subsection 901.9 is used for general works on civilization. As of January 1, 1975, however, the works formerly classed here are to be classed in section 909.[1] Sections 902 and 903 are used for miscellaneous works (e.g., chronologies) and for dictionaries, encyclopedias, and concordances.

Collected accounts of specific events of natural origin (e.g., earthquakes) and of human origin (e.g., battles, fires) are treated in 904. The next four sections, 905–908, respectively cover serial publications, organizations, study and teaching (including historiography), and collections of general history. Section 909 is assigned to general world history and works on ethnic, racial, or national groups not limited by continent, country, or locality. Also classified here are general works devoted to specific periods of time. The works classified here are not limited to specific countries. Recent changes in the DDC now call for works formerly classified in 901.9 and 910.03 to be placed here.

Division 910 is assigned to general geography and travel. The preliminary subsections cover general topics relating to geography, such as the philosophy and theory of geography, physical geography, and general works not limited by continents, countries, or locality. Subsection 910.03 has been reassigned to section 909. Subsections 910.2–910.99 are used for geographers, explorers, and travelers and for discovery and exploration by specific countries.

Section 911 covers historical geography, which is primarily the "growth and changes in political divisions." The next section, 912, is used for graphic representations of the earth's surface and of extraterrestrial worlds. Included here are atlases, maps, charts, and plans. Works relating to maps and maps of specific geographic areas and extraterrestrial worlds are classified in subsections 912.1–912.9.

The next seven sections, 913–919, are assigned to geography and travel in specific continents, countries, localities, and extraterrestrial worlds. General works on civilization in specific places were formerly classed in 913–919. Since January 1975, however, the Library of Congress is assigning these general works to 930–990 instead of 913–919.[2]

Section 913 deals with geography and travel in the ancient world. Archeology is assigned to subsection 913.031. This section, however, has also been revised and since January 1975 the Library of Congress is assigning archeology to 930.1 instead of 913.031. Also, subsections 913.31–.39, currently used for continents, countries, and localities, are being spread over 913.1–913.9. Sections 914 to 919 cover geography and travel in the modern world. Note the special table under the centered heading 914–919, which gives lengthy instructions for number building.

---

[1] See details of this change and other changes in this class in the following: U.S. Library of Congress. Processing Dept. *Cataloging Service Bulletin*, no. 112, Winter 1975 (Washington, Library of Congress, 1945–). Full details on these changes appear in: U.S. Library of Congress. Decimal Classification Division. *Dewey Decimal Classification Additions, Notes and Decisions*, v. 3, no. 6/7 (Washington, Library of Congress, 1959–) published in the spring of 1975.

[2] *Cataloging Service Bulletin*, no. 112.

The areas covered by sections 914 to 919 are, respectively: Europe, Asia, Africa, North America, South America, and other parts of the world (including Oceania and extraterrestrial worlds).

Subsection 914.2 was formerly used for the British Isles, but as of January 1, 1975, the Library of Congress is assigning the British Isles to 914.1. The British Isles, Great Britain, and the United Kingdom will all be represented by 914.1. This change is also reflected in the area notations (Table 2), where −41 (formerly −42) is being used for the British Isles and −411 (formerly −41) is being used for Scotland. As stated above, the number building examples will be developed from the *current* printed schedules (i.e., the 18th edition), since to do otherwise could lead to confusion.

Division 920 is assigned to general biography, genealogy, and insignia. There are provisions given at 920 for a preferred optional treatment of biographies of persons associated with a specific discipline. The preferred optional treatment is to "class biography of persons associated with a specific discipline or subject with the discipline or subject using 'Standard Subdivisions' notation 92 [092] from Table 1, e.g. biography of chemists 540.92; or, if preferred, class individual biography in 92 or B, collected biography in 92 or 920 undivided" (DDC, Vol. 2, p. 1536).

Subsections 920.1–920.9 and sections 921 to 928 are assigned to biography of persons in specific fields, such as librarians, philosophers, religious leaders, persons in social sciences, scientists, and persons in literature. The use of all these sections is optional, and preference is given to classifying the person with a specific discipline or subject using standard subdivisions notation - 092. Regardless of the option chosen for classifying biographies, it is important to be consistent and use the same method throughout the collection.

The final section, 929, covers genealogy, names, and insignia. Some topics included here are heraldry, royal houses, peerage, armorial bearings (e.g., coats of arms), and flags.

The remaining seven divisions, 930–990, are concerned with the history of specific continents, countries, localities, and extraterrestrial worlds. Note the table at centered heading 930–990, which provides for standard subdivisions and special numbers for persons, areas, and historical periods.

Division 930 is used for the history of the ancient world to 500 A.D. The geographic areas of the world are covered in specific sections: 931, China to 420 A.D.; 932, Egypt to 640 A.D.; 933, Palestine to 70 A.D.; 934, India to 647 A.D.; 935, Mesopotamia and Iranian Plateau to 642 A.D.; 936, Europe (excluding Italy) to 486 A.D.; 937, Italian Peninsula to 476 A.D.; 938, Greece to 323 A.D.; and 939, other parts of the ancient world to 640 A.D.

Section 938 has nine subsections devoted to geographical divisions of ancient Greece, which can be used with historical periods. This section is cited as an example of historical periods in the table at centered heading 930–990.

The numbers 940–990 cover the history of the modern world and extraterrestrial worlds. Division 940 is assigned to the general history of Europe from the fall of Rome (476 A.D.) to the present. Five main subdivisions cover the Middle Ages (476–1453), modern period (1453–), World War I (1914-1918), military history of World War I, and 20th century Europe (1918–). The subsections on World War I are lengthy and detailed. The last subsection, 20th century, is devoted mainly to World War II, although it is not as detailed as for World War I. Remember that World War I was primarily a European war, whereas World War II was a world war only partially conducted in Europe proper.

Section 941 is used for the history of Scotland and Ireland. There has been another major change in the schedule at 941: the British Isles, United Kingdom, and Great Britain will be classed in 941 preceding Scotland rather than in 942 with England.[3] Corresponding changes will be made in the areas notation in Table 2. When this change occurs, Scotland will be moved to 941.1. Ireland is assigned to 941.5 and Northern Ireland to 941.6.

Section 942 is now used exclusively for England in accordance with another recent change in the DDC. There are numerous subdivisions for specific historical periods and reigns of monarchs.

Central Europe, with an emphasis on German history, is assigned to section 943. The numbers for historical periods in German history start with Charlemagne and the Holy Roman Empire, which is here considered German history. Subsection 943.1–.1087 is used for East Germany and the German Democratic Republic. Other subdivisions cover the history of Austria, Czechoslovakia, Poland, and Hungary.

Section 944 is devoted to the history of France. Italy is assigned to section 945 and the Iberian Peninsula (Spain and Portugal) to section 946. Section 947 is assigned to Eastern Europe, with primary emphasis on Russia and the Soviet Union. Subsection 947.1 is used for Finland. Northern Europe (the Scandinavian countries) is covered in section 948. The initial subsections cover general Scandinavian history, with later subsections for Norway, Sweden, and Denmark. Section 949 is used for all other parts of Europe: Iceland, Netherlands, Belgium, Luxembourg, Switzerland, Greece, Turkey (in Europe), Albania, Yugoslavia, Bulgaria, Romania, and the Aegean Sea islands.

The general history of Asia, the Orient, and the Far East is covered in division 950. Subsections at 950 cover early history to 1162, the Mongol and Tatar empires, general works on the European exploration and penetration of Asia, and general works on modern Asian history.

Section 951 is used for China and adjacent areas. The subdivisions for China cover particular dynasties, the republic and nationalist period, and the People's Republic of China. The last subsection, 951.9, is assigned to the history of Korea.[4] Japan and its adjacent islands are assigned to section 952. The Arabian Peninsula, including Saudi Arabia, is covered in section 953. Section 954 covers South Asia including India, Pakistan, and Ceylon. Iran and Persia are treated in section 955. Section 956 is used for the Middle and Near East. There are subsections here for general works and for the various Israel-Arab wars. Subsections 956.1 to 956.9 are used for Turkey, Cyprus, Iraq, Syria, Lebanon, Israel (and Palestine) and Jordan.

---

[3] U.S. Library of Congress. Decimal Classification Division. *Dewey Decimal Classification Additions, Notes and Decisions*, v. 3, no. 4/5, April 1974 (Washington, Library of Congress, 1959–), p. 7.

[4] A new subsection, 951.2, for Southeastern China including Taiwan will be used by the Library of Congress and included in the 19th edition: *Dewey Decimal Classification Additions, Notes and Decisions*, v. 3, no. 2, September 1972 (Washington, Library of Congress, 1959–).

Section 957 covers Asiatic Russia (Siberia). Section 958, Central Asia, covers Afghanistan and the four Central Asian Soviet Republics. The last section, 959, is devoted to Southeast Asia, with subsections for Burma, Thailand, Laos, Malaysia, Cambodia, Vietnam, Indonesia, and the Philippine Islands.

The 960 division is used for the history of Africa. Section 960 is for general history of Africa. The next section, 961, is concerned with North Africa and the countries of Tunisia and Libya. The Nile countries, Egypt and Sudan, are found in section 962. Section 963 treats Ethiopia, while section 964 covers Northwest Africa including Morocco. Algeria is covered in section 965. Section 966 covers West Africa and the offshore islands, with subsections for the following countries: Mauritania, Mali, Upper Volta, Niger, Senegal, Sierra Leone, Upper Guinea area, Liberia, Ivory Coast, Ghana, Togo, Dahomey, and Nigeria. Next another lengthy section, 967, covers Central Africa and the offshore islands, with subsections assigned to the following countries: Cameroons, Gabon, the Congo (French Congo), Angola, Central African Republic, Chad, the Congo Republic (the former Belgian Congo, now Zaire), Rwanda, Burundi, Uganda, Kenya, Somaililand, Somalia, Tanzania, and Mozambique. Section 968, assigned to South Africa, includes the Republic of South Africa, Botswana, Transvaal, Lesotho, Rhodesia, Zambia, and Malawi. The last section, 969, is used for the South Indian Ocean islands, specifically Madagascar, now the Malagasy Republic.

A substantial division, 970, covers the general history of North America, which includes United States history. There are two changes in the 970's that should be pointed out. First, the "period of pre-history, discovery, and exploration of North America will be classed in 970.01 instead of 973.1 which will be used only for the topics in what is now the United States."[5] The second change is that "American Indians and Eskimos will be classed like other ethnic groups instead of in 970.1 and similar numbers."[6]

The first subsections at 970 cover general histories of North America for various historical periods, and these are followed by four subsections for the Indians of North America.

Section 971 is assigned to Canada. The first subsections cover specific historical periods and events in Canadian history, with subsections 971.1 to 971.9 used for the history of the provinces and territories from their early history to the present.

Section 972 covers Middle America, which is divided into three areas—Mexico, Central America, and the West Indies. Mexico is treated first from the earliest period to the present. Subsection 972.8 is assigned to the following Central American countries: Guatemala, British Honduras, Honduras, El Salvador, Nicaragua, and Costa Rica. Subsection 972.9 is used for the West Indies, including Cuba, Jamaica, Dominican Republic, Haiti, Puerto Rico, and windward and other southern islands (Trinidad and Tobago).

---

[5] U.S. Library of Congress. Processing Dept. *Cataloging Service Bulletin*, no. 112, Winter 1975 (Washington, Library of Congress, 1945–), pp. 16-17.

[6] Ibid.

The next seven sections, 973 to 979, cover in detail United States history. Remember that the first subdivision, 973.1, is now used only for discovery and exploration of what is now the United States. Discovery and exploration of America will be classed in 970.01, as stated above.

Subsections 973.1 to 973.9 encompass general works on specific periods in United States history (Fig. 11-1).

Fig. 11-1. Classification Schedule

973.1–973.9 Historical periods

Class comprehensive works in 973

SUMMARY

973.1	Period of discovery and exploration to 1607
.2	Colonial period, 1607-1775
.3	Revolution and confederation, 1775-1789
.4	Constitutional period, 1789-1809
.5	Early 19th century, 1809-1845
.6	Middle 19th century, 1845-1861
.7	Administration of Abraham Lincoln, 1861-1865 (Civil War)
.8	Later 19th century, 1865-1901 (Period of reconstruction)
.9	20th century, 1901–

The summary in Fig. 11-1 shows the historical period covered by each subsection from exploration and discovery to the present. A long subsection, 973.7, is used for Abraham Lincoln's administration, including the U.S. Civil War. Subsection 973.9 is further subdivided by Presidential administration. It will be helpful to study carefully numbers 973.1 to 973.9 for their detailed outline of United States history.

Sections 974 to 979 are assigned to the history of specific areas and individual states. The initial subsections in sections 974–979 are devoted to general history of the area, followed by historical subsections for each state. The coverage by each section is as follows: 974, northeastern United States (New England and Middle Atlantic states); 975, southeastern United States (South Atlantic states); 976, south central United States and the Gulf Coast states; 977, north central United States and the Lake states; 978, western United States; and 979, Great Basin and Pacific Slope regions and the Pacific Coast states. Notice that although Hawaii is a state it is classed in 996.9, for areas in the Pacific Ocean. Throughout these sections great use is made of the areas notations in Table 2 to provide for regional and local history.

The next division, 980, is assigned to the general history of South America. The subdivisions 980.01 to 980.03 are used for general works on broad historical periods in South American history. Subsections 980.1 to 980.5 are used for Indians of South America, including provisions for specific tribes and Indians in specific countries. The coverage of the following nine sections is as follows: 981, Brazil; 982, Argentina; 983, Chile; 984, Bolivia; 985, Peru; 986, northwestern South America (including Panama, Colombia, and Ecuador); 987, Venezuela; 988, Guianas (British, French, and Dutch); and 989, other parts of South America, including Paraguay and Uruguay.

The final division in the 900 class, 990, is assigned to the general history of other parts of the world including the Pacific Ocean islands and Oceania. Section 990 is used for general works on the Pacific Ocean islands. Sections 991 and 992 are unassigned. Section 993 is used for New Zealand and Melanesia, while Australia is covered in section 994. Sections 995 and 996 cover New Guinea (Papua) and other parts of the Pacific and Polynesia, respectively. Subsection 996.9 is used for Hawaii, including statehood. The final three sections cover the Atlantic Ocean islands (997); Arctic islands and Antarctica (998); and extra-terrestrial worlds (999).

NUMBER BUILDING, 900–999

Example 1

Where would a work on the exploration for the source of the White Nile be classified?

As usual, the classification process begins with a search of the Relative Index. The entry "White Nile River" provides an area notation −6293 while "Nile River" cites area notation −62. The entry "Explorations–geography" gives number 910.9. Checking the schedule shows that 910.9 is used for historical treatment and for general works.

Before proceeding it will be necessary to find out the geographic area involved. Checking Table 2 for area notations −62 and −6293 makes it clear that we are concerned with Africa. Looking through the schedules under the sections on geography, we find that section 916 is used for geography and travel in Africa. Therefore, the base number is 916.

Instructions under 916 direct the user to "add 'Areas' notation 61−69 from Table 2 to base number 91 . . . then to the result add as instructed under 914−919" (Figs. 11-2, 11-3).

Fig. 11-2. Classification Schedule

916   Africa

Add "Areas" notation 61−69 from Table 2 to base number 91, e.g., South Africa 916.8; then to the result add as instructed under 914−919, e.g., geography of mountain areas of South Africa 916.80943

Fig. 11-3. Classification Schedule

▶ **914–919 Geography of and travel in specific continents, countries, localities in modern world; extraterrestrial worlds**

Class here area studies; comprehensive works on ancient and modern geography of and travel in specific continents, countries, localities

Add "Areas" notation 4–9 from Table 2 to base number 91, e.g., geography of British Isles 914.2, of Norfolk, 914.261; then add further as follows:

001–008	Standard subdivisions
02	The earth (Physical geography)
03	Man and his civilization
	Class here prehistoric and ancient archeology of continents, countries, localities not in "Areas" notation 3 from Table 2
	Add historical period numbers (without 0) that appear in subdivisions of 930–990
	For civilization of specific ethnic, racial, national groups, see 06
04	Travel
	Class here discovery, exploration, adventure
	Add historical period numbers (without 0) that appear in subdivisions of 930–990

Now the area notations cited in the index can be used to build a number. In Table 2, notation −6293 is the proper area notation for the White Nile. Add −6293 to base number 91 to build 916.293. Now go to the centered heading 914–919 to see if any further number building is necessary. There notation −04 · is used for travel, discovery and exploration. This is added to 916.293 to build 916.29304. Now, still following the instructions at −04, go to 960—the section for general history of Africa—to see if there are any historical subdivisions. The subdivision 960.2 is used for early history (640–1900), which includes the period of the major explorations for the source of the White Nile. The 2 from 960.2 is added to 916.29304 to build 916.293042.

One could ask why the .403 in 962.403 for the Sudan was not used for the historical period, since the area notation −6293 is part of the span of numbers for the Sudan. The explorations of the White Nile, however, also cover many other African countries, the source of the river being in East Africa. This is the reason for using the more general historical number 960 for the historical notation. Also, a longer historical period was needed because the exploration for the source of the White Nile goes back earlier than the 1820 cited for 962.403.

The number building sequence developed as follows:

900	general geography and history and their auxiliaries
910	general geography, travel
916	geography and travel in Africa
.29	eastern and southern provinces of Sudan (from notation −6<u>29</u> in Table 2)
.293	Upper Nile including the White Nile River (from notation −6<u>293</u> in Table 2)
04	for travel (from centered heading 914–919)
2	the historical period number (from 960.<u>2</u> as instructed at −04 in the centered heading 914–919)
916.293042	a work on the explorations for the source of the White Nile

The abridged edition provides the area notation −62 in the Relative Index with the entry "Nile River." There is no entry for the White Nile. Under "Explorations—geography" number 910 is cited. A search of the schedule at 910 leads to 916 for geography and travel of Africa. There are instructions here to add from the areas notations −61–69 in Table 2 to base number 91. Notation −62 in Table 2 is used for countries of the Nile and specifically for Egypt. There are special instructions at notation −62 to see the instructions at −4–9 in Table 2. At −4–9 the classifier is told to "class comprehensive works on specific physiographic regions or features extending over more than one country, state or other unit and identified by * with the unit where noted in this table." There is no separate notation in the schedule for the Nile River or White Nile, so use the notation −62, which was cited in the Relative Index. Add −62 to base number 91 to build 916.2, which is the most specific number for this edition.

Example 2

How many ways can a biography of Herodotus be classified?

The Relative Index provides an entry to the schedules under "Biographies," citing number 920 and the standard subdivision −092. There is no entry for Herodotus, since few personal names are found in the Index. It will be helpful to know who Herodotus was and what he was famous for; a biographical reference work identifies him as a Greek historian and geographer who lived in the fifth century. Herodotus has been called the Father of History.

In the schedule at 920 instructions tell the cataloger to "class biography of persons associated with a specific discipline or subject with the discipline or subject using 'Standard Subdivisions' notation 92 [−092] from Table 1 . . . or if preferred class individual biography in 92 or B" (Fig. 11-4).

Fig. 11-4. Classification Schedule

920   **General biography, genealogy, insignia**

         Class here autobiographies, diaries, reminiscences

         Class biography of persons associated with a specific discipline or subject with the discipline or subject using "Standard Subdivisions" notation 92 from Table 1, e.g., biography of chemists 540.92; or, if preferred, class individual biography in 92 or B, collected biography in 92 or 920 undivided

These instructions provide three possible ways to classify an individual biography: the first two use 92, or B, along with book numbers for the biographee and author. A book number for the biographee is required so that *all* books about the same person can stand together on the shelf (see Chapter 12). Two biographies of Herodotus, by John Jones and Roger Smith, could have any of these numbers:

92	92		B	B
H559	H559	or	H559	H559
J77	S658		J77	S658

Notice that the number for Herodotus (H559) remains the same for every book, while the author numbers (J77 and S658) change; this allows all books on Herodotus to stand together on the shelves.

The third possibility is to classify the biography in a specific discipline. Since Herodotus was an historian, the base number will be 900. The instructions at 920 say to use the standard subdivision −092 from Table 1 and add this to the base number for the discipline (Fig. 11-4). In Table 1, −0924 is found to be a more specific notation for individual biography (Fig. 11-5).

Fig. 11-5. Standard Subdivisions (Table 1)

−092   **Persons regardless of area, region, place**

         Description and critical appraisal of work, biography, autobiography, diaries, reminiscences of persons associated with the subject

         If preferred, class biography in 920.1–928.9

         Class biography not clearly related to any specific subject in 920, belletristic diaries and reminiscences in 800

         Observe exceptions to use of −092 under 180–190, 739.22, 739.23, 739.3, 739.4, 741.5, 745.4, 746.3, 746.7, 747.2, 748.2, 748.5, 749.2, 750, 809, 810–890 (as directed in "Subdivisions of Individual Literatures" notation 09 from Table 3)

−092 2   **Collected**

         If preferred, class collected biography in 92, or 920 without subdivision

−092 4   **Individual**

         If preferred, class individual biography in 92 or B; or, if preferred, class individual biography of men in 920.71, of women in 920.72

Instructions at 900 tell the cataloger to use 900.1–900.9 for standard subdivisions. Therefore, to base number 90 add notation –0924, building 900.924.

A fourth option is mentioned in Table 1 at notation –0924 (Fig. 11-5): that is, to class biographies of men in 920.71. This is not the preferred treatment.

Another option is to use the span of numbers 920.1–928.9, although once again this is not preferred. Searching the schedule brings the cataloger to 928 for persons in literature, which includes historians (Fig. 11-6).

Fig. 11-6. Classification Schedule

928	*Persons in literature
	Writers and critics of belles-lettres, historians, biographers
.1	*Americans
.2–.9	*Others
	Add "Languages" notation 2–9 from Table 6 for language in which person writes to base number 928

*Use is optional; prefer treatment described under 920.1–928.9

The span of numbers 928.2–.9 covers persons other than Americans. Instructions tell the cataloger to add to the base number 928 the "Languages" notation –2–9 from Table 6 for the language in which the person wrote. Herodotus wrote in classical Greek. The notation –81 from Table 6 is used for classical Greek, so the number for an historian of classical Greece is 928.81.

To recapitulate, a biography of Herodotus can be classified in 900.924, 92, B, 920.71, or 928.81 depending on the requirements of an individual library. The most often used options are 900.924, 92, or B.

In the abridged edition, number 920 is cited in the index under "Biographies." In the schedule at 920 there is a summary of the three options used to classify biographies in this edition. Again, they include the use of 92, B, 928 (for persons in literature, including historians), and 920.71 for biographies of men. Another option is to class the biography with a discipline or topic; for Herodotus this will be 900 plus the standard subdivision notation –092 from Table 1, to build number 900.92.

Example 3

Where would a work on the history of the Chinese in Singapore be classified?

A search of the Relative Index provides two numbers that may help in building a number. Under "Singapore–state," area notation –5952 is cited; under "Chinese people," r.e.n. (racial, ethnic, national) notation –951 is given.

We need a base number for Singapore since we are concerned with the history of a people in a specific country. Mentally place a "9" in front of the area notation for Singapore: "9"59.52. Checking the schedule shows that 959.5 is the number for Malaysia, which now also includes the state of Singapore. The number 959.52 does not appear in the schedule, so it must be built from the specific area notation for Singapore. There are directions at 959.5 in the schedule to add as directed at the centered heading 930–990; the instructions at the centered heading are to add the areas notation −3–9 from Table 2 to base number 9 (Fig. 11-7).

Fig. 11-7. Classification Schedule

▶ **930–990 General history of specific continents, countries, localities; of extraterrestrial worlds**

(It is optional to class here general geography of specific continents, countries, localities, extraterrestrial worlds; prefer 913–919)

Add "Areas" notation 3–9 from Table 2 to base number 9, e.g., general history of Europe 940, of British Isles 942, of Norfolk 942.61; then, unless otherwise specified, add further as follows, e.g., general history of ethnic groups in Europe 940.04, in British Isles 942.004, in Norfolk 942.61004

001–003	Standard subdivisions
004	Specific ethnic [*formerly* 00974], racial, national groups
	If preferred, class in 909.04
	Add "Racial, Ethnic, National Groups" notation 01–99 from Table 5 to base number 004

Now add the area notation for Singapore, −5952 (given in the Relative Index and checked in Table 2), to base number 9 to build 959.52. This is the specific number for Singapore. Further instructions at centered heading 930–990 say to use subdivision −004 for specific ethnic, racial, and national groups and to add notation 01–99 from Table 5 to −004 (Fig. 11-7). In Table 5 notation −951 is assigned to the Chinese people. This notation was also cited in the Relative Index. Add −004 to 959.52 to build 959.52004. Then to 959.52004 add −951 to build 959.52004951.

The number building developed as follows:

950	general history of Asia, Orient, Far East
959	Southeast Asia
.5	Malaysia
.52	Singapore (from −59<u>52</u> in Table 2)
004	subdivision for specific ethnic, racial, national groups (as directed at centered heading 930–990)
951	Chinese people (from Table 5, as directed at 930–990)
959.52004951	a history of the Chinese in Singapore

The abridged edition's Relative Index entry "Singapore" cites area notation −595, but there is no entry for Chinese people and Table 5 is not used in this edition. Again we want a 900 class number for history, so mentally place a "9" in front of area notation −595 for "9"59.5. In the schedule, 959 is used for

Southeast Asia, with no more specific number for Malaysia or Singapore. There are instructions in the schedule at 959 to add as instructed at centered heading 930–990, where the cataloger is told to add to base number the area notation –3–9 from Table 2. Area notation –595 in Table 2 for the Commonwealth of Nations territories includes Singapore, as the Relative Index also indicated. Add –595 to base number 9 to build 959.5. No further number building is required for this edition.

Example 4

What classification number would be assigned to a work on the history of the native Hawaiians?

The Relative Index entry "Hawaii–state" provides area notation –969. We are interested primarily in the history of Hawaii, so we need a number in the 900's. Mentally place the 9 from 900 in front of area notation –969 to build "9"96.9. The schedule shows that 996.9 is indeed the number used for the history of Hawaii. The summaries at the end of Volume 1 of the DDC can be helpful in finding a number in the 900's for Hawaii. While 996.9 is the general number for Hawaiian history, we are concerned with the history of the natives of Hawaii. The standard subdivisions .9001–.9009 are used for groups, regions, persons of Hawaii (Fig. 11-8).

Fig. 11-8. Classification Schedule

996

.9	**North central Pacific Hawaii**	
	Add as instructed under 930–990, but use 996.90001–996.90009 for standard subdivisions, groups, regions, persons of North central Pacific	
.900 1–.900 9	Standard subdivisions, groups, regions, persons of Hawaii	
	As enumerated under 930–990	

The instructions say to add to these subdivisions as "enumerated under 930–990."

At the centered heading 930–990, subdivision –004 is used for specific ethnic groups. Add –004 to 996.9 to build 996.9004. Now to –004 add notation 01–99 from Table 5 for racial, ethnic, national groups. The Relative Index can be useful in finding the correct notation in Table 5. There is no number for "Hawaiian," but there is a reference to "Polynesian." Under the entry "Polynesian–people," the r.e.n. (racial, ethnic, national) notation –994 is given. Add this to –004 for –004994, and then add this to 996.9 to build 996.9004994. The number building sequence developed as follows:

990	general history of other parts of the world and Pacific Ocean islands (Oceania)
996	other parts of the Pacific and Polynesia
.9	north central Pacific and Hawaii
004	standard subdivision for specific ethnic, racial, national groups (from 930–990)
9	other racial, ethnic national groups (from Table 5)
994	Polynesians (from Table 5)
996.9004994	the history of native Hawaiians

The abridged edition's index entry "Hawaii" refers to area notation –969. Again, mentally place a "9" in front of –969, since we are looking for a history number. "9"96.9 in the schedule is indeed the number for history of Hawaii. The summary of the 1000 sections can also be helpful for finding a number. At 996.9 there are instructions to add as instructed at the centered heading 930– 990. Checking the schedule at 930–990, however, reveals that there is nothing applicable, so the final number remains 996.9.

PROBLEMS TO SOLVE

Try to build classification numbers for the following hypothetical works:

1) a work on the first 100 days of the administration of Gerald R. Ford
2) a work on sources for establishing family histories in England
3) a periodical on the history of the Peruvian Andean region
4) a work on India's military participation in World War II
5) a work on the role of Athens in the defeat of Xerxes
6) a work on the history of Suez and the Suez Canal since 1930

ANSWERS TO PROBLEMS

1) 973.925 (18th edition)   973.925 (10th abridged edition)

The Relative Index entry "Presidents of nations–biog. and work" has a reference to see the history of specific countries. The entry for the United States cites area notation –73. Another way to find a number for 20th century United States history is to look in the summary tables in Volume 1 and find 973 given for United States history. Searching the schedule one finds that number 973.9 is used for 20th century United States history. An additional approach would be to look in the index for another President who served in the same era. The index entry for "Nixon, Richard M.–U.S. hist." cites number 973.924.

The schedule has no number for Gerald Ford, the last assigned number being 973.924 for Richard M. Nixon. It is safe to assume that the next number in sequence (973.925) will be assigned to President Ford's administration. An edition of *Dewey Decimal Classification Additions, Notes and Decisions* will probably officially assign this number and the number will appear in the schedules of the next edition of the DDC.

The abridged edition's index has an entry under "United States" with area notation −73 and no entry for United States Presidents. The entry for "Nixon, Richard M. . . . ." cites number 973.924. The schedule again stops at 973.924, but we can assume here too that 973.925 will be assigned to the Ford administration.

2) 929.342 (18th edition)   929 (10th abridged edition)

The Relative Index provides two good entries to the schedule under "Families–history" (929.2) and "Genealogy" (929.1). When the schedule is checked this turns out to be the correct sequence of numbers. Remember that the problem is to find a number for the *sources* of family history, *not* a family history. The correct base number then is 929.3 and 929.33–.39 for treatment by country. There are instructions to add notation −3–9 from Table 2 to 929.3. The area notation for England (−42) is added to 929.3 to build 929.342 for a work on genealogical sources for English family histories.

The abridged edition's Relative Index provides the same entries as the unabridged edition, giving number 929. The schedule shows that numbers 929.1–.3 have been discontinued and number 929 is used for genealogy. There is no provision for geographic subdivision, so 929 is the most specific number.

3) 985.005 (18th edition)   985.005 (10th abridged edition)

The Relative Index entries for "Peru" and "Andes" provide area notations −85 and −8, respectively. Applying the knowledge gained in the previous examples, we can go to the schedule at 980 and 985. A physiographic region—the Andes—must be considered in building a number. Checking area notations −8 and −85 in Table 2 shows −8 to be for the Andes range. An asterisk refers to further instructions to "class parts of this physiographic region or feature as instructed under −4–9." At −4–9 the instructions say to "class works on a part of such a region or feature with the specific unit where the part is located." There is also an option to class works on part of a region with the region as a whole and then to add a physiographic region treatment as indicated (980.0943005: −8 for South America, −009 from the instructions at −4–9 in Table 2, −43 from the instructions at −3–9 in Table 2, and −005 from the instructions in the schedule at 930–990).

Following the first option (to class the work in the "specific unit where the part is located") return to 985 for Peru as the base number. At 985 once again an asterisk directs the cataloger to centered heading 930–990. Since we are classifying a journal, the standard subdivision −005 is added to 985 to build 985.005.

The abridged edition's Relative Index provides the same entries and area notations as the full edition. The number building sequence too is the same. The number for Peru, 985, has an asterisk that leads to a note to build

further from the instructions at the centered heading 930–990. There, the
standard subdivisions are 001–008. Subdivision –005 is for periodicals (serial
publications), so –005 is added to the base number 985 to build 985.005.

4) 940.540954 (18th edition) 940.54 (10th abridged edition)

The Relative Index entry "World wars–history–2" provides the number
940.53. For "India" there is an area notation –54, but no reference to World
War II. In the schedule, 940.53 is the general number for the war and 940.54 is
used for military history and conduct of the war. Looking further, 940.5409 is
assigned to the military participation of specific countries, and there are instructions to add the area notation from Table 2 to the base number 940.5409. We
already know from the index that –54 is the area notation for India, and this
number is now added to the base number to build 940.540954.

The abridged edition provides the same Relative Index entries and the same
number and area code. In the schedule 940.53 is the basic number for the war
and 940.54 is used for the military participation of specific countries. No further
number building is required; 940.54 is the most specific number necessary.

5) 938.503 (18th edition) 938 (10th abridged edition)

The first thing to establish is who or what was Xerxes, what Athens had
to do with this defeat, and which Athens? The Relative Index has three area notations listed for "Athens": –49512 for Athens, Greece; –385 for Athens in ancient
Greece; and –77197 for Athens County, Ohio. Xerxes is not cited in the index.
The work in hand would undoubtedly identify Xerxes and the correct Athens.
In our hypothetical problem, with no book in hand, we must use an encyclopedia
or biographical dictionary to identify Xerxes as an ancient Persian king whose
invasion of Greece was stopped at the Battle of Salamis by the Athenian fleet
in 480 B.C.

Proceed to division 930, for general history of the ancient world, and, more
specifically, to 938 for the history of ancient Greece. At 938.1–938.9 there are
subsections for the history of specific geographical regions of ancient Greece but
no specific mention of Athens. The area notation –385 is for ancient Athens. The
instructions at the centered heading 930–990 say to add the area notation to base
number 9. Adding –385 to 9 builds 938.5, which the schedule identifies as
Attica (which includes Athens). Instructions at 938.5 refer the classifier to subdivisions at 938.001–938.09. The historical period for the Persian Wars,
500-479 B.C., covers the defeat of Xerxes and is identified by .03. Adding 03 to
938.5 builds 938.503 for a history of Athens during the Persian Wars.

The abridged edition does not provide an entry for either Athens or Xerxes.
If the cataloger is unaware that the work is on ancient Greek history, a reference
work can be consulted. The index has an area notation under "Greece–ancient"
(–38). Mentally add a "9" (for the history class) to –38 for "9"38. In the
schedule 938 is used for the history of Greece to 323 A.D. There are no further
possibilities for number building, so 938 is the most specific number.

6) 962.1505 (18th edition)   962 (10th abridged edition)

The Relative Index provides a good start under "Suez—governorate—Egypt," with area notation —6215. Since a history class number is needed, go to the 900 schedule at 962.15. The closest number in the schedule is 962, so one can surmise that the number for Suez and the Suez Canal must be built from base number 962. Instructions at 962 direct the cataloger to add as instructed at the centered heading 930—990, and those at 930—990 say to add areas notation —3—9 from Table 2 to the base number 9. In Table 2, notation —6215 is used for the Isthmus of Suez and the Suez Canal. Add —6215 to base number 9 to build 962.15. Now the instructions —01—09 at 930—990 allow addition from the schedule for specific historical periods. In the schedule, 962.05 is the notation for Egypt that covers 1922 to the present. To 962.15 add 05 for the historical period, to build 962.1505.

In the abridged edition the Relative Index has no entry for Suez or Suez Canal. Under the entry "Egypt," area notation —62 is provided. Since we are interested in history, we want the 900 class number for Egyptian history, which is 962. At 962 there are directions to add as instructed at the centered heading 930—990. At 930—990 the cataloger is instructed to add the area notation —3—9 from Table 2 to the base number 9. In Table 2 the notation for Egypt, which includes Suez, is —62; when this is added to the base number 9, it builds 962. No other standard subdivision or historical period is applicable as instructed at 930—990, so 962 is the correct number for this edition.

CHAPTER 12

BOOK NUMBERS

INTRODUCTORY NOTE

The purpose of this chapter is to introduce the reader to the procedures and systems used to assign book or author numbers to a work after its DDC number has been assigned. Call numbers and book numbers are defined, and the functions of book numbers are listed. Three different book number schemes are described, with examples: Cutter-Sanborn numbers, Library of Congress author numbers, and the DDC book numbers for Shakespeare (which may be applied to any author if desired). Besides these three approaches, many local or home-made systems of book number codification can be used. It should be observed that any system of book numbers and work marks will have to be adjusted to fit into an individual library's shelf list, in order to maintain the deserved order on the shelf. A more extensive discussion of this problem can be found in Bohdan S. Wynar's *Introduction to Cataloging and Classification*, 5th edition, prepared with the assistance of John Phillip Immroth (Littleton, Colorado, Libraries Unlimited, 1976), pp. 277-280.

The DDC number by itself is not sufficient to identify a work for all the purposes required by a library. The book number is a notation used to create a *unique* call number for each work in a library. Each work that is classified is assigned a **call number**, which is composed of a **classification number** and an **author number** (also called a book number or cutter number):

call number: 973   classification number
               M361   author number

It is possible—indeed, very likely—that several books in a library will be classified in the same DDC number. It is necessary to use the author number to create a *unique* call number:

973	973	973	973	973	973	973
D888	D971	E58	J84	M959	P892	R974

The author number is *decimal*. Different works by authors with the same last name would stand on the shelves as follows:

973	973	973	973
D888	D8881	D889	D921

The initial letter in the book number is usually the first letter of the author's surname or the first letter of the main entry.

FUNCTIONS OF BOOK NUMBERS

The most obvious function of a book number is to create a unique call number for each work in a library. Some other functions have been pointed out by Bertha Barden in her manual *Book Numbers*:

"1) To arrange books in order on the shelves

2) To provide a brief and accurate call number for each book

3) To locate a particular book on the shelves

4) To provide a symbol for charging books to borrowers

5) To facilitate the return of books to the shelves

6) To assist in quick identification of a book when inventories are taken."[1]

BOOK NUMBER SCHEMES

Cutter Tables

The most popular book number scheme used with the DDC was devised by Charles Ammi Cutter. The notations are called cutter numbers and assigning them is referred to as "cuttering" or "to cutter." The most commonly used version of the Cutter scheme is the *Cutter-Sanborn Three-Figure Author Table*, altered and fitted with three figures by Kate E. Sanborn. The original Cutter Table had only two figures.

The Cutter Table consists of three or more initial letters from a surname, or a surname and a three-digit number. Letters J, K, E, I, O, and U are followed by two-digit numbers. The order is alphabetical except that S and the vowels are found at the end of the tables after all the consonants. The table is arranged as follows:

Bem	455	Chandl
Ben	456	Chandler, M.
Benc	457	Chanl
Bend	458	Chann
Bendo	459	Chant

The numbers in the center apply to the letters in each adjoining column. The cutter number includes the initial letter of the author's name and then the number. Find the letter group nearest the author's surname and combine the initial letter with the numbers. If the author's name "fits" between two cutter numbers, use the first listed in the schedule: Bendix is B458, *not* B459; because it falls between Bend and Bendo, the first of these is used. Thus:

---

[1] Bertha R. Barden, *Book Numbers: A Manual for Students with a Basic Code of Rules* (Chicago, American Library Association, 1937), p. 9.

Bemis	B455	or	Chandler, L.	C455
Benat	B456	or	Chandler, M.	C456
Bendix	B458	or	Channing	C458

Work marks or work letters are commonly used with cutter numbers to help maintain alphabetical order on the shelves and to create a unique call number for each work. The work mark is usually the first letter of the title of the work, including articles. The work mark comes *after* the book or cutter number. Thus, the call number for James Michener's *Hawaii* would be:

813.5
M623h

To maintain alphabetical order it is sometimes necessary to use two letters from the the title. Thus, Michener's *Caravans* and his *Centennial* would have these work marks:

813.5	813.5
M623c	M623ce
or	
M623ca	

In many libraries it is a policy to classify the literary works of authors with books *about* the author and his works. The books *by* an author are generally placed before the works *about* the author and his works. Usually a letter from the end of the alphabet is placed after the cutter or book number, followed by the initial of the author of the biography or criticism. Thus, Arthur Day's *James A. Michener*, which is a critical study of Michener's work, could be classified:

813.5
M623zD

Using the "z" ensures that the criticism will stand after all other works by Michener. (Another approach is that used in DDC 18 for Shakespeare, 822.33.)

Another commonly used work mark is the one provided to identify different editions of a work. For this purpose, either the date can be placed in the call number or a number can be placed after the work mark. Thus, if a library happened to have three different editions of Michener's *Hawaii*, the editions would be distinguished as follows:

813.5	813.5	813.5
M623h	M623h2	M623h3

or

813.5	813.5	813.5
M623h	M623h	M623h
	1970	1972

The use of work marks is a matter of cataloging policy in each library. Their use and application vary from library to library depending on the size of the collection and the patrons. In all cases work marks should be kept simple and should not be confusing.

Library of Congress Author Numbers

The author notations used with the Library of Congress classification can also be used with the DDC. [Editor's note: This usage is recommended only to small libraries with general collections, since the expansion to LC author numbers can be a most irritating shelf listing problem.] The author number consists of the initial letter of the author's name or main entry followed by a number derived according to the directions given in the tables that follow. The numbers are used decimally.

1. After the initial letter **S**,

for the second letter:	a	ch	e	hi	m o p	t	u
use number:	2	3	4	5	6	7-8	9

2. After the initial letters **Qu**,

for the third letter:	a	e	i	o	r	y
use number:	3	4	5	6	7	9

3. After other initial consonants, for the

second letter:	a	e	i	o	r	u	y
use number	3	4	5	6	7	8	9

4. After initial vowels,

for the second letter:	b	d	lm	n	p	r	st	uy
use number:	2	3	4	5	6	7	8	9

If the letters in a name do not appear in the tables, use the letter closest to it. Using this system, which is only a general outline, it is possible that an author could have different author numbers for works classified in different DDC numbers. The following examples illustrate the application of these rules:

1. Names beginning with the letter **S**:

Sabine .S15	Seaton .S4	Steel .S7
Saint .S2	Shank .S45	Storch .S75
Schaefer .S3	Shipley .S5	Sturges .S8
Schwedel .S37	Smith .S6	Sullivan .S9

2. Names beginning with the letters **Qu**:

Quabbe .Q3	Quick .Q5	Qureshi .Q7
Queener .Q4	Quoist .Q6	Quynn .Q9

3. Names beginning with other consonants:

Carter .C3	Cinelli .C5	Crocket .C7
Cecil .C4	Corbett .C6	Croft .C73
Childs .C45	Cox .C65	Cullen .C8
		Cyprus .C9

4. Names beginning with vowels:

Abernathy .A2	Ames .A5	Arundel .A78
Adams .A3	Appleby .A6	Atwater .A87
Aldrich .A4	Archer .A7	Austin .A9

DDC Book Numbers

At 822.33 in the DDC schedules there is a table of book numbers to use in arranging works by and about William Shakespeare (Fig. 12.1). The table can be adapted for use with any author. There are complete instructions for using the table in the schedule. For works about Shakespeare by others, an author number is still needed. For example, a biography of Shakespeare, *Shakespeare the Man*, by A. L. Rouse, will have either of the following numbers:

Cutter Number		**LC Number**
822.33B	or	822.33B
R863		R6

A work on general criticism of Shakespeare's writings, *Prefaces to Shakespeare*, by Harley Granville-Barker, will have one of these numbers:

Cutter Number		**LC Number**
822.33D	or	822.33D
G765		G7

Fig. 12.1. DDC Cutter Numbers

If desired, subarrange works about and by Shakespeare according to the following table, which may be adapted for use with any specific author:

A	Authorship controversies
	(It is optional to class here bibliography; prefer 016)
B	Biography
D	Critical appraisal
	Class critical appraisal of individual works in O–Z
E	Textual criticism
	Class textual criticism of individual works in O–Z
F	Sources, allusions, learning

APPENDIX

ADDITIONAL PROBLEMS

These problems represent books recently cataloged by the Library of Congress. They have been selected to cover all the main classes in the DDC and to provide number building problems of varying degrees of difficulty. For each problem the following information is given: author, title, and the assigned Library of Congress subject headings. This information is sufficient to build a basic classification number. Try to build a classification number for each, but do not spend too much time on a particular problem. Look up the answer and work backwards if you run into a "dead end." Also, do not be discouraged if you arrive at some incorrect answers. Learning to classify materials requires a great amount of practice over a few years. Segmentation marks have been included with the answers when appropriate. The answers are based on the 18th edition of the DDC and appear on Library of Congress cards.

PROBLEMS

Author/Title	Assigned Library of Congress Subject Headings
1) William Griffin, *The Irish in America*	1. Irish in the United States—History—Chronology. 2. Irish in the United States—History—Sources.
2) Robert Nisbet, *The Social Impact of the Revolution*	1. United States—History—Revolution, 1775-1783—Addresses, essays, lectures.
3) Brian A. L. Rust, *The Complete Entertainment Discography from the Mid-1890's to 1942*	1. Music, Popular (Songs, etc.)—Discography. 2. Vaudeville—Discography.
4) Nguyen Ngoc Bich, *A Thousand Years of Vietnamese Poetry*	1. Vietnamese poetry—Translations into English. 2. English poetry—Translations from Vietnamese.
5) M. A. Schnake, *Data-Processing Concepts*	1. Electronic data processing. 2. Electronic digital computers.
6) Desmond MacCarthy, *William Somerset Maugham; An Appreciation*	1. Maugham, William Somerset, 1874-1965.

7) Ruth Vesta Pope, *Factors Affecting the Elimination of Women Students from Selected Coeducational Colleges of Liberal Arts*

1. Education of women—United States.
2. College attendance—United States.
3. Women college students.
4. Universities and colleges—United States.

8) Gerhard Boldt, *Hitler; The Last Ten Days*

1. Hitler, Adolf, 1889-1945.
2. Germany. Reichkanzlei.
3. World War, 1939-1945—Personal narratives, German.

9) Samuel Enoch Stumpf, *Socrates to Sartre: A History of Philosophy*

1. Philosophy—History.

10) Alan Lockhart Douglas, *Electronic Music Production*

1. Musical instruments, Electronic.
2. Electronic music—History and criticism.

11) John Warham, *The Technique of Bird Photography*

1. Photography of birds.

12) James L. Smith, *Melodrama*

1. Melodrama—History and criticism.

13) Lewis B. Mayhew, *Reform in Graduate Education*

1. Universities and colleges—United States—Graduate work.

14) Francis Russell, *The Horizon History of Germany*

1. Germany—History.

15) Virgil Thomson, *The State of Music*

1. Music as a profession.

16) *Current Optometric Information and Terminology*

1. Optometry—Dictionaries.

17) Desiderius Erasmus, *The Correspondence of Erasmus*

1. Erasmus, Desiderius, d. 1536– . Correspondence.

18) Philip W. Davis, *Modern Theories of Language*

1. Linguistics—History.
2. Grammar, Comparative and general.

19) Mario F. Triola, *Mathematics and the Modern World*

1. Mathematics—1961– .

20) *Collier's Encyclopedia*

1. Encyclopedias and dictionaries.

21) John Frederich Waters, *The Mysterious Eel*

1. Eels—Juvenile literature.

22) Milton Rokeach, *The Nature of Human Values*

1. Worth.

23) Otto H. Theimer, *A Gentleman's Guide to Modern Physics*

1. Physics.

24) Frank Alonzo McMullan, *Directing Shakespeare in the Contemporary Theatre*

1. Shakespeare, William, 1564-1616—Dramaturgy.

25) David Warren Burkett, *Writing Science News for the Mass Media*

1. Journalism, Scientific.

26) Roger William Brown, *Psycholinguistics; Selected Papers*

1. Languages—Psychology.
2. Children—Language.

27) W. E. Burcham, *Nuclear Physics; An Introduction*

1. Nuclear physics.

28) Time-Life Books, *The Forty-Niners*

1. California—History—1846-1850.
2. California—Gold discoveries.

29) Glenn Kirchner, *Physical Education for Elementary School Children*

1. Physical education for children.

30) William V. Bangert, *A History of the Society of Jesus*

1. Jesuits—History.

31) Grace A. Bush, *The Mathematics of Business*

1. Business mathematics—Problems, exercises, etc.

32) Donald E. Kieso, *Intermediate Accounting*

1. Accounting.

33) Elden A. Bond, *Tenth-Grade Abilities and Achievements*

1. Mental tests.
2. Ability-Testing.
3. Tenth grade (Education).

34) Tom Wheeler, *The Guitar Book*

1. Guitar.

35) George Ogden Abell, *Exploration of the Universe*

1. Astronomy.

36) Dorothy J. Skeel, *The Challenge of Teaching Social Studies in the Elementary School*

1. Social sciences—Study and teaching (Elementary).

37) *The New Century Handbook of Greek Mythology and Legend*

1. Mythology, Greek—Dictionaries.

38) Gregory La Grone, *Basic Conversational Spanish*

1. Spanish language—Conversation and phrase book.
2. Spanish language—Grammar—1950— .

39) James Kirby Martin, *Interpreting Colonial America*

1. United States—History—Colonial period.

40) Mary Picken, *Needlepoint Made Easy; Classic and Modern*

1. Needlepoint.

41) George Robert Terry, *Principles of Management*

1. Industrial management.

42) Percy Wells Bidwell, *History of Agriculture in the Northern United States, 1620-1860*

1. Agriculture—United States—History.

43) Rodney P. Shearman, *Human Reproductive Physiology*

1. Reproduction.

44) Robert Glenn Gromacki, *New Testament Survey*

1. Bible. N.T.—Introductions.

45) Selwyn D. Ryan, *Race and Nationalism in Trinidad and Tobago*

1. Trinidad and Tobago—History.
2. Trinidad and Tobago—Race question.

46) J. Brandrup, *Polymer Handbook for Synthetic Polymers Including Cellulose and Derivatives*

1. Polymers and polymerization—Tables, etc.

47) Leslie V. Hawkins, *Art Metal and Enameling*

1. Art, metal-work.
2. Enamel and enameling.

48) Brice Carnahan, *Digital Computing and Numerical Methods*

1. Electronic data processing—Engineering.
2. FORTRAN (Computer program language).
3. Numerical calculations.

49) Thomas Courtenay, *Commentaries on the Historical Plays of Shakespeare*

1. Shakespeare, William, 1564-1616—Histories.

50) William A. Healey, *Basketball's Ten Greatest Defenses*

1. Basketball—Defense

51) Homer Hardwick, *Winemaking at Home*

1. Wine and wine making.

52) Richard Ketchum, *The World of George Washington*

1. Washington, George, Pres. U.S., 1732-1799.

53) Georg Wilhelm Hegel, *Hegel, the Essential Writings*

54) Jeanne Agnew, *Explorations in Number Theory*

1. Numbers, Theory of.

55) Frederick H. Hartmann, *The Relations of Nations*

1. International relations.
2. World politics.

56) Yu-wen Chien, *The Taiping Revolutionary Movement*

1. Taiping Rebellion, 1850-1864.

57) Pearl L. Ward, *The School Media Center*

1. Instructional materials centers—Addresses, essays, lectures.

58) George Rowell, *Late Victorian Plays, 1890-1914*

1. English drama—19th century.

59) Bible. O.T. Joshua. *The Book of Joshua*

1. Bible. O.T. Joshua—Commentaries.

60) Sheila Burnford, *One Woman's Arctic* 1. Eskimos—Baffin Island.

61) John Desmond Bernal, *The Extension of Man: A History of Physics before the Quantum* 1. Physics—History.

62) Philip Grant Davidson, *Propaganda and the American Revolution, 1763-1783*
1. United States—History—Revolution—Causes.
2. Propaganda, American.

63) Stephen J. Dearmond, *Structure of the Human Brain; A Photographic Atlas* 1. Brain—Atlases.

64) Francis A. Allen, *The Crimes of Politics*
1. Political crimes and offenses—United States.
2. Criminal justice, Administration of—United States.

65) M. M. Faktor, *Growth of Crystals from Vapour*
1. Crystals—Growth.
2. Vapors.

66) A. C. Greene, *Dallas: The Deciding Years—A Historical Portrait* 1. Dallas—History.

67) Monroe Upton, *Electronics for Everyone* 1. Electronics.

68) *Webster's New Students Dictionary* 1. English language—Dictionaries.

69) Albert Prago, *Strangers in Their Own Land; A History of Mexican-Americans* 1. Mexican Americans—History.

70) Brian Newton, *Cypriot Greek* 1. Greek language, Modern—Dialects—Cyprus.

71) Rex Gerlach, *Creative Fly Tying and Fly Fishing*
1. Fly tying.
2. Fly fishing.

72) John C. Rule, *Louis XIV* 1. Louis, XIV, King of France, 1638-1715.

73) Gerhard Schoenberner, *The Yellow Star; The Persecution of the Jews in Europe, 1933-1945*
1. Jews in Europe—Persecution.
2. Holocaust, Jewish—1939-1945.

74) Alice Henson Ernst, *Trouping in the Oregon Country: A History of Frontier Theatre* 1. Theater—Northwest, Pacific—History.

75) Minny Earl Sears, *Sears List of Subject Headings* 1. Subject headings.

ANSWERS TO ADDITIONAL PROBLEMS

1) 301.45´19´162073

2) 973.3´1

3) 016.7899´12

4) 895.9´221008

5) 001.6

6) 823´.9´12

7) 378.1´69´1

8) 943.086´092´4

9) 190

10) 789.9

11) 778.9´32

12) 809.2´52

13) 378.1´553´0973

14) 943

15) 780´.023

16) 617.7´5´03

17) 199´.492

18) 410

19) 510

20) 031

21) 597´.51

22) 121.8

23) 530 [Note: not 539]

24) 792.9

25) 070.4´49´5

26) 401´.9

27) 539.7

28) 979.4´04

29) 372.8´6

30) 271´.53´009

31) 513´.93

32) 657´.044

33) 153.9´4

34) 787´.61´2

35) 520

36) 372.8´3´044

37) 292´.08´03

38) 468´.2´421

39) 973.2

40) 746.44

41) 658.4

42) 338.1´0974 [Note that the number is for Northeastern— i.e., the first appropriate one.]

43) 612.6´4

44) 225´.6

45) 972.9´83

46) 547´.84´021

47) 739.1

48) 001.6´4

49) 822.3´3

50) 796.32´32

51) 663.2

52) 973.4´1´0924

53) 193

54) 512.7

55) 327

56) 951´.03

57) 021´.2

58) 822´.8´08

59) 222.2´077

60) 970.4´12´9

61) 530.09

62) 973.3´11

63) 611´.81´0222

64) 364.1´31

65) 548´.5

66) 976.4´2812

67) 621.38
68) 423
69) 301.45´16´872073
70) 489´.3
71) 688.7´9
72) 944´.033´0924
73) 296´.094
74) 792´.09795
75) 025.33

BIBLIOGRAPHY

Adams, Melba Davis. "Application of the Dewey Decimal Classification at the British National Bibliography." *Library Resources and Technical Services* 19: 35-40 (Winter 1975).

Advances in Librarianship. New York, Academic Press, 1970– . Annual.

American Library Association. *A.L.A. Glossary of Library Terms.* Chicago, American Library Association, 1943.

Bakewell, K. G. B., ed. *Classification for Information Retrieval.* Hamden, Conn., Archon Books, 1968.

Barden, Bertha R. *Book Numbers: A Manaul for Students, with a Basic Code of Rules.* Chicago, American Library Association, 1937.

Batty, C. D. "A Close Look at Dewey 18: Alive and Well and Living in Albany." *Wilson Library Bulletin* 46: 711-17 (April 1972).

Batty, C. D. *An Introduction to the Eighteenth Edition of the Dewey Decimal Classification.* Hamden, Conn., Linnet Books, 1971.

Bloomberg, Marty, and G. Edward Evans. *Introduction to Technical Services for Library Technicians.* 3rd ed. Littleton, Colo., Libraries Unlimited, 1976.

Coates, Eric James. *Subject Catalogues: Headings and Structure.* London, Library Association, 1960.

Custer, Benjamin A. "Dewey Decimal Classification," in *Encyclopedia of Library and Information Science*, Vol. 7. New York, Marcel Dekker, 1972.

Cutter, Charles Ammi. *Cutter-Sanborn Three-Figure Author Table.* Swanson-Swift revision. Chicopee Falls, Mass., H. R. Huntting Co., 1969.

Dawe, George Grosvenor. *Melvil Dewey, Seer: Inspirer: Doer, 1851-1931.* Library ed. Lake Placid Club, N.Y., Melvil Dewey Biografy, 1932.

"Dewey Decimal Bulletin Board." *Wilson Library Bulletin.* (An occasional column listing official additions and corrections to *Abridged Dewey Decimal Classification and Relative Index*. Corrections for the full edition are occasionally given.)

Dewey, Melvil. *Abridged Dewey Decimal Classification and Relative Index.* 10th ed. Lake Placid Club, N.Y., Forest Press, 1971.

Dewey, Melvil. *Dewey Decimal Classification and Relative Index.* 18th ed. Lake Placid Club, N.Y., Forest Press, 1971. 3 vols.

Foskett, Anthony Charles. *The Subject Approach to Information.* 2nd ed., rev. and enl. Hamden, Conn., Linnet Books, 1972.

Immroth, John Phillip. *Guide to the Library of Congress Classification.* 2nd ed. Littleton, Colo., Libraries Unlimited, 1971.

Library Literature. New York, H. W. Wilson, 1933– . Bimonthly. (An index to periodical articles, books and pamphlets relating to library science. Entries are under author and subject.)

Linderman, Winifred B. "Dewey, Melvil," in *Encyclopedia of Library and Information Science,* v.7. New York, Marcel Dekker, 1972.

Lydenberg, H. M. "Melvil Dewey," in *Dictionary of American Biography* XXI (Suppl. 1). New York, Scribner's, 1944.

Maass, John. "Who Invented Dewey's Classification?" *Wilson Library Bulletin* 47: 335-41 (December 1972).

Mann, Margaret. *Introduction to Cataloging and the Classification of Books.* 2nd ed. Chicago, American Library Association, 1943.

Maltby, Arthur, ed. *Classification in the 1970's: A Discussion of Development and Prospects for the Major Schemes.* Hamden, Conn., Linnet Books, 1972.

Merrill, William Stetson. *Code for Classifiers: Principles Governing the Consistent Placing of Books in a System of Classification.* 2nd ed. Chicago, American Library Association, 1939.

Needham, Christopher Donald. *Organizing Knowledge in Libraries: An Introduction to Information Retrieval.* 2nd rev. ed. London, Andre Deutsch, 1971.

Olding, Raymond Knox. *Readings in Library Cataloging.* Hamden, Conn., Shoe String Press, 1966.

Painter, Ann F., comp. *Reader in Classification and Descriptive Cataloging.* Washington, NCR Microcard Editions, 1972.

Rider, Fremont. *Melvil Dewey.* Chicago, American Library Association, 1944.

Samore, Theodore, ed. *Problems in Library Classification: Dewey 17 and Conversion.* New York, R. R. Bowker, 1968.

Sayers, William Charles Berwick. *A Manual of Classification for Librarians.* 4th ed. London, Andre Deutsch, 1967.

Trotter, Robert Ross. "Application of the Dewey Decimal Classification at the Library of Congress." *Library Resources and Technical Services* 12: 41-45 (Winter 1975).

U.S. Library of Congress. Decimal Classification Division. *Dewey Decimal Classification Additions, Notes and Decisions.* Washington, Library of Congress, 1959– . Irregular.

U.S. Library of Congress. Decimal Classification Division. *Guide to Use of Dewey Decimal Classification, Based on the Practice of the Decimal Classification Office at the Library of Congress.* Lake Placid Club, N.Y., Forest Press, 1962.

U.S. Library of Congress. Processing Dept. *Cataloging Service Bulletin.* Washington, Library of Congress, 1945– . Quarterly.

Workshop on the Teaching of the Dewey Decimal Classification. *The Dewey Decimal Classification: Outline and Papers Presented at a Workshop on the Teaching of Classification, Dec. 8-10, 1966.* New York, School of Library Service, Columbia University, 1968.

Wynar, Bohdan S., with the assistance of John Phillip Immroth. *Introduction to Cataloging and Classification.* 5th ed. Littleton, Colo., Libraries Unlimited, 1976.

INDEX

This index includes entries for the book topics used as examples in Chapters 2 through 11.